CRICKET – AN ADVENTURE

A History of English and Indian Cricket

with a bit of this
and a bit of that
thrown in for good measure

CRICKET – AN ADVENTURE
BOOK ONE

by

Dr M S Rao

A History of English and Indian Cricket

with a bit of this
and a bit of that
thrown in for good measure

Blackie & Co
Publishers Ltd

ISBN 1 903138 90 6

Blackie & Co Publishers Ltd
107-111 Fleet Street
LONDON EC4A 2AB

Acknowledgements

Although this section is customarily called 'acknowledgements', this word strikes me as being sterile, banal and inadequate; the only words that come close to what I feel are 'appreciation' and 'indebtedness'.

Bettina Croft, Jonathan Miller, Brian Jordan, Mike Richardson and Kevin Saunders of Blackie & Co. Publishers are the ones I know, but I am sure there are many behind the scenes to whom also I must extend my sincere appreciation and indebtedness for their indulgence and extraordinary innings of diligence, precision and alacrity in bringing this book out in time for the Cricket World Cup 2003 in South Africa. I recognize, too, Blackie's tremendous efforts involved in marketing the book to the eager cricket enthusiasts in England, India, South Africa and the rest of the cricketing world.

I also extend my appreciation and indebtedness to my friends Mike Glass and Madeleine Carson, who constantly restore my otherwise waning faith in human nature for their magnanimity, generosity and goodness extended to my wife and me over the years.

It is appropriate that I mention my inability to present a bibliography; a gross misdemeanour on my part, for which I ask to be pardoned. I have mentioned the reasons in the Prologue. But I sincerely hope that I will receive intimation of the sources of information from everyone concerned, if only to help other cricket-lovers to learn more of the game. I shall then be able not only to present a comprehensive bibliography in a subsequent edition but to express my appreciation, indebtedness and thankfulness personally to the people concerned.

One person to whom I can already extend my thanks is my sylph-like niece Anthara Mohan, who provided some of the statistics quoted.

Thank you.

Dr M S Rao

CRICKET – AN ADVENTURE
Book One

The evolution of cricket in England and India, English cricket
personalities, cricketing relations between the two great countries,
Indo-British history – and more . . . !

If the wild bowler thinks he bowls,

Or if the batsman thinks he's bowled,

They know not, poor misguided souls,

They too shall perish unconsoled.

I am the batsman and the bat,

I am the bowler and the ball,

The umpire, the pavilion cat,

The roller, pitch and stumps and all.

Andrew Lang

CONTENTS

BOOK ONE

PART ONE – A History of English Cricket

* * * * * * * *

PROLOGUE

When I told my wife, Ann, that I was going to write a book on cricket, she said, "Who is going to read about boring old cricket? You have to cater to the public taste...you know, a bit of oomph."

This was not just a dampener; it was veritable blasphemy, considering that she is a Yorkshire lass!

But that got me thinking...for – after all – I, as all authors, was writing to make a bit of lucre!

How does one inject a bit of Jeffrey Archer and Jackie Collins into cricket, for heaven's sake? An eminently difficult proposition indeed!

Well, I've cracked it...at least, I think I have.

A different mode of presentation, perhaps.

For the history of English cricket, I opted for the dialogue format and decided to write about personalities and incidents – not a boring description of every ball bowled and batted. The English are not really bothered about the depressing statistics of every game played. But the Indians are different. They like to wallow in the game; they like a bit more statistical information...even though they too might not have much to brag about, being quite often at the receiving end of the bat and ball. Accordingly, I have presented Indian cricket in a more traditional manner, though I have started off in the dialogue format.

I must also warn you that this is not a book filled with precise information about exact dates, venues, statistics and other records that titillate the avid cricket buff...though I have mentioned some of the more important milestones. My intention – or hope – in writing this book on cricket is that it may be interesting to both the cricket enthusiast and the general reader; it is for anyone to enjoy, not just the lovers of the game.

I am bound to be asked why I have chosen to present the histories of two cricketing nations in a single book. History has dictated that. If it were not for the British Empire, India would not have been a cricketing nation. Can you imagine the state of affairs if India had been conquered by France, Germany or Japan? What a frightful thought! The overwhelmingly colourful and noisy frenzy of Indian participation in the game, which swamps everyday life and daunts visiting teams, would have been absent. The very lifeblood of Indian sport would have been drained. Indeed, the Indian will have to ask whether life was worth living without willow and leather!

Politics pervades all aspects of life – including cricket. Peoples are often ignorant of their histories. I wish to fill in the blanks and show how politics and cricket have influenced each other.

I have written on virtually every aspect of cricket I could think of, from its rules and regulations, the Test and ODI matches, and cricketing personalities to the latest shenanigans of the 'Gentleman's game' and the future of cricket.

To fulfil Ann's need for 'oomph', I have had to broaden the canvas considerably to take in a bit of socio-political history, tourism, reminiscence, a bit of braggadocio…and sex. But Ann now says that she is scandalized at the naughty bits! Can't win. So, my cricket book is now infused with adventure, intrigue, skulduggery and erotica...not that cricket lacks any of these qualities by itself.

So there you have it!

I hope I have not offended orthodoxy. Well, if I have – hard cheese; I do not particularly care! The bookshelves are replete with more traditional interpretations. If one purchases my book and still wishes to stick to cricket, one is advised to skip the portions that do not pertain to it.

History spanning decades, different nations and hundreds of people cannot be gleaned by personal experience. It is a matter of 'appropriation' to a large extent...as any historical work inevitably is. As a general practitioner in England I practised wholistic medicine and had a very small independent practice with only 700 or so patients on my list. I had a lot of spare time. I used it to study various alternative therapies – and cricket. I visited libraries, where I made notes from various books, magazines and newspapers, and I spent countless hours on the Internet. When I returned to India, I saw to my dismay that I had quite a lot of information on cricket jotted about in a haphazard manner. I decided to put it all together in a book.

Unfortunately, I have not kept meticulous records of my work – which spans nearly 15 years – as it was not my intention at first to publish; it was just a hobby. Therefore I cannot give you details of the origins of the material. I can only humbly state that I am very much indebted to *anyone* who makes a claim of original authorship. After all, 'Imitation is the best form of praise,' said some bloke, whose name I cannot recall.

For the bluster, however, I take full credit.

3

For any omissions and errors – sorry.

Finally, this book has been written with one purpose in mind: enjoyment. May the reader enjoy it.

Dr M S Rao.

Well, there's one word that moved me when a boy
That moves me today.
It's when the umpire, to the general joy,
Pronounces, "Play"

Andrew Lang

Personally, I have always looked upon cricket as
organized loafing.

William Temple

PART ONE –
A HISTORY OF ENGLISH CRICKET

Thank God who made the British Isles
And taught me how to play.
I do not worship crocodiles
Or bow the knee to clay.

Give me a willow wand and I,
With hide and cork and twine,
From century to century
Will gambol round my shrine.

Rudyard Kipling

One fascination of cricket is that it never ceases to
fascinate. To become a devotee in childhood means
being hooked for life. Happily, it is an addiction for
which there is no need of legislation nor government
health warnings.

David Rayvern Allen

CHAPTER 1
Bombay to Melbridge

I refuse to say Mumbai.

The taxi – unusually spruce, tinted-glassed and air-conditioned – cocooned me from the professional squalor of the most populated city of India: 13 million people. For once the driver was civil, even helpful. At the hotel he had taken my suitcase from me with rare alacrity and placed it in the boot. He was pleasant company for the 35 minutes we wrestled through the conurbation of Bombay. I learnt that he owned his own cream-coloured Hindustan Ambassador – the ubiquitous Indian vehicle for half a century, in spite of modern foreign collaborations seemingly designed for dwarves or bilateral leg amputees; that he had just repaid the bank loan; that he lived in a rented house with 'proper' water and toilet facilities; that he was married with one male child who was attending a 'convent' school (which means English medium). Of course, his son was a darling genius; which Indian son is not! His wife commuted five miles every day, wading through the heavy carcinogenic air on buses gasping teratogenic fumes delivering tiffin-carriers to the canteen in a high-rise monstrosity in the city centre for 12 government sinecure-holders who probably delight in inflicting homicidal (or suicidal) tendencies on the people who pay their wages.

So, our friend was infinitely better off than most of his mates who, like himself, had migrated to the city from some village, romantic and picturesque to the artist, but oppressive and bereft of progressive opportunities for its residents. I asked him if he visited his people in the village. He replied that he hadn't taken a day off work for 18 years. I believed him.

Now it was my turn.

"You are not a Bambayite, sir."

"No. I am from Madras."

I also refuse to say Chennai. Bloody politicians.

"Madras is very good place. I like Madras food; *dosa*, *sambar* – excellent. My wife is very good cook. Where are you going, sir?"

"England."

"Very good, sir. Bizness or alliday?"

"Business."

"What bizness, may I ask, sir?"

"I am a writer. I am going to England to get some information."

"What are you going to write about, sir? Novels?"

"No. I am going to write about cricket."

"Cricket!"

And that was that. My friend, like every Indian, was a rabid cricket fan. I don't have to go on about what he said.

"I am going to learn about how cricket started," I said.

"So that is why you are going to England, sir – 'ome of cricket. Good. Good."

We had reached the airport. The meter showed the right fare. He had not demanded protection money. And he had retrieved my suitcase and placed it beside me...with a smiling face.

So I gave him a generous tip. He touched the soiled notes to his forehead. "Thank you sir…and very good luck."

It seemed like an auspicious beginning.

* * * * * * * *

I thought I was early but there were already some 50 people in the serpentine queue in front of the Air India counter. The usual conglomeration of adipose northern men and even more rotund northern women in their ungainly costumes; the token grim, proud 'Queen Mother' being wheeled about by her dutiful son; awkward adolescents in exasperating denim; little monsters running amok, hastening Armageddon; undernourished, nervous, ill-attired southerners; a few suited businessmen; and a cohort of Westerners masquerading as famished beggars.

I put my suitcase through the X-ray machine; the female official in khaki was looking over her shoulder and yawning – I could have got away with a tank. The usual charade with passport, tickets and luggage; I came in at the regulation weight. Boarding card; non-vegetarian, non-smoking. I watched my suitcase disappearing, prayed that it would not end up in Hong Kong, and made my way to security. Another khaki official, only this time of the other gender, waved what looked like a fancy kitchen gadget all over me, stamped my boarding card and let me through without speaking a word. I made my way to the duty-free. There was nothing there that I wanted. I window-shopped the Indian arcades stacked with pinchbeck jewellery and other garish rubbish. I strolled into the bookshop.

Cheetal Walk, by E R C Davidar. The name sounded familiar. I picked it up. Imagine my amazement when I discovered it had been written by someone I knew. He and his son run a charming guest house in Mudumalai Wildlife Sanctuary. I had visited them on several occasions. I bought it.

I avoided the careering monsters, cursed their parents who were quite unconcerned at the havoc caused by their malicious spawn, settled down in a chair and opened the book. I was in the jungle... Barely audible, raucous, unintelligible messages undoubtedly uttered by a raucous, unintelligent female grated on my tympanum at irregular intervals. I adopt the sheep mentality in airport waiting rooms. I follow fellow passengers hoping that they know what they are doing. When I see them collectively getting up and making for some secret exit, I de-chair myself.

A silly sareed girl with an even sillier ersatz smile – which is really a grimace – says, *"Namaste,"* the Indian form of greeting by placing the palms together. I respond with equal inanity. Boarding card again. K29. I struggle through the passengers trying to stuff their oversize hand luggage into the overhead lockers. I have a window seat. I settle down, buckle up and look around. All the stewardesses are uniformly ghastly. I pray that strangers to India boarding Air India in their country of origin do not conclude that we are a nation devoid of pulchritude.

"Excuse me. Can we swap seats, please?"
"Why?"
"I like a window seat...for the view, you know."
"Which is your seat?"

"The aisle seat."

"OK."

Why did he want a window seat when we were travelling almost the entire journey in darkness? I didn't follow the logic. In fact, I was happy for an aisle seat, as I am – for an Indian – tall, with long femurs. Now I could poke my legs out. I saw my friend undo his gleaming leather briefcase, extract the *Economic Times of India* and a pocket calculator, and start punching it...the calculator, not the paper. One of those city whizz-kids with imitation brains. I wasn't going to hobnob with that species. A fat, sweaty specimen inserted himself into the baby-seat between the metropolitan kid and me.

My fate is such that I always have a bipedal monster behind me. After the third kick on my spine, I turned round and told him that, if he didn't sit down and behave himself, I would hit him. It works unfailingly.

In-flight magazines are usually full of glossy rubbish and what to do in case the pilot mucks things up. The usual idiotic spiel about what to do in an emergency was enacted by a ghastly robot. No one listens to the rot. Who is going to work out how to harness himself into the flaming life jacket? Besides, how do we know when it was last checked? Everyone knows that we are going to scream and die if anything goes wrong. Some more idiotic announcements over the intercom in English and Hindi. Why does the Hindi version always sound so grim? Why does the Hindi for 'thank you' sound like an expletive? Why do not our announcers sound warm and courteous? We can never answer these questions.

A ghastly robot comes around with sweets. I take two.

The aircraft works itself into a frenzy that must surely frighten the daylights out of the novice. After a last desperate shudder the aeroplane shoves off, and within 30 seconds it is airborne. It never ceases to amaze me. I open my book. The pilot comes on the intercom and informs us of the route, altitude, speed etc. As if that is vital for us! It must be the automatic pilot talking, as it sounds robotic. No sense of humour or humanity; mind you; you cannot expect those qualities from Indians.

I can never sleep on flight. I doze, read, doze, read. *Cheetal Walk* is good. Just when I am about to doze, it is time to eat; comestibles are always good with Air India. And then it is duty-free time. I don't purchase anything. The question always pops up in my head: why can't the airlines allow people to bring their own food? It would save them a lot of hassle and bring down air fares – a bit. And why should they have in-flight duty-free when all airports have duty-free? If the airport of embarkation stocks rubbish, why can't they allow us to stroll through the duty-free on disembarkation? Surely that would save the airlines a lot of weight – which they could then pass on to the passengers instead of restricting luggage to a measly and impractical 20 or 25kg.

* * * * * * * *

We are approaching Heathrow. Within 30 seconds of touchdown, the massive aircraft is walking. It always fascinates me. Passengers are already getting up and pulling their oversize luggage from over their heads. Where do they think they are going? It takes ages for the aeroplane to taxi to the right spot; and then it takes aeons for the luggage to trundle along. I sit tight – but I have to get up to make way for the two morons who are in a terrible hurry to get nowhere. I scream silently. After the aisle is clear, I move out. My fate is such that my suitcase is always the last to appear: 20 minutes of agonizing tension. Where is it? Don't tell me that it *has* gone to Hong Kong, for God's sake! It appears eventually, almost like a long-awaited Messiah. I start to breathe again. I yank it off, place it on a trolley and join the exodus.

The privileged EEC fellows sail through passport. We wait endlessly. Hell! I have forgotten to fill in my disembarkation card. I fill it in now.

It is my turn.

"Good morning," says a smiling official, almost like a long-lost friend. How do they train them to be so? Why cannot Indians be so trained?

"Good morning."

"Are you a resident here?

"Yes."

"Welcome. Have a nice holiday."

"Thank you. You wouldn't know how Liverpool is doing in the league, would you?"

"Not too well, I'm afraid. Sixth in the league."

I grimace.

You see, I have been a general practitioner in Liverpool for 17 years. I have the coveted 'indefinite visa' for Britain that I can maintain if I visit the country once in two years. And I am a rabid Liverpool Football Club fan.

I make my way to the tube station at Heathrow, purchase a ticket to Victoria and board the clean, cushioned train. Once we surface to ground level, we see the English topography: landscaped countryside; quaint Victorian terraced houses; millions of TV antennas; manicured gardens; washing on the line; motor car junkyards; well-mannered roads; omnipresent juggernauts crashing through the speed barrier; massive red, brown, grey brick warehouses and factories; supermarkets; car parks, car parks, car parks; high-rise buildings; ...not one specimen of wildlife about, not even a bird; and, of course, food fields which seem to miraculously produce whatever it is they produce without human presence – I strongly suspect that invisible, nocturnal, alien goblins do the necessary work and present us human beings a nicely packaged product in the mornings.

London is another conurbation ravenously devouring all in its way like some prehistoric dinosaur. There will come a time when the only uninhabited parts of Britain will be the hills of Wales and the highlands of Scotland, what with periodic baby booms amongst the autochthons, Asians trooping in by the thousand in search of golden pavements and fabled trees with currency notes for leaves, and the flotsam and jetsam of refugees from all over trying to escape tyrannical governments, real or imagined.

I got off at Victoria, pummelled my way out and walked along Buckingham Palace Road to Victoria coach terminus. The next bus to Melbridge was in an hour. I purchased my ticket. A thank you and a smile from the man behind the counter. I went to the coffee shop. £1.20 for a paper cup of liquid that masqueraded as coffee! I bought a copy of *The Independent* and looked up the football results. Liverpool had lost to – of all teams – Wimbledon, and were placed sixth in the Premier League, which by Liverpool standards was disastrous and totally unacceptable. I had to do something about that. Maybe I could send some positive thoughts to the management and players and gee them up, or give everyone a swift kick up their behinds.

I threw the paper into the bin as everything else is a litany of lies. I looked around. Everyone was waiting patiently in orderly queues. Complete silence. All were probably deaf and dumb.

Contrast that with a bus stop in India. Everyone is rushing about as if they had new batteries that they were frantically trying to test for endurance: Duracell! Queue! Pshaw! Shove, push, pull. Hawkers hawking everything under the sun – newspapers, coffee, tea, ginger sweets that cure everything from common colds to cancer, exotic fruits, flowers, neem sticks to brush your teeth. Beggars trooping in and out with regimental regularity and mouth-watering aromatic delicacies. And, to counter the esculent victuals, the pervading essence of kidney and rectal excretions. Good fun!

I handed my suitcase to the immaculately uniformed driver, who placed it into the cavernous bowels of the bus. He checked my ticket and I boarded the bus; clean cushions, white linen to rest oily heads, not a speck of dirt on the floor, the lever for the push-back chair in working order. Punctually, on the dot of 9:15 a.m., the engine was gunned into life and we glided smoothly out of the terminus. By 'we' I mean me and six others. How do they make it pay? I wonder. Imagine a bus leaving with that number in India!

I settled back. The driver announced the route. I would arrive at Melbridge village at 10:45 a.m. Melbridge is a small hamlet in West Sussex. At exactly 10:45 a.m. the bus pulled into the tiny coach station. I alighted, picked up my suitcase and strode along the only main street till I came to a Halford's supermarket. I turned left into James Street and, ten minutes later, I was knocking on the solid oak door of 'The Victorian Guest House', owned and managed by Mr and Mrs Peter Edmondson. They were expecting me and showed me to my room.

The first thing I did was to have a nice hot shower. Then I unpacked my suitcase and arranged everything in its proper place in the wardrobe and chest of drawers. I shall describe the room. It was like going back in time 150 years. It was about 16 feet by 14 feet, and maroon carpeted; the wallpaper was dark maroon with tiny white spots, with a flowery border about 4 feet above ground level. The bed was walnut, sprung with a six-inch mattress. The duvet was maroon, the pillows cream with frilly edges; the sheets were white flannelette. Thank God for that, as I can't abide cold cotton against my skin. The curtains were maroon and cream. The double wardrobe was walnut with a huge drawer at its bottom, all silk-lined. It had wooden coat hangers and a full-length mirror on the inside of one door. The dressing table was again walnut with a tilting mirror in the centre with half a dozen small drawers and two big ones. The chest of drawers was mahogany with lovely brass handles. The mahogany writing table was 4 feet by 3 feet and had some more drawers. The upright chair had maroon upholstery. Two large cane chairs and an occasional table made up the rest of the furniture. On the occasional table were a glass jug with two glasses, an electric kettle, coffee, tea, brown sugar, milk, two cups, saucers and spoons. A television spied on me from a corner. The walls were adorned with exquisite Victorian prints. The fireplace had an ornamental dried-flower arrangement in the hearth, for the room was centrally heated. Bowls of pot-pourri gave out a lavender scent. I looked out of the bow window onto yellow fields of rape, which stretched as far as the eye could see.

I stepped out onto the landing, where there was a chair and table with a dried-flower arrangement, and came down the steps into the hall and then into the sitting room, where I found Mr and Mrs Edmondson.

"Good morning, doctor," they said; "I hope you had a pleasant journey."

"Yes, thank you," I said.

"Is your room alright? If you need anything, please ask. Would you like us to make you some sandwiches or something?"

"Oh no. Thank you. No sandwiches. I think I'll stroll into Melbridge and discover it. And the room is fine…it does live up to the name. Thank you. Do you mind if I potter about?"

"Oh no. Potter about all you like."

"Can I make a telephone call to Mr Landrum, please?"

"Yes. The payphone is in the hall on the right. Have you got some change?"

"Yes, thank you. What about incoming calls? Would they be a nuisance?"

"Provided they are not at ungodly hours."

"I'll make sure they are between 8 a.m. and 8 p.m."

"That's fine."

I went to the telephone.

"Hello! Can I speak to Mr John Landrum, please. This is Dr Mohan calling...Good morning, Mr Landrum. How are you? I'm fine, thank you...Just got in...Yes, I am speaking from 'The Victorian Guest House' you recommended. Lovely place...Mr and Mrs Edmondson are charming, thank you...Oh no. I want to get over the jet-lag. I am going to take a walk around Melbridge in the afternoon...No, I can never sleep on the flight...If I have a good sleep tonight, I will be fine tomorrow. When can I see you? Yes, yes, ten o'clock will be fine. Well, see you then...and thank you very much."

I went down the garden path. It was a typically English garden – some parts of it precise and geometric and some parts semi-natural with a rockery and privet hedges. It had a few apple trees in the back under which there were some cast-iron garden chairs and tables. To the left there were similar red brick Victorian houses, to the right a field of potatoes – the guest house being the last house in the lane. I went into Melbridge peering through the windows of the semi-detached houses and bungalows. I love peering into houses. I notice the net curtains, the vases on the window ledges, the fireplace in the sitting room on which there is usually a clock of some sort and other knick-knacks; I seldom see anyone in the sitting room. I wonder where they are and what they do. Surely they can't be hiding from me! I surmised that quaint old Melbridge would be mostly composed of the retired population.

On the main street, I found a florist, a butcher, a grocer, a bakery, a launderette, a betting shop, a stationer's cum post office, a 'fish'n chip' shop and an off-licence. I decided to investigate Halford's supermarket. It had everything one needed, the difference between it and the other small shops being that it had more variety. I bought myself a pork pie, a Scotch egg, bananas and a carton of apple juice. I saw a church at the bottom of the village; where there is a church there is a cemetery and I love cemeteries. I sat on a 'Mr A. Fothergill, 1812-1884' and had my lunch. It was a lovely clear day, a bit chilly. I went into the church and wandered around admiring the woodwork. I can never understand why the West loves to have plaques of the locally renowned dead – especially those dead due to war wounds – all over the church walls. I sat in one of the pews and admired the stunning stained-glass window behind the altar that bore a brass cross. I was the only one in the church. I sat till I felt a bit dozy and then made my way back to Halford's, where I bought a loaf of wholemeal bread, a chunk of Cheddar cheese, butter and a few tomatoes. I ambled into the off-licence and took down a bottle of Jamieson's Irish whiskey. I returned to my quarters and asked Mrs Edmondson if I could have some cutlery and if it was permissible to eat in the room. I assured her that I would not stink the place out. She smiled and gave me the necessary implements. After leaving my booty in my room I went out for a long walk along the road leading out of town amongst the fields. You see, I hadn't slept properly for 48 hours and I had to avoid sleeping in the daytime; the only way to avoid jet lag is to sleep at the time that's appropriate to the place you are in. I had my dinner at 8 p.m. – shepherd's pie, roast potatoes, boiled peas and cauliflower, and an apple pie – and slept till 8:00 the next morning.

* * * * * * * *

CHAPTER 2
The Landrums; C Aubrey Smith;
The Graces of Cricket

After a breakfast of toast, butter, jam, mushrooms, tomatoes, sausages, orange juice and coffee, I set off to meet John Landrum at no. 6 Canal Bank, Melbridge.

It is about time I told you how I came to be in Melbridge on the 14th of July 2000.

I am from Madras, south India. I came to England in 1979 and settled as a general practitioner in the maritime city of Liverpool. I lived in the northern outskirts of the city in Maghull and my medical practice was in adjoining Kirkby. After starting up as a single-handed practitioner, I had a small list size…compared to my colleagues. To fill in time I learnt various alternative therapies – homoeopathic medicine, acupuncture, hypnosis, the Bach flower remedies, reflexology, the importance of diet, and something that is rather uncommon nowadays called common sense. Thus I came to practice what is referred to as wholistic medicine, which is treating the whole person, the causes and the symptoms with 'appropriate' medicine, as no one system of medicine is a panacea for all illnesses. When the priorities of the NHS started to change, inflicting on us poor doctors the onerous task of being managers and all the mechanization and technology that that entailed, I decided to opt out. I did not have the wherewithal to fight it. Pointless doing something you do not want to do every day till you retire; it is bound to drive you bonkers.

So, in 1996 I decided to pack it in and settle in the Nilgiris, a hill station in south India at the confluence of the three States of Tamil Nadu, Kerala and Karnataka. To keep myself busy I opened up a guest house. I had brought all the stuff that I had collected when I was in England in two large containers by sea.

I had written three books; they were with various publishers for approval. Eventually they were published by Blackie & Co. Publishers. I decided that my next effort would be a sort of 'cricket novel', something which is not just about cricket players and statistics. One of our guests during the cricket World Cup of 1999 was a young lady called Clare, an interior designer from Portsmouth. All India is cricket-mad. During our various chit-chats, she happened to tell me that her great-grandfather was a living encyclopaedia on cricket. I managed to wangle an interview with Mr John Landrum through her. They had arranged for me to stay with the Edmondsons during my visit to Melbridge. They gave me precise directions and instructions – and, so, here I was.

John was 94 years old and lived with his wife Shirley, who was 88. For the past four years their granddaughter – Constance, aged 46 – was living with them. She had lost her husband, a victim of cancer; she was a schoolteacher. Clare was her unmarried daughter.

John's house was beside a canal, and it had ducks majestically gliding across the green water. A couple of hundred yards away was a romantic hump-backed footbridge across the canal. I am always a bit wary about fancy addresses. 'Green Pastures' usually is a hunk of concrete with not a blade of grass for miles; 'Jasmine Drive' is totally devoid of jasmine; 'The Wooded Glade' is famous for the total absence of woods and glades; 'The Rook's Nest' hasn't seen a rook for yonks; and 'Meadow Lane' turns out to be a sickening gully in the city centre.

The Landrums' place was, indeed, beside a canal.

I knocked on the door at precisely 10 o'clock.

"Good morning, Mrs Landrum."

"Good morning, Dr Mohan."

I enter the hall and am showed into the sitting room.

"Good morning, Mr Landrum."

"Good morning, Dr Mohan."

I sit in a single-seater sofa opposite the couple.

"Would you like a cup of coffee, please?"

"Only if you are having one too."

Mrs Landrum scuttles off with agility belying her age.

Let me describe them to you.

John Landrum is, as I said, 94. He could have been the twin of C Aubrey Smith, the cricketer who later went on to become an accomplished character actor in Hollywood. Head full of rusty hair, bushy eyebrows, slightly glazed eyes with a hint of authority, Roman-ish nose, full lips, a military moustache, a furrowed forehead. He stood a couple of inches above me at six feet; he must have been taller in his prime as he now had a slight stoop. I was to discover that he was never without his pipe and Clan tobacco. He was immaculate in his tweed trousers and burgundy sweater.

Mrs Shirley Landrum, aged 88, was a bit more stooped and stood at five foot seven, I would say. Her hair was a brilliant white, and I was to observe later that, if she stood with the sun's rays glinting on it, it would actually glow. She had not a wrinkle on her face; they all seemed to have congregated on her neck. Blue eyes, a nose that maybe was just a little too big for her oval face, and a mouth that always gave one the impression of a smile.

Both were physically wonderful; they attributed it to gardening and daily walks. His astounding knowledge was due to his stint as 'secretary's secretary' – the legman – to Surrey Cricket Club for 30 years.

Their house was typical of other pensioners' houses in Britain – a mixture of good, solid, old furniture, excellent cutlery and crockery…and tacky nonsense of the post-war era.

"Many people must have told you this, Mr Landrum, but, unless I get it off my chest, I am not going to feel completely comfortable."

"Since you are going to be a frequent visitor here, let us first dispense with the formal stuff. You can call me John and my wife Shirley. What is your first name?"

"Rajesh."

"Now, you can't teach an old dog new tricks. Do you mind if we call you 'doc'?"

"Not at all."

"Right. Now, what is it that you wish to get off your chest?"

"That you are the spitting image of C Aubrey Smith."

"It is more than 30 years since anyone told me that. Nowadays people have forgotten about him. Now that you mention it, let me test you. What do you know about Aubrey?

"Charles Aubrey Smith was a Cambridge man in love with both the theatre and cricket. He played for Sussex between 1882 and 1896, captaining a team to Australia in 1887-88. In 1889 he captained a certain Major Wharton's team to Port Elizabeth, South Africa; a very successful tour due to very poor opposition. In fact, it was so poor that the South Africans were allowed to field 22 players. Smith took seven wickets. He caught a local illness at the end of the tour, was later bitten by the gold speculation bug and went into the stock market business with a chap called Bowden. The stock market collapsed. Smith contracted typhoid. Upon recovery he threw in his lot with the Johannesburg Cricket Club and challenged the Kimberley Club, the only side that had done well against the tourists. Smith's Transvaal XI easily won the newly instituted Currie Cup. Smith's challenge established the annual contest that survives to this day.

"He had a rather peculiar delivery action which earned him the nickname 'Round-the-Corner' Smith. After he left Sussex he became a star on the London stage, where he played the villain Black Michael with gusto in *The Prisoner of Zenda*. He also played Shakespeare, *As You Like It,* and Professor Higgins in Shaw's *Pygmalion* opposite Mrs Patrick Campbell. When he eventually went to Hollywood he took his cricket bat and ball with him, named his house 'The Round Corner' and started the Hollywood Cricket Club. Later Los Angeles honoured him by naming a cricket ground after him. He was the leader of the British film people there. C B Fry, dashing cricketer-scholar and friend of Ranjitsinghji, once played in Smith's side alongside David Niven, Basil Rathbone and Nigel Bruce in Hollywood against a local club.

"If one is to believe David Niven, who was given to excessive embroidery, Smith dropped a catch at slips, asked his butler to fetch his spectacles and dropped another one and said, 'The damned fool brought my reading glasses.' His physical stature and his 'Britishness' pigeon-holed him as unofficial royalty, a part he played with exactitude in many of his films. In 1944 he was knighted for his role in Anglo-American relations. In 1948, when he was about to play Old Jolyon in *The Forsyte Saga*, he died at the age of 86. He is buried in Hove."

"Shirley," John screamed, "Shirley."

Shirley came in hurriedly.

"This blighter knows more than me!"

"Sorry, sir…John. I am a movie buff. It wasn't fair of me."

"He is staying for lunch. Is that alright?"

"Er…yes, it would be an honour."

"Now, stop acting like a lunatic, doc. We are going to have a great time," said John.

I believed him.

"When can we start?" I asked.

"Start what?"

"I've come to learn about the history of cricket from you."

"Oh. That can wait. Tell me something about yourself. What sort of cricket book are you going to write?"

"Most cricket books are about cricketers and statistics, and the few history books are pretty bland. I want to write a book about cricket with a human element. It must cover interesting episodes of history (both English and Indian), the people involved and the game. The climax is the next World Cup."

"And who is going to win the next World Cup – according to your book?"

"India, of course!"

"You have a good team. As individuals they are probably the best players around. But they don't seem to gel together for some reason. They should be winning all the time, but they seldom do. Look at the fiasco in '99."

"Yes. So I will have to make some drastic changes with administration, players, training, strategy etc."

"It is a tall order. How are you going to go about it? Have you written any books?"

"I have written three books. They are with the publishers."

"None have come out in print?"

"No."

"Don't let that worry you. They are a bunch of idiots. They wouldn't know a good book if it was handed to them on a flaming plate."

"I know that it is terribly hard for a first-time author to get published anywhere in the world. I write because I like to. Get something off my chest."

"What are your three efforts?"

"One is about health matters…being a doctor."

"Not another book on health, for God's sake. You fellows are a horrible lot. We get letters all the time from our GP asking us to come for this and that…hypertension clinic, diabetic clinic, well-man and well-woman and well-bloody-dinosaur clinic. We ignore them. The last time I saw one of your kind was in 1944 when I was wounded in the war."

"I agree with you that we are a dodgy lot. That is why I have written the book. It is all about how to short-circuit the doctor and look after yourself. And, if you have to see a doctor, how to grill him intelligently before submitting yourself to medical procedures."

"That sounds alright."

"It also contains information about some alternative methods of therapy."

"So, you are into all that hocus-pocus, are you?"

"Yes. Any method of treatment is acceptable if it does not cause any harm. How and why it works is of no concern really."

"That is not very scientific, is it?"

"I am up to here with all this scientific nonsense. What we modern doctors practise is more unscientific than witchcraft."

"Shirley! Did you hear that? A doctor saying that doctoring is twaddle!"

"Yes. I heard that. You two will get on well, by the looks of it."

"I am beginning to like this fellow. What are your other books about?"

"The second one is about my interpretation of my religion, Hinduism. I have cut through the nonsense and presented it in a practical and logical manner."

"How did you do that? As far as I am concerned religion *is* impractical and illogical."

"I approached it from the agnostic's and atheist's point of view."

"That's interesting. So you manage to prove that religion is logical?"

"Yes."

"Are you a practising Hindu?"

"No. I am, without intending to sound fustian, a man of the world. I happen to have been born into a Hindu family. But all religions say the same thing: be good."

"I suppose they do. What is your third book about?"

"It is an interview with Jesus."

"What?"

"You see, no one knows what on earth Jesus did before he suddenly appeared on centre stage...or, should we say, bat in hand on the centre pitch!? How did he prepare for the match? The best way would be to get the story straight from the 'horse's mouth'. So I get him to come down and give an interview. I ask the questions and he fills in the blanks."

"This I should read. Have you got a copy with you?"

"Have you got a computer?"

"Catch a schoolteacher without one – you know that Connie, my granddaughter, is a schoolteacher, don't you? – yes, we have."

"I have all three of my efforts on floppy disks. I could give them to you."

"Let me have just the one about Jesus. I want to see your style before we start to talk."

"Fine. I'll drop it in this evening."

"Your eyesight is not very good, John. You can't sit in front of the computer and read," said Shirley.

"But we have a printer. Constance can get a print out and I can read, can't I?"

"Well. That's alright."

We had finished our coffee. They took me into the garden and Shirley introduced me to all her botanical friends. I can appreciate beauty...of any sort. But botanical names...pshaw. We have a good garden at home in Coonoor, Nilgiris, but I'm damned if I know the names of the plants. I had to do pharmacology in my third year at medical college; generic names drove me nuts.

"Clare told us about your place in India, doc. If we were a few years younger, we would have come."

"What's wrong with now?"

"Getting a bit long in the tooth."

"He won't admit it, but he does get a bit breathless and tired sometimes," said Shirley.

"What's wrong with getting a bit breathless and a bit tired after a two-mile walk, for God's sake?"

"Tell me something about yourselves, please," I said.

"Well. We were both born in Henfield – about 12 miles from Brighton," said John, "The world went crazy for a few years during our childhood. Both our fathers went off to fight the bloody war. Mine returned with a bullet through his shoulder and Shirley's returned with poison gas in his lungs. When I was older I saw documentaries and films about the war and they were horrific. My father said that it was ten times worse in reality...even the documentaries were cleaned up for public consumption. He said that, if it weren't for the cock-ups, the war would have been over in 18 months. I believed him when I had to go to Europe when we had the second round of unpleasantness. Many a time, I felt like shooting our commanders rather than the enemy.

"When I was in school, I started to play cricket. W G Grace and Ranjitsinghji were over the horizon. It was the time of Jack Hobbs. I was a bowler-batsman. I represented a local club and eventually Surrey Cricket Club, and played county cricket for 20 years. When I was 40, I was recruited to be the man behind the scene at Surrey Cricket Club and..."

"Hold on. Tell us about your cricketing career."

"Nothing much to brag about. Medium-fast bowler with the ability to swing the ball. Five down as batsman. I once saw even the great Ranji play. Lissom fellow with wristy shots...like many of your players. I saw or played against all the great names post-1930s."

"Don't be modest. Any outstanding moments?"

"Once took 14 wickets in a match against Lancs. and made a couple of centuries here and there. Nothing spectacular."

"How did you become the man behind the scenes at Surrey Club?"

"We were playing Lancashire. 1946. They made 348 in their first innings. We replied with 285. Second innings, Lancs. collapsed for 189. We had to score 253 to win. I went in at five down. When I came to the crease, we were 194. As the shadows lengthened, we were 249 for eight with me 84 n.o. The ball was pitched outside the off stump, good length. I padded up and played it to mid on. The fielder stumbled. We ran for a single. The fielder recovered and threw the ball to the bowler's end. It missed the stumps and the bowler and went to fine leg. We ran for another single. My eye was on the ball and I ran straight into number ten. I fell. I heard a crunch. I had broken my ankle. When I was convalescing, I was approached by the secretary of Surrey and asked if I was willing to do some desk-work till I got on my feet. I needed the money. At first it was part-time. Once my playing days were over I was made full-time and stayed on for nearly 30 years."

"What was your profession then?"

"I was an accountant."

"What do you mean by 'secretary's secretary'?"

"I used to do the accounts and wages and fix the accommodation for players, administrators etc."

"General dogsbody."

"That's right."

"You were all amateurs then."

"Don't you believe it. I was an amateur...for I had a profession. But, if you were a good cricketer, you could get paid on the side. The great W G Grace regularly pocketed anything between £20 and £40 for every match."

"How was that?"

"W G was a character. He embodied all that was Victorian. You know that he was a doctor like you. He came from a family of doctors. Because of his cricketing exploits, he was in great demand. He was, what you would call, a star. The public was charged threepence for a match, but if W G played it was charged sixpence. Can you imagine something like that now? If your Tendulkar played you could charge an extra fee!"

"Quite unthinkable."

"But that was how it was. Do you know why he demanded and got his fees…as an amateur? He said that he had to pay the locum doctor when he could not attend his clinic due to his cricket commitments. It may even be true that he was out of pocket despite this reimbursement, but still it was illegal for a 'gentleman' to accept money. It was assumed that 'gentlemen' could afford their pastimes without having to be paid. In 1893, when he went on his second tour of Australia, he received £3,000, which was a considerable amount in those days."

"Then you could also have demanded a fee."

"Ah. But I wasn't a star! I wasn't the instantly recognizable figure W G was – over 6 feet tall, 20 stone, pouchy eyes and a great bush camouflaging his face. If you can imagine Henry VIII in flannels, you have W G. I did not belong to the famous Grace gentry…riddled with cricketers...who could make up entire male and female teams with members of the family. I did not play for England…and I wasn't the great and flamboyant cricketer W G was."

"Tell me something about W G."

"William Gilbert Grace, born 1848, fourth son of Dr Henry Mills Grace and Martha at Downend, near Bristol. It is said that Martha and a maternal uncle called Alfred Pocock were instrumental in encouraging the Grace brothers to become such exceptional cricketers. By the way, Martha is the only woman to be mentioned in the obituary column of *Wisden's Almanack.*"

"Hold on, there. Can I have a piece of paper, please? I must take notes."

John gave me a notebook.

"Let us not forget W G's elder brother, Dr. Edward Mills Grace, who was the most admired cricketer of his day despite his unorthodoxy, autocracy and eccentricity. Unorthodox because he was the Victorian equivalent of Vivian Richards, thrashing the ball with great force all over the field many a time using the cross-bat freely; autocratic because he would refuse to obey rules when it suited him – indeed, he may have started the shenanigan referred to nowadays as 'gamesmanship'; eccentric because he would run off to do an autopsy in the middle of a game – he was a coroner.

"E M once caused a riot at the Oval when he contrived and got a batsman out by lobbing a ball high in the air to land on the stumps. It had never been done before and the crowd did not approve. The match was stopped, and the players tore up the wickets and had a free-for-all. Eventually the batsman had to go.

"In 1863 he was the only amateur to be invited to tour Australia. In first-class matches his batting average was above 60. From 1870 to 1909 E M was secretary to Gloucester Country Club at a salary of £60 per annum, in which position he made himself indispensable. On his retirement he received £600 from the Duke of Beaufort. Two years later, he died.

"W G was an all-round athlete. In his younger days when he was not so bulky he could do the 100-yard dash in under 11 seconds, the 200 yards hurdles in 28 seconds, and 440 yards in 52.2 seconds. After retirement he was the first captain of the English bowls team. He was also a formidable pugilist, in which sport he nearly killed an opponent once. W G was the reason why half the cricket pavilions were built in this country. Such was his drawing power. I mentioned to you about his match payments. If only he had gone openly professional, we would have had professional cricketers right from his time. It would have avoided the hypocrisy of the two-tiered social structure of cricket that eventually came to an end some 100 years later. He was as obdurate as his brother. He would refuse to walk if he thought he was not out. He would have a tantrum if his bowling was whacked. Once he tried inducing a young batsman to hit him for a catch by bowling donkey drops. When the batsman did not oblige, he threatened to walk off. We chastise players today for undue appealing. W G indulged in it a lot. He would appeal vociferously and, if the umpire gave the batsman out, he would whisper to the batsman on his way to the pavilion, 'You weren't out, you know'."

"A good story...but I get the feeling that you don't entirely like W G, John."

"I admire his cricket; I don't have to like him. W G was the greatest cricketer of his time, and he knew it. He took advantage of it and was pretty mercenary. Can't really blame him, for his father died young. The mother had to take care of the large family under straitened circumstances. W G followed in his father's footsteps and qualified as a doctor in ten years. W G and his two cricketing brothers could have become professional cricketers and made a fortune, but having descended from a 'gentleman's background' they wished to be gentlemen and played as amateurs. W G joined Lord's and, because he knew that he was the main draw at the games, his average was twice that of the next man…forced them to turn a blind eye to his demands for exorbitant 'expenses'. Besides playing for Lord's, W G joined and soon took over the United South of England XI, an itinerant team. He organized the matches, paid his team-mates and kept the rest. He even organized matches abroad. When the Australians invited him, he demanded and got £1,500 for the tour, paid his team £175 per head, and pocketed the rest. I'll give you another example of W G's piratical propensities. He auctioned off a fixture to Yorke's Peninsula Association, then wangled an unscheduled match at Adelaide and refused to play for Yorke. The story doesn't end there. The contract stated that, if the match against Adelaide finished within three days, W G would play a free exhibition match. He refused unless paid an extra £10. He was up to all these shenanigans under the guise of 'amateur' and 'gentleman'. Because he was a star attraction, he was always paid more than the other players. Whilst the professionals were being paid £5 in *wages*, the amateurs were being paid £10 *expenses* and W G £15 *expenses*. Finally, in desperation, the MCC arranged a testimonial match in 1879 at Lord's, raised £1,458, and set him up in his surgery at Bristol once he qualified. But what did good old Grace do? He employed a locum and played even more cricket all over the place and persuaded Gloucestershire to pay his locum fees!".

I had to laugh.

"You may well laugh. Even in 1896 W G demanded and got £40 whilst the others got ten. Such were his prodigious abilities with bat and ball and his universal popularity."

"Well, nothing wrong with that. Players get paid according to seniority now."

"Seniority is one thing; popularity is another. Tendulkar is junior to Azharuddin but more popular. Does he get paid more?"

"I get your point."

"W G began by playing for the Gentlemen of the South against the Players of the South. He was stumped for a duck but bowled unchanged through both the innings, taking 13 wickets for 84 runs. His first hundred in first-class cricket was when he played for England against Surrey, where he made 224 out of a total of 521. Three weeks later he scored 173 after bowling unchanged, taking seven wickets.

"When both the brothers opened the innings people would travel miles to come and see them. More than once their calling as doctors was wanted on the field. A certain C J M Fox sustained a dislocated shoulder while fielding; E M sat on the man and W G jerked it back into place. Another time, a chap called A C C Croome was impaled on the fence and had a terrible gash on his neck. W G held the edges of the wound together for nearly 30 minutes while waiting for the needle and thread to suture it.

"He worked hard at batting, bowling and fielding. He could never teach people, though; he didn't know how to. Since it was so natural for him to perform, he couldn't understand the others' difficulty. When asked how he felt while batting he replied that he did not think or feel anything! Modern batting, stroke play, forward and back play techniques are more or less the invention of W G. He was the first one to score 1,000 runs and take 100 wickets in a season; first to score a century on his debut against Australia; first to score a triple century – 344 against Kent in eight hours – and the first to score 100 hundreds.

"Between 1868 and 1874, he topped the English batting averages. In 1871 he averaged 79 runs per innings. Only Bradman has bettered that record. You will see how great he was when I mention that the next man averaged under 40.

"Let me give you some statistics to show you his stunning achievements in first-class cricket: 54,211 runs, 2,808 wickets, 874 catches, five stumpings. He captained England 13 times, touring Australia twice and North America once; captained Gloucestershire for 30 years before switching to London County. His final match was at the Oval in 1908 against Surrey.

"He was a prodigious eater, and always had one large whisky and soda with a touch of angostura bitters during the lunch break and another when play ended.

"1914. The Great War. You would think that County Championships came to an end. No. They carried on virtually undisturbed throughout the first year of the war. W G wrote a piece in *The Sportsman,* questioning the ethics of able-bodied men playing and watching cricket while a war was on. It seemed as if cricket was incompatible with patriotism. Immediately there was a flood of volunteers deluging the War Office, who found themselves in the unenviable position of finding lodging, boarding and arms for the multitudes. They could not. Men were billeted under canvas, and drilled in civilian togs using walking sticks for rifles and living on rationed food. It was the beginning of their disenchantment. Little did the beggars know of the horrors that awaited them across the Channel.

"In October 1915, while he was pottering about the garden, the old duffer suffered a stroke. He dragged himself into the house. He had many visitors. To one of them he mentioned how he hated the Zeppelin raids. 'How can they bother you when you played all the fast bowlers of your time with ease?' W G replied, 'Ah, I could see those beggars; I can't see these'."

"WG died on the 23rd of October 1915 during the First World War. His friend Arthur Conan Doyle maintained that he died of a broken heart, unable to witness the madness of humankind. I think we can discount that; after all, Doyle was his friend and admirer. I think the great big fellow died of 'excess' – excess of eating, drinking and playing."

"That is truly incredible. How can you remember all those figures from over a century?"

"That is my aptitude. I love cricket.

"I'll tell you about Doyle. He indulged in all sorts of things – football, boxing, golf, billiards, skiing, flying, whaling, rugby *and* cricket. He represented his university at rugger when he was in medical school; he was a fast forward.

"He was a middling cricketer. Once when he played against the Gentlemen of Warwickshire he accomplished a hat-trick. One of the batsmen protested that he had been put off because Arthur had suddenly bowled with his right arm instead of his usual left! Arthur was a trickster. Another of his victims said that he just couldn't bat seeing a bowler dressed in crude pink shirtsleeves! He started playing first-class cricket in the early 1900s. In one of the matches, he handsomely on-drove W G Grace for a four. He stepped out to drive the next ball that looked exactly similar, but W G had disguised it…it rose a little higher and dropped a little shorter…and Arthur was comprehensively stumped. A P Lucas of Cambridge once tossed up a 30-foot lob. As the ball descended on him like a bomb Arthur was caught in several minds. In desperation, he decided to slash it past point. In doing so he knocked down two of his stumps, the bat flew out of his hands – and the descending ball neatly landed on the one remaining stump. No one was more comprehensively dismissed. Another time W M Bradley bowled a vicious ball that slammed into his thigh. There was a sharp pain that became suddenly unbearable. 'My word, sir,' said the wicketkeeper to Arthur, 'you're on fire.' The ball had ignited his matches in a tin box! W G lumbered in from point and said, 'Ho, couldn't get you out. Had to set you on fire'."

My head was reeling. I said goodbye to John.

"Don't forget to give me *Jesus*," he said.

I went to my room and put together in longhand the impromptu notes I had made while John was narrating. I transferred a sort of first draft onto the portable computer. The next day I decided to take my tape recorder.

I returned in the evening and gave him the floppy, *Interview with Jesus*.

I was still a bit stunned when I went to sleep that night.

CHAPTER 3
Interlude – Day Trip to Brighton

At 8:00 the next morning Mr Edmondson informed me that John was on the telephone for me.

"Good morning, John."

"Good morning, doc. Don't come today."

I missed a beat. I had offended him.

"Why? Are you unwell...or have I offended you? If I have, I'm sorry."

"What are you blabbering about?"

"*Interview with Jesus.* If I have upset you with what I have written, I apologize."

"Now look. Constance got a printout of *Jesus*. I want to finish reading it. Great stuff. Better than ploughing through the Bible."

I heaved a sigh.

"Good God. I was visualizing myself packing up and returning home."

"No, no. I've now got an idea of what sort of bloke you are. Right up my street. Now, get lost! Go to Brighton or somewhere for the day. We'll see you tomorrow."

"OK. Thanks. Fine."

I asked Peter how to get to Brighton. He said that there was a direct bus to Brighton at 9:00 a.m. I had my breakfast, made myself some cheese-and-tomato sandwiches, took a flask of hot coffee (I always travel with a flask just for such occasions) and boarded the bus. I reached Brighton at 10:30 a.m.

It is a raucous town. I have never liked seaside resorts. When I was in Liverpool, it took me about 15

42

years to go to Blackpool on the west coast, even though it was only an hour's drive from Maghull. I have also been to Scarborough on the east coast. I hated them both. Amusement arcades for the brainless, funfairs for people with a twisted sense of humour, gambling dens for the vacuous, and meretricious gift shops for country bumpkins. Southport, which is only 30 minutes from Maghull, is a much better and relatively unspoiled alternative, for, though it has all the above-mentioned iniquities, it also has a main thoroughfare, Lord Street, where it is a pleasure to promenade; and lovely buildings, shops, hotels and tea houses, bookshops etc. And now, here I was, in the queen of the resorts on the south coast.

Brighton is where Britons with retarded brains – or should I say who are cerebrally challenged – go to barbecue themselves during the fleeting days that pass under the euphemism 'summer'. It is where people with diseased brains go to lose their money in the gambling dens. These people confine their 'holidays' to about a square furlong of Brighton. But there is another side to the resort. It has around 1,200 acres of parks and gardens. Stanmer Park covers 537 acres and Moulescombe Wild Park comprises 143 acres. Adjoining the parks is the University of Sussex, splendidly designed by Sir Basil Spence with a lot of pink bricks. There are bowling greens, tennis courts, golf courses and a racecourse. We have all heard of the famous Veteran Car Run from London to Brighton, held every November, and the annual Arts Festival when famous musicians perform classical music, jazz and pop. This is where established and striving artistes from all over Britain gravitate to prance about in operas, plays and variety performances.

I visited the shingle beach and the promenade that was extended by an undercliff walk built by a crew of unemployed Welsh miners in the 1930s. The aquarium has fish from all over the world. Though I do not like to see any animals in confinement, I did purchase a ticket and join the queue. It was not as bad as some of the places I have been to. I refused to see the equally famous Bird Museum that has a collection of 3,000 stuffed birds. And, of course, all seaside resorts must have their waxworks. The Brighton one was devised by a great-grandson of Madame Tussaud. Somehow I am always a bit disappointed with wax exhibits. I like the realistic eyes and I admire the clothes and the props. But the figure itself is so evidently wax. With appropriate lighting, the figures could be made to appear more realistic. But, personally, I wish Madame Tussaud would emulate our Vincent Price in the famous 3D film *House of Wax*, where he stumbled upon the much easier alternative of murdering real people and dipping them in a cauldron of exquisite wax. After all, most of the models were of politicians and members of the royalty, who are universally held to be better dead than alive!

In 1754 a Dr Richard Russell arrived at Brighton and prescribed brine bathing and brine drinking as a panacea for all ills. Of course, everyone believed the idiot, and soon Brighton became a spa town. In 1783 the Prince of Wales, who later metamorphosed into King George IV, built the famous Regency terraces and a holiday home in the classical style with a Chinese interior. Between 1815 and 1822 John Nash rebuilt the Royal Pavilion in the Moghul style – onions, carrots, radishes and all. Queen Victoria took one look at the place, screwed her nose up and sold it to the Brighton authorities in 1845. The interior is garishly and greenishly Chinese. The ceiling in the banqueting hall is 45 feet high and painted to represent an oriental sky. Chandeliers, each weighing a ton, are everywhere and must look breathtaking when lit. I liked the kitchen; 550 pieces of copper ware belonging to the Duke of Wellington, who used to serve up to 116 dishes at his banquets!

I didn't have time to visit the Museum and Art Gallery. I don't care much for art nouveau and art deco, but I would have liked to see the paintings by the English and continental artists and the famous Willett collection of pottery.

I returned to Melbridge at 8:00 p.m., had my dinner and went to bed exhausted.

* * * * * * *

CHAPTER 4
The Origin and Evolution of Cricket

Pray, cricketers, remember, if you want to play with me,
How you carry on your little conversations.
You must give up your wicked swear words and abjure
the big, big D,
And moderate your hasty exclamations.
Should a ball rise unexpectedly and take your wind
away,
This is no excuse for making such a pother;
You must bear it like a Christian, for I certainly shan't
play
If there is any stronger language than a 'bother!'

You must all be good teetotallers. Beer savours of the
pit,
And is, of every thing, symbolic.
It's ruin, moral, physical – I would as soon admit
The fiend himself as liquor alcoholic.
And as for gin and whisky – pour the filthy stuff away!
Who drinks these deadly, poisonous pig-washes?
Bring tea and ginger beer instead! I certainly shan't
play
If there's any stronger drink than lemon squashes.

Of course, you musn't gamble! (When we once begin to
bet
No power on earth can ever check or turn us.)
Nor smoke, for the insidious, seductive cigarette
Is the facilis descensus to Avernus.
But if you'll follow me; and fling your vices away,

Observing my conditions well and duly,
Why, then; it is just possible I may consent to play,
If there is no stronger batsman than yours truly.

May 1898

I presented myself, with portable tape recorder, at John's at 10:00 the following morning.

"Good morning, John. Good morning, Shirley."

"Good morning, doc," said both of them.

"What did you do yesterday?" asked John.

"As you suggested, I went to Brighton."

"Did you like it? The weather was good, anyway."

"Yes. But it was mad; too crowded. I was glad to get back to good old Melbridge. Have you finished with *Jesus*? I'd like to get on with cricket, you know."

"Say, listen," said John; "you have done your homework on it. All that you say in your book *could* have happened...as you mentioned in the frontispiece."

"Yes. The thing about Jesus is we can say anything. No one can prove or disprove it."

"Correct. You have accounted for everything from the logical point of view...from today's point of view. I did like the way you presented his teachings in dialogue form; witty and pertinent...and logical."

"I hope I didn't offend you in any way."

"No, no. Even the bit where Jesus has an affair. You put it in such a natural way that only a bigot would take offence."

"I showed it to a Protestant minister in India. He was not pleased. Most Christians in India belong to the evangelical ilk. Thanks for your appreciation, John. Now – can we get down to brass tacks, please?"

"By which you mean cricket. OK. What do you want to know?"

"The history of English cricket."

"As in human history, the history of cricket also has to do with characters. Characters make cricket. People make history. If it weren't for that particular person at that particular place at that particular time, history would not have been made. You have to understand that. You can't talk about Indian cricket without mentioning Tendulkar, Gavaskar, Kapil Dev."

"Yes. I understand that. How did it all start?"

"No one can answer that question, I'm afraid. As far as generic terms are concerned we have the French *criquet*, Anglo-Saxon *crec*, Danish *krykke*, German *krucke*. The obstetrical wards of cricket could be anywhere; it could be where a couple of kids hit a ball about with a stick."

"In India we have a game called *gilli-dandu* which is akin to cricket. It is played by urchins in the streets and waste grounds all over India."

"You see. It could have evolved from that or from *stoke ball, handyn and handoute* or the Persian *chugar*. Who knows? Lost in the mists of time, if you want a cliché."

"How did the game evolve from its humble beginnings to its present state, John?"

"The MCC was in charge of administering the laws of the game. In the 17th century you could hit the ball and then charge across the field and wallop the fielder with the bat if you were in danger of being caught. That was amended in 1744 when you were allowed to charge at the fielder and throw him down by bodily contact."

"In other words, you couldn't hit him on the head with the bat!"

"That's right. In 1727, the length of the pitch was 23 yards. In 1744, it was made 22 yards. C T Studd played for Eton, Cambridge, Middlesex and England, became a missionary and went to China, India and the Belgian Congo – where he helped build a church; he made sure that the aisle was exactly 22 yards! It was also the year when the red ball and the lbw law were introduced.

"There were two stumps with one on top. 22 inches by 6 inches. Round about 1775, three stumps came into force as batsmen were not out if the ball whizzed in between the two stumps, which – as you can imagine – happened very often. Slowly the dimensions grew to 27 inches by 8 inches, and so on until the present one of 29.5 inches by 9 inches. But in the old days, just to make the game more interesting, the 'gentlemen' (amateurs) defended wickets 22 by six and the 'players' (professionals) defended wickets 27 by eight. Great fun...

"They used 4lb curved, one-piece, unsprung bats. Imagine the shock travelling up your arm when you hit the ball! It slowly evolved into blades with wooden handles, then the 'spring handle', and then the 'whalebone handle'. In 1835 Thomas Nixon, a craftsman-cricketer, fashioned the springy cane handle. In 1841 he introduced cork knee pads; in 1862 he and Lillywhite patented the bowling machine called the

'Balista'. Pads were experimented with round about 1836; by 1860 pads and gloves were a necessary fashion.

"A Mr White of Reigate played with a bat the same width as the wicket! When the bowlers howled in anguish, it was decreed that in future the width of the bat should be 4½ inches. In 1835 the length of the bat was fixed at 38 inches. In the same year follow-on was made compulsory after a deficit of 100 runs.

"In 1838 the circumference of the ball was fixed at 9 – 9¼ inches, which was again amended to between 8 and 13/16th and 9 inches.

"I told you it was underarm bowling in those days and that ladies played cricket. You may wonder how they did it. They used to force the ball away at the level of the armpit. A chap called Brown of Brighton bowled underarm with such speed that he once killed a dog on the boundary…if you can believe that!"

"How did the present overarm bowling evolve, John?"

"Well, there are many stories about that, but the most romantic is this. Christina, a woman cricketer…or cricketress…took to bowling in a wide arc to avoid hitting against her billowing hooped skirts. Her brother, John Willes, noticed the trajectory of the ball and thought that it had potential. He imitated her and thus became the first and leading advocate of round-arm bowling. But this new style was hooted down. The showdown came at Lord's, where, in 1822, he bowled round-arm. He was immediately no-balled. He threw the ball down in disgust and rode off on his horse, never to play again.

"Five years later, William Lillywhite and James Broadbridge restarted round-arm bowling for Sussex, but it was not until May 1828 that the MCC legalized the round-arm action – the hand was permitted to be raised as high the elbow and the arm to be extended outwards and horizontally. Using round-arm, a 6-foot 15-stone player called Jackson nobbled a poor chap by the name of Ludd on the leg, and appealed for leg before. The umpire said, "Not hout!" but poor Ludd was in such agony from the blow that he said, "Mebbe not, but I's a-going," and hobbled off.

"In 1835 the hand was allowed to be raised as high as the shoulder. The new bowling action became a rage; Mynn, Lillywhite and Caffyn were the best exponents of this form of 'modern' bowling. Finally, in 1864, the MCC revised the law and overarm bowling became the vogue."

"Can you tell me something about the evolution of the present-day helmet, John?" I asked. "What sort of headgear did people wear in the olden days?"

"It was ordinary everyday wear: tricorne hats and postilions' caps in the 18th century; high toppers, bowler hats and tasselled caps in the early 19th century. Then we had the white felt hats that evolved into cloth caps."

"In India, we had the topi."

"And then, of course, we had the straw hats with colourful bands. I used to like them…In the 1930s Patsy Hendren was hit by Larwood. He designed the comical three-peaked hat, which was quite ineffective really. George Brown of Hampshire appeared to face Larwood in what looked like a German helmet…that later turned out to be a lady's cloche hat!

"The modern helmet may have had its origins in the 1974-75 tour of the MCC to New Zealand, when Peter Lever bowled a vicious short-pitched delivery to the number 11 batsman, Ewan Chatfield. It took off the pitch like a bolt of lightning, grazed Chatfield's glove and slammed into his temple. He fell to the ground and started to twitch and his heart stopped. The MCC physiotherapist Bernard Thomas and the St John's ambulance men gave him mouth-to-mouth and heart massage and brought him back to life. After Chatfield was carted off, the next man in was a chap called Richard Daft. He had swathed his head in a towel. Everyone laughed at him because he looked ludicrous. But he set about Platt with a vengeance. Maybe the adjective 'daft' derives from him!"

"That is a curious story..."

"Well, people started to think about protective headgear thereafter. When the fibreglass caps began to be worn in the 1970s, ex-cricketers squirmed. Compton, Close, Benaud, Larwood, Laker etc. said that they would rather be found dead than be caught with that 'unmanly' thing on their heads. And later, when the headgear came with protective visor and grill, cricketers were dubbed as Martian sissies! There's a little ditty...

> *There was a young fresher called Jessop*
> *Who was pitching 'em less up and less up,*
> *Till one of the pros got a blow on the nose*
> *And said, "In a helmet I'll dress up."*

I laughed.

* * * * * * *

CHAPTER 5
Cricket and the Clergy

John said, "A chap called Josephus Oscanus, a 12th-century cleric of Exeter, wrote a ditty:

> *The youth at cricks did play*
> *Throughout the livelong day.*

In 1330, another man of the cloth, William Pagula of Winkfield, wrote:

> *Bat and bares and such play*
> *Out of chyrche-yarde put away.*

In 1300, King Edward I paid his chaplain, John de Leck, for equipment for a game called *creag,* which is supposed to be a forerunner of cricket."

"How do you remember all this?"

"I had a lot of spare time when I was with the MCC. I used to delve into libraries. I was nuts about cricket. I can remember anything about cricket."

"I read somewhere that people of the cloth took up cricket in a big way. Since you have brought up the subject, can you tell me about the association between the Church and cricket?"

"You see, in those days, they didn't have any playgrounds as such. It was all marshy and slushy. The only open and possibly flat ground was within the precincts of the local church that had gardeners to tend the lawns. So naturally people sneaked in there for a game of cricket. But you were not allowed to play on a

Sunday; God's day. Besides, cricket was synonymous with gambling...and gambling was frowned upon by the Church.

"In 1622 nine people of Boxgrove in Sussex were prosecuted for playing in 'God's acre' on a Sunday. In 1629 players were arrested for a similar charge in Ruckinge, Kent; amongst those arrested was the local curate, Henry Cuffin, who was playing truant. In 1654, in Kent, players were fined for playing on a Sunday. Between 1550, when a match was played at Guildford school, and 1700, when a 'mini-Test' series was played on Clapham Common with a prize money of £600, there are some 60 references to the game of cricket. It is known that, around the time of the Civil War, the Royalists took up cricket as a pastime. After the war, Cromwell proscribed it throughout Ireland.

"But, as the years progressed, the clergy took a keen interest in cricket. Two chaps with names beginning with 'F' were influential. Frederick Farrar, a religious fool who later became Dean of Canterbury, and Frank Fisher, who later became Archbishop of Canterbury, wrote books relating cricket to religion, equating God with the 'one great scorer' and the 'straight bat' as a symbol second only to the cross.

The Venerable Archdeacon Alexander Colvin brought about the Somerset County Cricket Club. Reverend Gilbert Harrison invented the catching practice device, the 'cradle'. Reverend Walter Fellows struck a ball a record 175 yards. Reverend George William Gillingham, when the river Severn flooded the county ground, swam across the pitch to the pavilion and retrieved the account books. You won't catch me doing that! Father William Ignatius is the only cricketing monk to be mentioned in *Wisden*. Reverend Clement Eustace Macro Wilson mastered the art of bowling with either arm. Reverend John Charles Crawford once hit the stumps so hard as to send the bails flying a record distance of 51 yards, and, if the opposition were poor, he would offer to play left-handed. His father, Andrew Crawford, scored his only century in 1926 when celebrating his 100th birthday. His son, Vivian Frank Shergold, scored a century in 19 minutes against bowlers of the highest class. Another son, John Crawford, drove a ball through the amateur's dressing room, very nearly decapitating the secretary of Surrey Cricket Club, and a few days later made a hole in the mirror of the visitors' dressing room. So, some of the people of the cloth were pretty good at cricket."

"I still cannot believe that anyone can remember all these anecdotes with names, dates etc!"

"There was one scoundrel called Reverend Lord Frederick Beauclerk, vicar of St Albans. He was a violent, intolerant, short-tempered bigot. He was avaricious, a cheat and a gambler. He was instantly recognizable in white stockings, nankeen breeches, scarlet sash and white beaver hat, and he dominated cricket for 35 years. He didn't have an ounce of compassion or piety in him. He belittled and bullied and humiliated everyone whom he came across. He had to win by any means. Like W G, he was an autocrat with a short fuse and indulged in gamesmanship. As captain he was feared. Once, when he was bowling himself for too long, he was asked if it was time for a change, to which he answered, 'Certainly; I'll change ends.'

"He would hang his gold watch on the stumps and challenge the bowler to get him out. A phlegmatic country fellow called Tom Watkins once refused to get out to his bowling. Beauclerk ranted and raved to intimidate him. Walter remarked, 'I doan' care what ee zays,' and batted on."

"Good for him!"

"I'll tell you something else for your book...probably the first fatality in cricket. In 1686 a chap called Jasper Vinall was accidentally killed when the batsman tried to hit the ball twice to avoid being caught."

"What do you mean?"

"Oh yes. In those days, you could hit a ball and, if it was liable to be caught, you could run after it and clobber it again. You could even clobber the fielder with the bat or just throw him down!"

"Good God! Can you imagine that today?!"

"I'll tell you another story. In 1739 a crazy Croydon farmer bowled his way to London Bridge with 455 deliveries!"

" So there were crazy people even then."

"There have *always* been crazy people, mate. They make life interesting. I'll give you a ballad about the clergy."

I bowled three sanctified souls
With three consecutive balls!
What do I care if Blondin trod
Over Niagara Falls?
What do I care for the loon in the Pit
Or the gilded Earl in the stalls?
I bowled three curates once
With three consecutive balls!

I caused three Protestant 'ducks'
With three consecutive balls!
Poets may rave of lily girls
Dancing in marble halls!
What do I care for a bevy of yachts
Or a dozen or so of yawls?
I bowled three curates once
With three consecutive balls!

I bowled three cricketing priests
With three consecutive balls!
What if a critic pounds a book
What if an author squalls?
What do I care if sciatica comes
Elephantiasis calls?
I bowled three curates once
With three consecutive balls!

Cricket Songs, 1896

* * * * * * * *

CHAPTER 6
Hambledon Cricket Club; Timeless Cricket;
England versus South Africa

Village Cricket

*Young William on his village green was frolicsome and
free,*
To watch him bat the village came and sat in ecstasy,
*For fielders flinched and bowlers bold recoiled when he
appeared*
*And quivers of excitement ran through every ancient's
beard.*
Full many a gentle village maiden's heart went pit-a-pat
*With longing to walk out with him when he walked in to
bat.*
*He wore no pads, he took no guard, 'twas all the same to
him;*
*He swung a swift and valiant bat and smote the ball with
vim.*
*He smote it oft and hard and high, loud rose the village
yells*
To peals of ringing merriment from all the village belles.
*With last man in and two to win a slip claimed a doubtful
catch;*
*Their umpire took a chance and cried, "Out! And we
wins the match."*
*He spoke too soon; the scorer (ours) countered his little
tricks*
*And swore he'd only put down four for William's final
six.*
*So both sides claimed the match and went home happy,
which is rare.*
Some say it wasn't cricket, but the village doesn't care.

1939

"What is this about Hambledon being the birthplace of cricket?"

"Ah! Cricket was flourishing all over England well before Hambledon village came on the scene. The first printed evidence of the village is in 1776. But it was Hambledon Cricket Club that first *recorded* its matches. History always starts with written records of events. Those revered Hambledon score sheets were stored by a certain Stephen Leacock's mother's family, the Butlers, at Bury Lodge. They are as sacred to the cricketing fraternity as the Dead Sea Scrolls."

"Whilst the former are open to the public the latter are not."

"Hey, that's right! I wonder if the reason is what you have written. Suppose Jesus really had his groundings in India – can you see what that will do to Christianity?"

"It would totter, I suppose. But I can't see why it should. Jesus, whoever and whatever he may be, is still a remarkable man. Anyway, which Hambledon is this? There are three in England."

"Hambledon in the Hampshire hills, 12 miles from Portsmouth. It was in windswept Broadhalfpenny Down that the glorious game of cricket was played, by plebeians and patricians alike."

"Do you mean to say that cricket was played by the common people? I thought that it was a game of the upper classes."

"We are talking about the mid-18th century. Richard Nyren was captain of the local club; amongst his players was a certain Richard Purchase, the local blacksmith and the 4th Earl of Tankerville. In 1746, when Kent defeated the All England team by one run, Lord John Sackville played under the captaincy of his gardener!"

"Labourer, landowner, squire, farmer, butcher, curate, grocer, miner, lords and laymen – who was this Richard Nyren?"

"He learnt his game from a chap called Richard Newland of Slindon, West Sussex. Richard moved to Hambledon and established the game to the extent that in 1780 some 20,000 people thronged to see the matches."

"Much more than today's turnouts in England."

"Yes. It fielded the best side in the country. The ambition of the other clubs was to beat Hambledon. All England XIs regularly came to try to best Hambledon…in vain. By the end of the 18th century, the club's achievements had dwindled. Hambledon's fame is due to Richard Nyren's son John Nyren, 1764 – 1837, who preserved the memory of his father's great teams on paper. In 1833 he published *Young Cricketers' Tutor* with a postscript entitled 'Cricketers of my Time' – possibly the work of another character called Charles Cowden Clarke, who had a way with words. John Keats, eight years his junior, said of him, 'I learned from him all the sweets of song'."

"A great tribute, indeed."

"A few Hambledonians of note. John Small was a shoemaker/gamekeeper. It was he who abandoned the curved bat and invented the straight bat – which has become the English symbol of probity. William Fennex was the first batsman to step out of the crease and clout the ball. In 1790, Tom Walker was vilified when, one day, he decided to raise his arm to bowl; it was underarm bowling then.

"Let me finish with the Sackvilles of Knole. When the Duke was appointed as ambassador to the court of Louis XVI, he thought of introducing the game to the French by arranging the first overseas tour. But – alas! – it was 1789; the Bastille had fallen. He scuttled back to England in time to notify the team waiting at Dover that the game was off...due to circumstances beyond his control!"

"Beautiful story. What next?"

"Next we have a cup of coffee. Shirley."

"Coffee coming up," said Shirley. "So, how is it going, doc?"

"Great. John is saving me a lot of trouble and research."

"Where are my glasses?" asked John.

"On top of your head, you dope," said Shirley.

"Do you too like cricket, Shirley?" I asked.

"What? Isn't it enough to have one nut in the family? I like the one-day matches better. More interesting."

"But that is not real cricket, I keep telling her," said John. "If I had my way I would have Test Matches with no limitations. The four innings will go on till both the sides are out...till we get a result. No drawn matches due to rain or lack of time. That will show who has the endurance, the technique, the concentration, the true ability."

"I believe there was one such 'timeless cricket match' between England and South Africa some time back," I said.

"Yes, there was. I wish we could have them back. 1938-39 winter tour of South Africa. SA made 530, taking their own sweet time over three days. England replied equally slowly, with 316 over the fourth and fifth days. At the end of the sixth day SA made 481. Now England had to make a mere 696 runs to win. End of seventh day – 253 for one; next day was Sunday, no play. By this time the people of Europe were getting ready for another bloody confrontation and the ship *The Athlone Castle* had to sail from Cape Town back to England to be refitted for war duties. It would take the team three days to travel from Durban to Cape Town. So they had four days in which to complete the match. Ample time. Eighth day – rain. Ninth day – 496 for three. Tenth day – England passed 600 and the clouds opened. 42 runs were needed. But time, tide, rain and *The Athlone Castle* wait for no man. The two captains agreed to abandon the match as a draw. Do you know that Len Hutton made 364 in that match? Also a 16-year-old called Sheriff, from Melbourne, scored an incredible 1,004 in seven innings in the season without once being dismissed."

"What is more incredible is that you remember these figures. You pluck them out of the blue."

"To me they are interesting. Interesting because, in spite of it being a 'timeless match', we still could not produce a result...because of circumstances beyond anyone's control."

"They surely are. So, we would have three types of cricket. Five-day Test Matches, one-day matches and 'timeless matches'."

"Great, isn't it? Supposing we had a real World Cup, where all the sides had to play all three types of cricket."

"If we had one-day and 'timeless cricket', we would not need conventional five-day Test Matches," said Shirley.

"Yes, John, she is right."

"It would be tough on the players but the result would be fair. It would depend on fitness, concentration, ability."

"That's right. Just one-dayers and 'timeless matches'."

Shirley burst out laughing. "You are both crazy. You are talking as if you are in charge of world cricket," she said. "Finish your coffee, will you. If you two have nothing else to do, I have to do the washing and cooking."

"We would do a better job than the idiots in charge now, wouldn't we, doc?" said John.

"I'm sure we would."

"Call me when you come down to earth," said Shirley and went into the kitchen.

* * * * * * *

CHAPTER 7
Thomas Lord; The MCC; George Osbaldeston

"The scene now shifts to London," said John. "It is early in the 19th century. London was the first city in the entire history of humankind to have a population of one million. It stretched for four miles from east to west and two miles from north to south. Much of today's London was in Middlesex. It was the centre of the civilized world. We had great writers, painters, architects, inventors, entrepreneurs; we ruled the seas; we had an Empire covering most of the globe.

"Most of the patricians were either patrons or players of cricket. It is said that the Duke of Hamilton married his wife because he was smitten with her stroke making!"

"I didn't know that ladies played cricket in those times."

"Of course they did. When I spoke to you about the Graces, I mentioned that they made up ladies' and men's teams. Ladies up and down the country were playing cricket as it was the 'in' thing to do; it was an 'English' game."

"Yet, today, hardly any women play cricket...though it is a more genteel game than hockey, football or tennis."

"Ah. You need brains to play cricket."

"I heard that," said Shirley from the kitchen.

"You were meant to," said John. "Though the rich had their country seats, London was the centre of business; the centre of the universe. Business demanded their presence for extended periods of time in the city.

They needed a change from hunting down poor foxes, slaughtering pheasants and persecuting cocks, rats and dogs. What is more natural than to start cricket in the city! Thus did London become the new centre of the new national game. They were members of The Star and Garter Inn in Pall Mall. They used to drive along muddy St Marylebone to White Conduit Fields to indulge in their favourite pastime. The White Conduit was exclusive to 'gentlemen'; the rabble was not allowed to watch the gentlemen play in their frilly short waistcoats, top hats, breeches and buckled shoes. So the toffs proposed to purchase a piece of land away from the prying eyes of the commoners.

"Two people were instrumental in the establishment of the new premises. One was the Earl of Winchelsea, whose dedication to cricket never wavered even though he suffered large losses through bets on cricket, and the other was Charles Lennox, who later became the fourth Duke of Richmond. Charles was a right character. He fought personal duels with people who maligned his character; later he fought alongside Wellington against Napoleon at Waterloo; he was Governor General of British North America and Lord Lieutenant of Ireland. But all these posts did not deter him from playing cricket. In 1819, when visiting a military post in Canada, he was bitten by a fox and died a horrible death from hydrophobia.

"The attendant at White Conduit Fields was a certain Thomas Lord, 1775 – 1832, son of a Yorkshire Catholic yeoman farmer who had lost his property in the Jacobite rebellion of 1745 and suffered the indignity of having to work for a wage on his own land. Young

Thomas decided, early in life, to make his own mark. He worked hard to fulfil his ambitions. He was a moderate all-rounder, a real estate agent dealing in property all over London, and had a lucrative business supplying wines and spirits to the lords and ladies. He was one of the burghers of St John's Wood, claimed George IV as a 'friend', and was frequently seen in the company of royalty.

"To such a person did the Earl of Winchelsea entrust the job of finding a new home for his cricketing pals. Tom leased a tract of land, Dorset Square, from the Portman family and erected a large perimeter fence to keep out the riff-raff. In May 1787 the ground was baptized with a match between the Earl and his friends. Within weeks matches were being played for sums ranging from 100 to 1,000 guineas. In 1791 there was a match between 22 of Middlesex and 11 of Hambledon for 1,000 guineas that the former just managed to win. Such was the quality of Hambledon. By 1800 people were paying sixpence to watch matches. Lord's was different then. Lord staged foot races, hopping contests, balloon ascents, pigeon shooting, velocipede riding...anything to entertain the spectators and make the ground pay...he wouldn't have turned his nose up at one-day cricket.

"There is a story of the brother of George III who died of internal injuries having been struck by a cricket ball; but that did not deter the King and Queen from celebrating the marriage of their daughter with a cricket match – for which the winning team received a round of beef and a riband.

"Thus was the famous Marylebone Cricket Club established. It was the premier club in all England and rightfully assumed the responsibility for administering the laws of the game."

"So MCC started the snobbery which exists to this day?"

"You bet it did."

"How can one explain the paradox? In Hambledon they didn't mind playing with or even under the plebeians; but when they got back to London they didn't even wish their game to be witnessed by the working class."

"London is a funny place. It does things to you."

"Who were the members of the cricket club?"

"Bunch of toffs. They don't exist any more. They represented a type of Englishman that has become extinct. Times have changed. The difference between the classes has been blurred. Social security, media influence and daft policies have equalized people. The first members were people of independent means who did not have to work for a living – 'gentlemen'; they held positions in society and parliament; they saw themselves as dominant personalities and staunch patriots. But in reality most of them were uncouth, with little culture, and many were *arrivistes*. They indulged in 'sport'…slaughtering wildlife. Since they could not do this in London, they turned their attention to cricket. They were inveterate gamblers; they brought their vices into the cricket grounds."

"And Lord's cricket ground is named after this Thomas Lord?"

"Yes and no. The present cricket ground *is* named after Thomas Lord, but it is not the one about which we are talking now. London was becoming a gigantic conurbation; the price of property was escalating. The lease at Dorset Square was expiring. Portman upped the premium. Lord told him to get lost and moved; he rented from Samuel Eyre two fields, called Brick and Great, further to the north. When he moved he took the turf with him from Dorset Square. In 1812, Lord heard that the Grand Junction Canal from Paddington Basin that formed the northern boundary of Regent's Park would cut through his cricket field. He pocketed a £4,000 compensation, rolled up the turf again and plonked it on farmland close to Punker's Barn. This was to become the permanent home of MCC. But there were problems. A duck pond close to the field would cause drainage problems for generations. An accidental explosion in a pub close by marred the auspicious opening ceremony.

"Did you know that the grass was not mowed at Lord's in those days? On Saturdays four or five hundred sheep were driven onto the ground on their way to Smithfield Market; they did a marvellous job. Though the mowing machine was invented in 1850 it was not used at Lord's. For the first time a heavy roller was used in 1870. In 1872 somebody thought up the idea of covering the pitch with a tarpaulin on rainy days.

"In 1825 Lord was thinking of selling part of the land to build houses. Alarmed members approached William Ward, a banker-cricketer who bought the grounds for £5,000. Ward was elected a director of the Bank of England at the age of 30, and by 1826 was Tory

Member of Parliament for the city of London. His 278 at Lord's was not bettered until 1925. Disaster struck immediately in the form of a fire that completely gutted the clubhouse, taking with it the irreplaceable records and trophies. In 1835, Ward transferred the lease for £2,000 and an annuity of £425 to James Henry Dark, who made many splendid renovations."

"Quite a yarn. I thought that Lord's was named after some lord or other."

"A common presumption... Have you heard of George Osbaldeston?"

"No."

"Well – he was a character. George was born in 1777. He was one of those self-appointed leaders of the community who made Lord's his private club. He probably qualifies as one of the great 19th-century sportsmen. He was a brilliant rider to hounds and participated in every classic race of the season, beat the French and Italian real tennis champions, was a formidable pugilist (taking on opponents 4 stones heavier than himself), was a crack shot with the rifle and once slaughtered 90 pheasants in 100 shots, and he once won a wager for 1,000 guineas to ride 200 miles in ten hours – a feat he achieved by the stratagem of changing horses every four miles; he did it in less than 9 hours. He refereed the Caunt-Bendigo heavyweight championship match in 1845, rode 50 miles to deliver a choice bloom to a lady at a ball, rescued a drowning boy and renounced a seat in parliament, stating that it was not according to his tastes. He fought a duel with Disraeli's friend, Lord George Bentinck, who fired and missed, whereupon George fired into the ground in chivalry.

When he was 66 years old, he played billiards for 72 hours and in his 80th year, just before he died, he won a bet for a sovereign by sitting without moving for a whole day. But his passion was cricket. He was one of the fastest bowlers and the hardest hitters of the ball of his time."

"Today's sportsmen pale in comparison."

* * * * * * * *

CHAPTER 8
Homerton Cricket Club; Kent Cricket Club

"A third cricket club has to be mentioned when talking about the history of cricket," said John, "Homerton Club, just north of London, came into prominence as Hambledon was waning. It attracted a lot of good players who don't mean anything to anyone now: Sir Henry Martin, F Ladbroke. But when telling a story one has to mention the wine merchant Benjamin Aislabie, later to become the first secretary of MCC. He weighed 20 stone and had to have a runner while batting and fielding. Another Homertonian was Lord Frederick Beauclerk, grandson of Charles II...whom I mentioned before. Though he was a rotter, he was a fine all-rounder; he smacked eight centuries at Lord's and took 66 wickets in 1797 – a record that lasted 34 years."

"There were some colourful characters around then."

"You bet there were. The only one of recent times was Ian Botham," said John. "If you know your history, you will know that between 1790 and 1820 England indulged in a bit of fisticuffs with Spain and France. So the sound of leather against willow was overshadowed by the sound of cannon. But not completely so. The warriors formed the Garrison Cricket Club in 1816."

"No wonder that the Duke of Wellington ascribed his victories to the 'playing fields of Eton'."

"Oh, you know about Wellington."

"Of course I do. We were taught English history in school. Well before he became famous at Waterloo he fought against Tipu Sultan of Mysore, who was given French troops by Napoleon. And it was he who told the notorious Harriet Wilson, 'Publish and be damned,' when she wrote her memoirs exposing Regency charades."

"I am not very well up on political history, doc. I'm sure they were up to all sorts of shenanigans. Thomas Arnold, the headmaster of Rugby School, invented 'gentlemanly conduct' and placed it higher than knowledge or ability. Other public schools imitated him. By the end of the century 'the gentleman's kit' had evolved – gentlemanly etiquette, accent, morality, religion and games. But it was the Clarendon commission that really got sport going in the schools. Lord Palmerston appointed the commission in 1861 to investigate why the great public schools were turning out imbeciles. The commission proposed, amongst other things, that team games be made an intrinsic part of education. It thought that gentlemanly behaviour and proficiency at games would somehow automatically lead to better diplomats, administrators and soldiers. This daft correlation of the playing field and the battlefield was tragically exposed during World War I, when thousands of public school graduates at the head of rustics rushed over the top to ignominious deaths. It also proved that playing the game had nothing to do with good administration or diplomacy."

"So, good old Wellington got it wrong!"

"A curious tale to Eton, though. The headmaster, Dr Heath, in 1803 flogged his team for playing cricket!"

* * * * * * * *

"Kent, the fourth club that came into prominence around the 1830s, owes its renaissance to three players." continued John, "The inimitable Alfred Mynn, who stood at nearly 20 stone – brilliant batsman, slip fielder and perhaps the fastest bowler of his time, despite his bulk. Once, when this colossus was asked how many balls there should be to an over, he replied, '100'. He was a humourous, generous, gentle sportsman; he died in 1861.

"W J Prowse wrote a verse to Mynn in *Bell's Life:*

With his tall and stately presence, with his nobly moulded form,
His broad hand was ever open, his brave heart was ever warm,
All were proud of him, all loved him. As the changing seasons pass,
As our champion lies a-sleeping underneath the Kentish grass,
Proudly, sadly, we will name him – to forget him were a sin –
Lightly lie the turf upon thee, kind and manly Alfred Mynn.

"I wonder how many of today's cricketers would inspire such warmth?" I mused.

"Mynn's team-mate was Fuller Pitch, who invented the forward lunge to convert every fast delivery into a half-volley. After his cricketing days were over, he set up as a tailor, went bankrupt and died in 1870.

"Nicholas Wanostrocht was a Flemish emigrant who found himself suddenly as headmaster at Camberwell when his father and uncle both died. He played under the pseudonym of Felix and, as the name would suggest, he was one of those lovable clowns on and off the field. Once, when he floored a catch off Mynn's bowling, he rolled himself into a ball on the ground whereupon Mynn strode up, caught him by the scruff of his neck and lifted him off the ground with one hand. Unfortunately Felix suffered a stroke early in life and had to give up the game. But this was when he became famous. He designed the first tubular batting gloves and the mechanical bowling machine, the Catapulta, and wrote the first thorough book on cricket, called *Felix on the Bat*, with illustrations by an old pupil of his school, George Frederick Watts. Felix then became a cricket reporter for *Bailey's* magazine."

* * * * * * * *

CHAPTER 9
William Clarke; John Wisden

"What do you know about railways?"asked John.

"Railways?" I was a bit thrown.

"Yes, railways. Steam locomotives."

"Well...I know that the very first steam locomotive was made by a Frenchie called Nicholas Cugnot in 1770 for use on roads. The railway line was, of course, in operation in the coal mines, the trolleys being pulled by mules or little horses. And steam engines were used to pump water from the mines. A Cornishman, Richard Trevithick, built the first locomotive to haul a ten-ton load in the Welsh mines.

"In 1769 James Watt patented his high-pressure steam engine. But it was George Stephenson who was the 'father of the railway'. In 1825 he designed *The Locomotion* between Stockton and Darlington and *The Rocket* between Liverpool and Manchester. Queen Victoria showed her approval by travelling in a train."

"Just imagine it," said John; "no one in the entire history of humankind had ever travelled faster than a horse until then. No one had even dreamt of anything else. And suddenly there were 'iron horses'."

"*The Rocket* puffed along at a leisurely pace of 24 mph. In 20 years trains were travelling at 70 mph. Now they go at a fantastic 250 k.p.h. We would like to assume that, once the railway was invented, all other modes of transport were made redundant. Not so. The equestrian lobby fought on for another 100 years. Lord Palmerston was the last Prime Minister to arrive on horseback in the 1860s. The last London-to-Brighton

Royal Mail was in 1905. The London fire brigade used horses until 1911. Horse-drawn coaches plied around London until 1916."

"In 1902 the Australian tourists travelled to Birmingham by coach and horses... Now – why are we on about railways and horses?"

"I heard about the 'Travelling XI' who called themselves the All England XI. I suppose this was possible only because of the facility of efficient public transport."

"That's right. Every period calls for a man to make his mark. Now it was the turn of one William Clarke, a Nottingham bricklayer...his father was one too. He was born in 1798 and, though he played for his county from his teens, he was 50 when he was called to Lord's and employed as a practice bowler. He lost his eye playing squash. He was shrewd. When everyone had switched to round-arm bowling, he reverted to underarm. This must have befuddled the players. I mention Clarke because he was the first to do his homework on the opposition. He knew exactly how to bowl and how to place his field for each member of the opposition. 'Without headwork, I should be hit out of the field,' he said. Once, he asked a batsman if he was Harrow and, on it being confirmed, he said, 'Then we shan't want a man down there.' He once dismissed Felix for nought. In 1846 Clarke made his master stroke. He organized a troupe of travelling professionals called the All England XI, of which he was manager and captain, and toured the country playing local sides. He and Lillywhite once took all 20 wickets against Sheffield."

"That's something!"

"It is more than something when I tell you that these chaps played against sides of 20 or 22 because they were too good for the local amateurs. Imagine batting against 22 fielders! Between 1847 and 1853, Clarke took 2,385 wickets – 340 per season. There's a little story about one of Clarke's players. He was about to be arrested for non-payment of a debt of £12. He asked the creditor to come to the ground on the morning of the match. Alarmed at the prospect of losing a star player at such short notice, the other players passed a hat and raised the money and paid off his debt!

"Clarke was an arrogant taskmaster and pocketed the profits. In 1852 his gladiators rebelled and formed the United England XI. The leaders of this splinter group were two Sussex men, Jemmy Dean and one John Wisden. The All England XI v United England XI matches were the rage of the day, with attendances of nearly 10,000. A little titbit for your book. In 1854 crusty old Clarke brought his side to Bristol to play West Gloucestershire on the Downs of Durdham. W G Grace, aged six, was a spectator. The following year, Clarke returned and was so impressed with the batting of W G's elder brother, E M Grace, that he presented Grace's mother with a copy of his book."

"Didn't the ginger-haired, mutton-chop-whiskered George Parr, known as 'the lion of the north', take over from Clarke?"

"Yes – fancy you knowing that! Parr was a powerful and fearless hitter of the ball, especially on the leg side. A branch from George Parr's tree at Trent Bridge, where he hit most of his shots, was placed on his grave at Radcliffe-on-Trent when he died in 1891."

$$* \quad * \quad * \quad * \quad * \quad * \quad * \quad *$$

The next day.

"What shall we talk of today?" asked John.

"You were going to tell me about John Wisden," I replied.

"Oh yes – John Wisden. He was a character. Wisden was one of William Clarke's men who broke away to form the United England XI. He was born in Brighton on the 5th of September 1826, but he played for the Northerners because he acquired some property in Leamington. He was only 5 foot 4 inches and weighed 7 stone, earning him the sobriquet 'the little wonder'.

"He was a bowler. He took all ten wickets in an innings – all clean bowled – at Lord's in 1850. He once bowled unchanged through two innings at Lord's, took six wickets in six balls on the 1859 American tour, and in the 1851 season took 455 wickets. By the time he retired he had taken 1,300 wickets. He was also a reasonably good batsman and once scored a century for Sussex against Kent.

"But his real fame was to come *after* retirement. He was an entrepreneur and a wit. When he was crossing the rolling waters of the Atlantic, he remarked, 'What this pitch needs is ten minutes of the heavy roller!' In 1855 he and Fred Lillywhite opened up a cricketing and cigar business in New Coventry Street, Leicester Square, London. It didn't do too well. In 1864 he created a landmark in journalism by bringing out the *Cricketer's Almanack*. The first edition was 112 pages and was poor in quality, information and circulation. He panicked and padded his editions with all sorts of nonsense – equestrian results, University Boat Race results, the rules of bowls, quoits, the length of the British canals, dates of principal battles, foundation dates of antiquarian, astronomical, horticultural societies etc. By 1866 he had learnt his lessons. He published full scores of the previous season's matches. In 1867 he introduced 'Births and Deaths of Cricketers'. In 1870 came the first match reports; in 1872, match records. The *Almanack* was established as *the* cricketing manual. John died in 1884. In 1887 his bible included the full list of batting and bowling averages of the past season and the full fixture list of the next. In 1888 came photographic illustrations; 1892, obituary notices. 1899, averages computed to the modern two decimal places. In 1900 it included more than 500 pages of editorial text."

"John Wisden's *Cricketer's Almanack* bestows authenticity on achievements, giving them a sort of immortality. Now cricket is a circus, commercialism taking its toll," I said.

"You think commercialization of cricket is a thing of the present? You have to see everything from the social point of view, doc. In the late 19th century, the period we have been talking of all this time, Britain was making unprecedented history. It was the beacon of the world; it set the standards for others to follow. As much as 70 percent of all commodities in the world market were British. The new education bill fostered literacy. The nouveaux riches were always looking for ways to augment their coffers. Cricket was the 'in thing'. Sporting journals grew from 14 in the 1860s to 87 in the 1890s. The power of the written word created the accoutrements of commercialism. Staffordshire figures,

Doulton jugs, ceramics, presentation plates, bronze busts, silverware, glass bottles, cigarette cards, pub signs, beer mats, matchbox labels, belt buckles, coat buttons, gentlemen's ties, cartoons, children's games, oil paintings, lithographs, sculptures, woodcuts, spirits, soaps, photography with action shots, coloured drawings, club logos; anything and everything to do with the cricketing motif was exploited by the shrewd businessman.

"Once you have all this paraphernalia, the path is laid for 'collectors'. Reverend R S Holmes, a Yorkshireman, was a legendary collector of cricketing artefacts. A Charles Pratt Green had in his possession 151 cricket bats of all the leading batsmen until 1914."

"They would be worth a fortune now."

"You bet they would. So, you see, all this sponsorship that is going on now is nothing new. People who say that this sort of nonsense did not exist in the old times are talking poppycock."

"We are still in the 19th century. Were there any more colourful characters around beside the Grace family, Wisden and others?"

"There were many. The trouble with today is that there are not enough colourful players around. There are good players creating records but we do not know anything about them as people...with possibly the exception of Ian Botham, but even he belongs to the past now. Talking about the Graces, Martha's sister had a son called Walter Raleigh Gilbert who played alongside the famous Graces. W G would place him at long on to catch the poor blighters off his bowling. Once Gilbert played the ball into his shirt-front and started running endlessly between the wickets. The bewildered opposing captain appealed to the umpires, who at last realized what had happened and ordered Gilbert to stop running and accorded him six runs. Suddenly, in 1886, no mention is made of Gilbert by anyone; the Graces had disowned him. He appears on the scene many years later in Canada. What happened?

"It is the 5th of June 1886, East Gloucestershire versus the Stroud XI. Gilbert walks into the pavilion at Cheltenham. No one there. He sees all the coats hung up. He rifles the pockets. But someone sees him. And that was the end of the poor idiot."

"Was there much of match rigging in those days, John?"

"You bet there was. Lord's was the watering hole for gamblers and all sorts of skullduggery went on in the taverns across the country. There was talk of deceitful players throwing a match. William Ward, who made the first 200 in 1820, said that one of the ways to keep a player from playing was to tell him that his wife had died! William Lambert was accused of fixing a match to keep the hucksters happy and was involved in an argument at Lord's. The outcome was that he was banned forever from Lord's."

* * * * * * * *

CHAPTER 10
Interlude – Dinner with the Landrums

"Have you finished for the day then, gentlemen?" asked Shirley.

"I would like to go on and on," I said; "John is incredible. But I have to go back to my room and listen to all this again, make notes and type it into the computer."

"It has been a long time since anyone has grilled John. So he is liking it too," said Shirley.

"Keeps my brain ticking," said John.

"Doc," said Shirley, "do you mind if I asked you for the health book you have written?"

"Not at all. I have it on a floppy. So you will have to get a printout like the other one."

"Connie will manage that. By the way, you haven't met our Connie. If you are not doing anything tonight, why don't you join us for dinner?"

"That will be splendid...but the problem is that I cannot eat early. I know that the English eat between 5:30 and 7:00 p.m. I eat after 8:00 p.m. I don't want to put you to any trouble."

"Nonsense. Sometimes Connie doesn't get back from school after her meetings till half past eight. We always wait for her. So it will be alright. Shall we say 8:00 p.m. then?"

"Yes, thank you."

* * * * * * * *

I had put all the information into the computer by 7:30 p.m. I had a hot shower and went to John's.

"Hello there!"

"Hello, doc.   This is our granddaughter, Constance."

"Connie, if you don't mind," said Connie and extended her hand.   "I have heard so much about you…from my daughter and this lot."

"Just believe the bad bits."

"Dad hasn't stopped speaking about *Interview with Jesus*. I haven't had time to read it."

"Ah…you are a schoolteacher! So, you are busy putting all sorts of things into peoples' heads…and then you have teacher meetings, parent-teacher meetings, teacher-pupil meetings. But how can you stand it? It would drive me crazy."

"It drives me crazy sometimes. I keep telling myself that I am going to give it up, but then something nice happens in school and I say to myself that maybe it is all worth it."

"What sort of nice things?"

"Oh. Some of the children turn out to be really good…at studies and as people. And some parents appreciate the work we do and become friends."

"From guarded scepticism to satisfying trust."

"That's it."

"I told you that he has a way with words," said John.

"After all, I am a writer. We have to be a bit flowery now and then…if only to impress the odd schoolteacher," I said.

"But you are a doctor and a hotelier too," said Connie.

"Never mind that.   I brought a bottle of Jamieson's. Anyone willing to share it with me?"

"We will all share it," said Connie.

"I hope I am not delaying dinner." I said. "This is the health floppy for you, Shirley, and a bouquet for you, Connie."

"Thank you very much. Lovely flowers," said Connie.

So we settled down and chit-chatted.

I haven't described Connie to you. She was in her mid-forties, 5 foot 4, auburn hair, brown eyes, slight snub nose, cute lips, dimpled cheeks, flawless skin, compact and smart. On the 'attraction scale', I would say about eight.

"I bet your students don't do too well," I said.

"What do you mean?" said Connie.

"Too much distraction."

"Pardon?"

"You are a bit glamorous for a school ma'am," I said. "What age group do you teach?"

"14- to 16-year-olds."

"Whew! I bet one or two make eyes at you!"

"'Make eyes at you!' You sound positively archaic."

"Never mind paying each other compliments... Connie, could you put this through the printer, please," said Shirley.

Connie disappeared for a few minutes.

"Doc," continued Shirley, "you know that Connie lost her husband a few years back...cancer of the bowel. She hasn't recovered fully yet. She used to be a lively

84

girl – still is, but not as before. She decided to come and live with us. We were glad of that."

"You must count yourself lucky. There are too many people banished in nursing homes in this country. You two are very fit, but still it is nice to have someone around," I said.

"Last year, John had an angina attack. We would have been devastated if Connie had not been with us."

"What about her parents – your daughter and son-in-law?"

"They don't get on. You see, Connie married Colin against her parents' wishes. Since then they have not spoken to each other."

"Sounds a bit like Indian society. What happened?"

"We are Protestant. Colin was Catholic."

"Colin was a good lad," said John. "He had a nice and secure job – British Rail – and he was very good to Connie and us. We didn't mind his being Catholic. We have always treated people as people. But, unfortunately, my daughter and her husband – he is to blame really, he is a religious bigot – were very stubborn."

"What about now...when Connie is alone?"

"They tried to make up. But Connie told them in no uncertain terms where they should go."

"She seems to be happy here. Clare comes up now and then. But sometimes we wish that she would find someone nice."

"I'm sure she will." I said. "Do you think she is afraid to leave you?"

"We have told her a thousand times that she should live her own life and not worry about us. We can always manage. If we can't, there is always the nursing home. After all, we have paid our taxes all our lives. Why shouldn't we get something back?"

Connie returned.

"Have they been telling you about me?"

"Yes."

"What?"

"I'm sorry, Connie. It is none of my business."

"Make it your business. After all, they have confided in you."

"Well…it boils down to happiness. If you are happy doing what you are doing – for whatever reason – fine. But if you are sacrificing your life for the sake of some ideal – sense of duty or obligation – to anyone, your grandparents or late husband…which means that you are not 100 percent happy – then you are a fool."

"You took the words out of my mouth, doc," said John.

"He doesn't mince his words, does he?" said Connie. "Let's say I am happy for now. I am not a complete fool."

"Good," I said.

"What about you?" asked Connie. "Have you a family?"

"No family. I was married once…for a whole year. Didn't work out."

"Why haven't you married again?"

"Well. 'Once bitten, twice shy', as the saying goes."

We had a lovely dinner. Roast chicken, roast potatoes, boiled peas and cauliflower with mint sauce and gravy, followed by apple pie.

"Do you like Indian food?" I asked.

"I like it," said Connie, "but these two are not too keen."

"You don't like spicy food?" I asked.

"We don't mind the spices; it is the chilli we don't like," said Shirley.

"I am a good cook. If you wish I can cook you an Indian meal without the chillies...if you will let me use your kitchen."

"That would be nice," said Shirley.

I shook hands with John, kissed Shirley and Connie, and returned to 'The Victorian Guest House'.

* * * * * * *

CHAPTER 11
Australia; Thomas Wills; William Midwinter

"Now, let us go out of England for a bit," said John. "Let us travel to Australia, for it has something to do with English cricket. What do you know about it?"

"About what?"

"About Australia."

"The 19th of April 1770. A Yorkshire sea captain, James Cook, takes his frigate *Endeavour* on to the Great Barrier Reef, sights the south-east coast of Australia, docks at Botany Bay and claims the continent for Great Britain. Time was running out for the Brits in America. In a few years you would lose it. A new dumping ground had to be found for criminals and a new mercantile base had to be found to command the eastern seas. By 1786 you decided to colonize Australia. The great Industrial Revolution was rearing its head and bringing in its wake the spectre of crime. The country's jails were overcrowded. The 'bad'uns' had to be got rid off – no point trying to rehabilitate them as they were just 'born wrong.' So, a brisk transfer of felons and petty and hardened criminals got under way. By 1830 more than 50,000 convicted criminals had been dumped onto the new continent; 8,000 of whom were women and girls. All of them were cheap labour, 'employed' by the government to build homes, bridges, roads etc., and many were sold as 'slaves' to the private sector – ordinary non-criminal folk who had left Britain in search of adventure and fortune. Initially there were no pardons; a criminal was a criminal for life. Later 'pardon' was introduced, inventing the 'ticket-of-leave' men (or women) who were employed as field or house hands. In 1850, when inexorable contingents of criminals had swelled the population to 150,000, the export of Britain's bounders ceased."

"I don't know how you remember all this daft history!" said John.

"Same as how you remember anything to do with cricket."

"Hardly had the Brits arrived in Australia than they started to play cricket," said John. *"The Sydney Gazette,* noted for its journalistic prolixity, dated the 8th of January 1804 reports a game of cricket between two amateur teams that was held despite the intense heat. A generation later, Sydney had a gentlemen's cricketers' club and hosted games in Hyde Park."

"How did they organize themselves so quickly in an alien, desolate and hot land?"

"Let us follow the fortunes of a family. 1799; Mr Edward Spencer Wills, being a younger son of a wealthy English county family, resenting the rule of primogeniture, decided to seek his fortune in Australia far from the constraints of the society in which he had been born. He set up as a merchant in Sydney. But he could not cope; he died in 1811, aged only 32, leaving behind a widow and six children. The shrewd lady promptly married the editor of *The Sydney Gazette,* George Howe – known for his sesquipedalian propensities. This must have driven poor 15-year-old Horatio mad, as he ran away to sea and got embroiled in adventures like the fabled Sindbad. After being marooned on an island and being rescued by a princess – so he says – he returned to the bosom of his family, who had given up the prodigal son for dead, and was given a job in the publishing house. 21-year-old Horatio married Elizabeth Wyre, begot a son (Thomas, with whom we have business), and in 1835 disdainfully scattered the local inhabitants out of his way and settled in Victoria with 5,000 sheep and 500 head of cattle."

"For 'disdainfully scattered' read 'massacred'?"

"Exactly."

"Horatio must have had the aplomb of the perfect pioneer, confident in his rights as a white Christian and perhaps thanking God that he had been given a chance at clearing the land of rabble."

"You are probably right. We – or they – thought that they were right to wipe out anyone who dared to stand in the way of the progress of the British Empire. Coming back to the story: Thomas was sent to Rugby School in 1852, where he flunked his exams but became captain of both cricket and rugby football. After a stint at Cambridge, he returned home in 1856 and, finding the standard of physical fitness below Rugby standards, invented the game of Australian Rules football and pioneered the game of cricket."

"In 1851 Australia went mad," I said. "Gold was discovered at Clunes, Arrendyte and Ballarat. It became a focus of international interest. Overnight there was an exodus. Everyone left their families and businesses and headed for the world's richest surface goldfields."

"That's right. Within a short time Horatio found himself without any help, all having departed to fill their pockets. The aborigines had their revenge. They swooped down and massacred the entire party. Tommy escaped only because he was away from home collecting stores.   The whites retaliated, killing three times the number of aborigines.   In 1864 Tommy returned to Victoria when sanity once again prevailed.   The administrators of Australian cricket thought it would be a good idea to teach the aborigines a less warlike occupation.   Tommy took over as coach.   In 1868 the Aborigine cricket team toured England."

"It certainly says a lot about Tommy's character."

"Yes…seeing that the first white tour of England was in 1878.   Tommy was the first fluent all-rounder in Australian cricket and had a good throwing arm from the deep, was elected secretary of Melbourne Cricket Club, played his last game in 1869 and died in 1880 in a mental asylum.   He died of softening of the brain; in one of his fits he stabbed himself with a pair of scissors."

"What a story!"

"I'll tell you another one.   Once upon a time, in the village of St Briavels, Forest of Dean, England, there lived a labourer called William John Midwinter and his wife Rebecca.   On the 19th of July 1853 Rebecca gave birth to a son, whom they christened William Evans Midwinter.   One day the father found himself without work and moved to Cirencester in the vain hope of finding employment.   Alas, there was none.   Then he heard about the gold rush in Australia.   Frustrated and desperate, he took the plunge and set off for Australia in 1861, hoping to strike it rich.   Alas again! He did not find any gold.   Poor William settled in a small town called Sandhurst and became the proprietor of a butcher's shop.   It was fortuitous, for it was here that young Billy made friends with a lad called Harry Boyle. The two boys practised cricket assiduously and quickly blossomed into fine players representing the Melbourne district.

"It is Boxing Day 1873. The great W G Grace was on his honeymoon tour. The tourists' first match was against Eighteen of Melbourne. Billy was out for seven...not a distinguished beginning. Three months later was the return match. Billy clean bowled W G. W G was impressed. He got talking and found out that Billy had been born in Gloucestershire, like the Graces. He looked at Billy – who stood at 6 foot 2 inches, weighed 14 stone and was recognized as the best quarter-miler in the state, a good shot and a skilled billiards player – and told him that, if he ever wished to play in England, he would be welcome to play alongside him for Gloucestershire.

"W G didn't know what...or whom...he was taking on! In 1876 Billy played for Australia against England. In 1877 Billy arrived in England and played for Gloucestershire. In 1878 the Australian tourists arrived at Liverpool, from where they went by train to Nottingham. A huge crowd awaited them. On seeing them, a burly blacksmith exclaimed, 'Well, I'm damned! They aren't black after all. If I had knowed, I wou'na come.' Another onlooker, on seeing the swarthy, bearded Australian captain, exclaimed, 'Ah, 'ere's one's a 'arf-caste any'ow!'"

"The citizens of Britain apparently did not have any idea of the citizens of their Empire. I suppose they were expecting a kind of freak show."

"I suppose they were. Let's come back to Billy. When the Australians landed, he was a contracted Gloucestershire professional. But Conway, the

Australian manager, claimed him for his side...as our Billy had told him that he would play for Australia! The 20th of June 1878. Gloucestershire's first fixture of the season at Kennington Oval. Also, Australia was to play MCC at Lord's. W G took it for granted that Billy was with his team at the Oval. Conway picked Billy. Billy was at Lord's, padded up and ready to do battle. In his pocket were two sets of fees – one from Gloucestershire, the other from Australia. The susurrus of the crowd was now and then accentuated by roars of cheering or disapproval.

"Meanwhile, away to the south-east, W G discovered that he was one player short – Mr William Midwinter! W G knew exactly where to find him. He mustered a raiding party consisting of himself, his brother Edward Mills and his wicketkeeper Arthur Bush, jumped into a cab, raced to Lord's, dashed into the dressing room, apprehended Billy and took off for Kennington Oval. The Australian management, upon recovering from shock at witnessing one of their players being abducted by a 20-stone bearded giant and company, hailed a cab and...must have said to the petrified driver, 'Follow that cab!' in true Hollywood fashion. We shall not go into the nature of the speeches made between the two parties at the Oval. Suffice it to say that, after a prolonged epistolary campaign, W G had to make a magisterial apology to Billy and the Australians."

"What a story! Sounds like something out of a comic book."

"The story doesn't end there. Despite everything, Billy continued to play for Gloucestershire. By 1880 the

Gloucestershire committee, realizing his value after a successful English season, attempted to pin him down by offering him £100. Billy turned it down with cool sarcasm. He sailed for Australia in the *SS Lusitania*, made some prudent mining investments, got rich and metamorphosed into a 'gentleman'.

"In April 1881 he sailed back to England in the same boat and played for Gloucestershire for the season. The same year, 1881, the England selectors took Billy to Australia where he played four matches – for England against Australia, much to the chagrin of the latter. After the Test series he returned to England and represented Gloucestershire for the 1882 season, ending his association with W G with a match against the Australian tourists. When these tourists sailed home, Billy went with them, officiating en route as an umpire in the matches they played in America! Billy then went on to represent Australia against England six times between 1882 and 1886! During this period, when he played against his old team-mates at Cheltenham and at Clifton there was no tomfoolery; he played as an Australian for Australia.

"Thus, by criss-crossing the seas, he managed to play six cricket seasons between 1880 and 1882. In 1883 he married and retired from cricket. And then Fate caught up with him. In 1888 his ten-month-old daughter died of pneumonia; in 1889 his wife died of apoplexy; three months later his three-year-old son died. In 1889 poor Billy lost his mind and was admitted to Kew Asylum in Melbourne. He died on the 3rd of December 1890.

"Haygarth wrote one of the saddest epitaphs to a cricketer: 'May the death of no other cricketer who has taken part in great matches be like his.'

"It is a terrific story! Midwinter bent the rules to suit himself. During the course of his turbulent life he must have faced the wrath of a great number of people – fellow cricketers, the press, patriots, administrators and selection committees. He was the Artful Dodger of cricket, who had no sentiment or loyalty. He was perhaps the precursor of some of the dodgy things that happen today – England recruiting the likes of Alan Lamb, Graham Hick and Basil d'Oliveira. And maybe he was the first to realize that, if one was prepared to be footloose, one could hop from one part of the world to another and live an entire life in summers playing cricket... As is being done today."

* * * * * * * *

CHAPTER 12
Exporting Cricket

"Can you tell us when cricket was introduced into the colonies, John?"

"I can't remember the dates. But I have them written down somewhere. Let me forage."

John foraged and found the information.

"I must read to you the opinion of a wag in *Punch* about foreign cricketers," said John.

> *The game is essentially English and, though our countrymen carry it abroad wherever they go, it is difficult to inoculate or knock it into the foreigner. The Italians are too fat for cricket; the French too thin; the Dutch too dumpy; the Belgians too bilious; the Flemish too flatulent; the East Indians too peppery; the Laplanders too bow-legged; the Swiss too sentimental; the Greeks too lazy; the Egyptians too long in the neck and the Germans too short in the wind.*

We had a good laugh.

"I have various dates here. No one can be sure when cricket was actually introduced in these countries. Some of the dates may record when a match was documented or when a cricket club was first started or when a foreign tour graced their shores.

"Let's start with India.

"1721 – cricket was played by the seamen of the East India Company at Cambay, India.

"1797 – the British military played at Bombay and Seringapatam.

"1848 – Parsees form Orient Club in Bombay.

"1864 – match between Madras and Calcutta.

"1886 – Parsee tour of England.

"1911 – All India side under Maharaja of Patiala tour England.

"1932 – first three-day Test at Lord's under C K Nayudu.

"1750s – Ireland.

"1850s – Scotland and Wales.

"1736 – Lisbon.

"1751 – New York, Maryland, Connecticut, Boston, New England, Georgia. I wonder how it didn't catch on in America? Bloody barbarians, anyway!

"But I later found evidence that cricket was not only played in Philadelphia regularly right till the Wall Street crash but that there were *two* monthly cricket journals in the city; one of them, the *American Cricketer*, was probably the best cricket magazine of any time. The leading clubs of Philadelphia played in exquisite surroundings in front of some 20,000 spectators a game. Domestic cricket was highly organized...though they were still experimenting with eight- or ten-ball overs when England was bowling five. Perhaps it was from the Americans that the Australians adopted their eight-ball over. One great Philadelphian player is mentioned, one John Barton King, who headed the English bowling averages in 1908: around 10.05 – a figure not to be excelled for another 50 years – and he set up a North American record for batting, too.

"Between 1896 and 1914 Haverford College toured England five times to play other schools and clubs – many years before any English school toured America. Three Philadelphian clubs toured England. Kent had Ranji when it toured America. The Americans also toured Bermuda and Jamaica and Australia.

"How did the game die there? The amateur could not be sustained indefinitely by the leisured and the wealthy. Wall Street collapsed. The magnificent American clubs were turned into tennis or country clubs. And there was very little junior cricket; the players of the 1890s played on for 20 years, after which no one remained to take over."

"It is too leisurely a game for the Americans," I said. "They do not have the patience to follow a game over five days. They would rather be making money – which they seem to be doing in an unholy frenzy. Before we leave America, didn't George Parr take an All England XI in 1859?"

"Yes and no. Six were from Clarke's All England XI and six were from Wisden's United England XI. Besides these 12, there were 11 more. They played to 10,000 people in New York and more in Philadelphia. They won all the matches and returned to England with a nice profit of £90 per player. The second visit to America was in 1868. The captain was Edgar Willsher, who was no-balled five times for bowling over the regulation shoulder height, threw down the ball in disgust and left the Oval, then appeared the next day to continue to bowl in the same manner, but after the umpire was sacked! His side drew against the 22 of Canada and beat the 22 of the United States. The third tour was in 1872 and it had a 24-year-old W G Grace as the star batsman."

"Were there any great American cricketers? With their blatant nationalism and staunch belief that anything is possible, I sometimes think that they would be world champions if they launched themselves into the game."

"You may be right. I have often wondered why they look down upon cricket when they play baseball, which is somewhat similar to it. Probably because it is not played over five days, as you mentioned earlier. Let me tell you something about American cricket – a subject not many know of. They toured England five times between 1895 and 1908. They played the various counties and various touring sides, including the Australians. They had many good players but the king amongst them was undoubtedly John Barton King. He was from the true-blood town of Philadelphia and was born on the 19th of October 1873. Like most Americans, he played baseball in his childhood. At the age of 15 he was 6 feet tall and still growing and played for the Tioga side for the Halifax Cup, the cricket championship of Philadelphia. He started off as a batsman but was tried as a bowler because of his height. In his first year he took 37 wickets at an average of 2.40 with his medium pacers. A few seasons later, he developed into a genuine fast bowler. He could deliver 'the hook' in baseball, a ball that would travel straight and fast for most of the way and then towards the end of its journey would swerve viciously. If only he could do that with the legitimate cricket bowling action… King worked at it until he mastered both the out- and in-swinger and could bowl them at will. Not many bowlers can do that – far less *explain* how they swung the ball. But, in doing so, King had the most awkward and terrifying bowling action, charging up to the bowling crease like a demented giant windmill and releasing the ball over his left shoulder. He plundered wickets against Canada, Ireland and the visiting Australians, against whom he also scored a goodly number of runs. Let us come to the 1897 tour of England. The Philadelphians against Sussex at Brighton. The tourists made 216, largely due to a 109 stand between King and Lester. Sussex to bat. All out in less than an hour for 46. John Barton King, ten overs, five maidens, seven for 13. More importantly he had clean bowled not only the great Ranji first ball, but Murdoch and Vine too. Sussex followed on. This time, Ranji scored 74, and King had to admit that he didn't have the answers. Sussex made 252 and the Philadelphians won by eight wickets. But it wasn't all success. When they played Gloucestershire at Bristol, King was up against W G Grace and Jessop and ended up with figures of two for 100 in a total of 363. I'll tell you about the Americans' sportsmanship. In a game against Somerset at Bath the pitch was dangerous and the tourists took King off – an act that gained applause and friendship throughout England. By the end of the tour, King had taken 72 wickets at an average of 24.02. Many English counties approached King offering what were then known as 'cricket clerkships' that guaranteed money outside the game. King refused. One county desperately offered him a rich widow worth £7,000 a year to marry; King politely declined. During the 1901 England tour of Philadelphia, King took 23 wickets in four innings at 10.30. In 1903, he took 78 wickets at 16.06. Between 1904 and 1908 he won the Batting Cup three times and the Bowling Cup four times; he was blossoming into an all-rounder.

"Now we come to the most famous episode in John Barton King's career. He was playing for Belmont Club against Trenton at Elmwood in the Halifax Cup. The Trenton captain missed his train and, when he arrived at the field, found himself going in at number 11 and his team in dire straits. He apologized to the Belmont captain for his unpunctuality and also muttered, 'If only I had been here on time, we would not have been in such a mess.' King overheard the mutterings.

"There was a famous baseball pitcher called Rube Waddell around at the time who would dismiss all the catchers to show that he could dismiss the striker without any help. King called his fellow men together and persuaded them to leave the field. King walked up to his starting point and turned around. He saw the wicketkeeper behind the stumps. 'Why, Eddie,' he called, 'what are you doing there?' The wicketkeeper left the field.

"By this time, of course, the Trenton captain was turning into a mass of jelly. He appealed to the umpires. After a huddle, the umpires told him that the law demanded that the fielding side should not comprise more than 11; there was no law, however, to prevent the fielding side from deploying fewer than that number. King smiled and went back to his starting point. He twirled the ball in his hands and leaned forward into his run. Abruptly he stopped and gestured to the pavilion that he wanted one fielder. King caught the volunteer by the hand and led him with elaborate courtesy to a point some 20 yards behind the wicket and four paces to the leg. The Trenton captain blurted out, 'What do you want him for?' King answered, 'He is there to pick up the bails.'

"By this time, of course, the batsman was jelly. King roared up and bowled a stinging in-swinger. The bails landed at the feet of the single fielder, who picked them up, walked up to the umpire and handed them to him."

"Is that true?"

"Who knows… But it is a great story."

"That it is."

"Let's get back on track. 1785 – Montreal.

"1766 – Paris.

"1768 – Austria.

"1790 – Rome.

"1811 – Naples.

"1860 – Denmark.

"1855 – Netherlands.

"Before the 1917 revolution – Russia played cricket. Nicholas II liked it.

"1803 – 1808 – Australia, South Africa, West Indies.

"The first English team to Australia in 1861 was sponsored by Spiers & Pond and captained by Ned Stephenson. They won six and lost two matches out of 12, all against odds. They returned to Australia in 1863, won all their matches against odds. E M Grace was in the side. W G Grace led a side to Australia in 1873-74. We now come to the first recognized Test Match."

"Melbourne, 1877. Australia won by 45 runs. The centenary Test in 1977 was again won by Australia by the same margin."

"Correct. Who was captain of England in 1877?

"James Lillywhite. He was promoter, manager, captain."

"Correct…"

"Before we leave Australia, were there any Aborigine cricketers, John?"

"There were. There was a chap called Lawrence in the 1860s who played for Middlesex and Surrey. He went to Australia with Stephenson's team and stayed on to coach Albert Club in Sydney. Four gentlemen of Sydney sponsored Lawrence's aboriginal team tour of England. They belonged to a now extinct tribe called the Werrumbrook somewhere in Victoria and were supposed to be related to the Maoris of New Zealand. There's a picture of them at Lord's Museum. Big, black, bearded, wiry, bare-footed, armed with boomerangs and spears. When they arrived after what must have a terrifying sea voyage for them in a tub called the *Paramatla* they had no fixtures. The MCC courteously offered them the hallowed grounds of Lord's. Thereafter all the counties invited them – though I suspect that it was more for the novelty factor rather than their cricket. The first game, however, was at the Oval against Surrey Club. Surrey won by an innings but the crowd was mesmerized after the game by a stirring display of boomerang-throwing. Mullagh, the best tourist batsman, was presented with a golden sovereign. One titbit for your book. After the ceremony, a young fellow called W G Grace participated in the cricket-ball-throwing exhibition and threw 116, 117 and 118 yards. After this the visitors were taken to witness the Derby at Epsom, where I am not sure if they placed any wagers... They played 47 matches, won 14, lost 14 and drew 19."

"Pretty good, I would say. I wonder if India would have fared better..."

"Very creditable if you consider the travelling they had to do, criss-crossing a cold and windy country in horse carriages over potholed roads. One of them, King Cole, died – probably of pneunomia. Johnny Mullagh made 1,670 runs and took 250 wickets. Johnny Cuzens made 1,000 runs and took 100 wickets. He was a terrific sprinter. A race was organized between him and an Englishman. Cuzens was slow off the mark and fumbled but then he kicked off his cumbersome shoes and swept past the opposition. Then there was a Jimmy Mosquito, who was wizard with a whip. He could whip a shilling off your outstretched hand without you feeling it."

"I don't know how you remember these things!"

"Big brains, my lad; just simple big brains..."

"Point taken and accepted, John... Can you tell me something interesting about South Africa?"

"Yes. The whites had their South African Cricket Association. In 1950 the Coloured, Indian and Black cricket boards amalgamated into the South African Cricket Board of Control. They applied to the ICC for full membership but the SACA blocked it. 1951, Dadabhai Trophy Tournament, but no whites participated. 1956, the SACBOC captained by Basil d'Oliveira played their first Test Match against the touring Kenyans. The coloured South Africans won the series 2-0. In 1958, they toured East Africa. The South Africans demolished Kenya and East Africa."

"I know something about the East Africans, John. They were an able side and had played against the Pakistan Cricket Writers' Club that included the great Hanif Mohammed and against the Indian Sunder Cricket Club that included many famous names – Mustaq Ali, Vinoo Mankad and Jesu Patel – and against Freddie Brown's MCC featuring Mike Smith."

"Back home, things were worsening. 1960, Sharpeville massacre. 1961, severance of Common - wealth ties."

"It all started in 1902 with the Treaty of Vereeniging after the Boer War. Britain turned a blind eye to racism then. And in 1910 the Blacks were removed from the Common Voters' Roll. By cutting relations with the rest of the world in 1961 the white South Africans thought they could now get on with their apartheid policies without external pressure. The plan backfired and the world boycotted them."

"The 1960s saw the exodus of sportsmen to the West: Albert Johanneson, the Leeds United winger; Green Vigo, the rugby player; Cecil Abrahams, whose son captained Lancashire; and, of course, Basil d'Oliveira."

"Tell me about d'Oliveira, John," I said.

"He was a good right-handed batsman and could bowl both medium pace and off spin. He left South Africa at the age of 25 and played for Lancashire and Worcestershire. He made his debut for England in the second Test at Lord's against the West Indies and played his last one in the fifth Test against Australia in 1972. He was *Wisden* 'Cricketer of the Year' in 1967.

"Statistics – 44 matches, 2,484 runs at an average of 40.06. Highest score: 158. He took 47 wickets at 39.55. He also had good first-class figures. 18,918 runs at 39.57 and 548 wickets at 27.41. For some reason that has not been satisfactorily explained, he was left out of the squad to tour South Africa in 1968-69. He was tagged on only when Cartwright dropped out. The South African government objected and that was that. For 25 years no one played cricket with them."

"Any other South Africans of note?"

"There was a family of four brothers, the most famous of whom was Suleiman 'Dik' Abed, who was recommended by d'Oliveira to the Lancashire Club, Enfield. In 1967, in the company of such stars as Clive Lloyd and Charlie Griffith, Dik scalped 70 wickets at 13.23 and made 358 runs at 21.99. The following year Dik took 120 wickets and belted 600 runs and Enfield walked away with the title. But, for reasons unknown, Dik just faded. In 1970 he returned to South Africa as a press reporter to cover the Springboks' Test against Australia. He was herded into the non-white stand. The fourth Test was the last the Springboks would play in a long, long time. In 1971 he married Janny, a white Dutch girl, and was exiled from his country. He continued to play for Enfield until 1976, when he retired with a tally of 969 wickets and 5,528 runs. He moved to Holland with Janny and managed a sports complex and became a cricket coach."

"1832 – first cricket club in Sri Lanka.

"1842 – first cricket match in New Zealand.

"In the last two countries cricket was played well before clubs and matches were installed.

"1840 – Hong Kong.

"1893 – a cricket match between China and Japan! Can you ever believe that?

"1837 – Singapore.

"1890 – Thailand.

"1851 – Egypt, Alexandria Club.

"1951 – an Egyptian side played the MCC at Lord's. The actor Omar Sharif was one of the players. There's one for your book.

"1966 – it took the Israelis this long to organize themselves to form cricket clubs.

"In the Fiji islands the natives played in calf-length skirts. Here is another bit of trivia for you. The cricketer with the longest name ever – Talebulamaineiilikenamainavelaniveivakabulaimainakul alakebalau."

We simply laughed for a good five minutes.

"What is happening? Have you both gone mad?" asked Shirley, coming in from the back garden.

"Oh, Shirley, you must see this. Can you pronounce this cricketer's name?" I said.

"Ta..le..bula…main…e.i..i..liken..a..main… I give up." And she started laughing as well.

When sanity prevailed again, John told us about him.

"He was called 'Bula'. It means 'greetings' and 'life'. The rest of his name tells his family history. Something about a forefather recovering from some wretched illness…returning from the dead, marrying and begetting eight children. Well, Bula was the finest batsman to emerge from the 300-odd Fijian islands. He was born in a thatched hut in 1922 and was coached by Tuinaceva and Cakobau; that gave him the happy admixture of orthodoxy and unorthodoxy. He was often compared with the greats – Sutcliffe, Hammond, Constantine and Crompton – for his elegance and power. If he had been born in England he would have been an automatic choice and would have overshadowed the others. But in his country he had a limited role. He was kept as a secret weapon to be unleashed on the opposition in times of dire need. He was often sent in late to clock up the required runs in double quick time – 60 runs in 15 minutes. New Zealand thought of drafting him into their side. It was technically feasible for Fiji players to be eligible to play for the nearest country, New Zealand, which was 1,000 miles away – but I don't think the local New Zealanders would have liked that. One of Bula's greatest innings was against Canterbury captained by Hadlee. He scored 63 with four sixes and six fours in the first innings. Fiji had to make a formidable 354 runs to win the match. Bula came in at seven for two. He made 120 and brought Fiji within a whisker of a win; they lost by 36 runs. Soon after the match he came out of the pavilion and sang his native songs to his adoring fans. At first he used to sign his full name for autograph-hunters. He soon realized that it was an impossible task and shortened it to 'I L Bula'. In spite of his achievements, he was a shy and simple man. After matches, he would return to the pavilion and relieve the twelfth man of making the South Seas drink called yaqona. It was ceremoniously offered first to the princes – who, incidentally, were descendants of the cannibal king Cakobou and who now played cricket – and then to the rest of players and visitors to the soft clapping of hands. He was a true hero – self-effacing, humble. He fell to pieces after the unfortunate accidental death of his brother, Waqabaca, at sea and ended up as a clerk in the Native Lands Commission."

* * * * * * * *

I asked the Landrums when they would like to try an Indian meal. They said that the next day would be fine – Connie did not have any after-school meetings. We said our goodbyes.

I went to Halford's supermarket. Unfortunately, they did not stock the spices I needed. There were no Asians in the village. I had to go to Hartington town.

I returned to my room and finished my homework on the portable computer.

Exhausted, I slept like the proverbial log.

* * * * * * * *

CHAPTER 13
Interlude – 19th-century History

Now that we know what transpired in the world of cricket, let us look at what was happening in the world at large.

Politics

The British were expanding their territories all over the world, threatening, frightening, cajoling, blackmailing and slaughtering.

The Americans were acquiring tracts of land as big as continents by buying, blackmailing and slaughtering.

Whilst the British were fighting in Europe, Asia and Africa, the Americans were fighting with each other, the Spanish, the French, the Blacks and the American Indians, depriving all of certain fundamental rights.

Besides all that the two peoples of Britain and America found time to fight each other.

The 49th parallel was established between America and Canada in 1818.

In 1834, Spain officially ended its heinous Inquisition, and Lincoln entered politics.

In 1836, Davy Crockett was killed at the Alamo and Texas became a republic, with General Samuel Houston as its first President.

In 1837 Victoria came to the throne in Britain, whilst, across the Atlantic, Chief Sitting Bull was born.

Events moved rapidly in the 1860s in America. Lincoln was elected President in 1860, and the next year the Civil War broke out; 1863 saw Lincoln's 'Gettysburg

Address'; 1865, Lincoln was assassinated and the senseless Civil War ended.

In 1869 Neville Chamberlain and a certain Mohandas Karamchand Gandhi were born, little knowing that they would meet at a momentous time in their respective nations' history at a later date. Victoria was crowned Empress of India in 1877.

Mussolini was born in 1883, Hitler in 1889.

1857 – the Great Indian Mutiny.

The first Indian National Congress was inaugurated in 1886.

The personalities of the century were Napoleon, the Duke of Wellington, Disraeli, Queen Victoria, Bismarck, Garibaldi and Abraham Lincoln.

Whilst all sorts of unpleasantness was happening all over the world, one would justifiably wonder how anyone had time to do anything else. Yet great and beautiful things were happening; human efforts that cannot be bettered by anyone at any time by any stretch of the imagination.

Literature

I shall mention only those authors with whom you may be familiar. That will suffice to emphasize my statement that the 19th century gave us priceless gifts.

Hans Christian Anderson; the brothers Grimm; Alexander Dumas; Chateaubriand; Alexis de Tocqueville; Guy de Maupassant; Emile Zola; Edmond Rostand; Romain Rolland; Victor Hugo; Goethe; Pushkin; Dostoyevsky; Anton Chekhov. Leo Tolstoy; Sir Walter Scott; Elizabeth Barrett Browning; Robert Browning; Lord Byron; H W Longfellow; William

Wordsworth; Shelley; Keats; Lord Tennyson; Jane Austen; Charlotte and Emily Brontë; Elizabeth Gaskill; Thackeray; Charles Dickens; R L Stevenson; Ibsen; Hawthorne; Ruskin; Trollope; Coleridge; Eliot; Thomas Hardy; Jules Verne; H G Wells; Anthony Hope; Lewis Carroll; Charles Kingsley; G B Shaw; Oscar Wilde; Arthur Conan Doyle; Wilkie Collins; William Morris; Samuel Butler; Rudyard Kipling; John Galsworthy; Jack London; Disraeli; Lew Wallace; Rider Haggard; Mark Twain; Louisa Mary Alcott; Thoreau; Poe; Harriet Beecher Stowe; James Fennimore Cooper; Herman Melville; Oliver Wendell Holmes.

The list goes on and on. Their works are classics enshrined for all time for all peoples everywhere.

How many such stalwarts has the 20th century produced? I can only think of Somerset Maugham.

Music
The music of the Gods was composed in the 19th century.

Beethoven; Chopin; Schumann; Schubert; Liszt; Verdi; Wagner; Weber; Johann Strauss; Berlioz; Brahms; Dvořák; Mahler; Rachmaninov; Offenbach; Tchaikovsky; Elgar; Bellini; Rossini; Paganini; Puccini; Gilbert and Sullivan.

Visual Art
Turner; Constable; Nash; Morse; Waterhouse; Goya; Gauguin; Vincent van Gogh; Rousseau; Delacroix; Rosetti; Renoir; Monet; Manet; Millet; Cezanne; Degas; Gustave Dore; Pissarro; Toulouse-Lautrec.

Most, if not every one, of the composers and artists had terrible lives steeped in impecuniosity, prejudice, physical and mental illness. Yet they were blessed by the Gods.

Today, the rich are speculating with the lifeblood of these artists.

Science and Technology
Almost everything we use or need or luxuriate in or take for granted has been invented or discovered or explained by stalwarts in the 19th century. To enumerate them all would be a stupendous task.

* * * * * * * *

CHAPTER 14
20th Century; Ranji; Bosanquet; Rhodes; Jessop

At the turn of the century England was upbeat. It was master of a lot of real estate all over the world. It strode forth with imperial pride and lorded it over the natives of the acquired countries, convinced of its divine destiny.

There is a Freudian interpretation to the export of cricket by the English. Undoubtedly one of the more obvious reasons was that the Englishman wished to recreate part of his English life in the lands he conquered. As soon as he unfurled the Union Jack, he also set about unfurling a piece of turf on which to play his dear cricket. It was an escape from the mundane efforts of administration that carried him, a solitary figure, to far-flung and inhospitable areas of the Empire; it was an oasis where people of his own kind could congregate, chit-chat, get inebriated and participate in team games. Cricket was a sort of safety valve that helped them retain their sanity.

But under that veneer the Victorians equated cricket with Christianity. Somewhere along the line the Christians had confused virtue with abstinence; sexual sublimation was therefore called for. One of ways to curb unbridled passion was thought to be through physical effort. After the Indian Mutiny of 1857, the sergeant majors screamed, "Sweat the sex out of you," and threw cricket balls and footballs at each other in the heat of the Indian plains. They somehow bludgeoned their logic with the false syllogism: Christianity means chastity; cricket is chaste; therefore cricket is synonymous with Christianity. Thus 'playing the game' acquired some deeper, almost mystical significance.

Today even the barbarous Americans know that cricket stands for probity; 'this is cricket' means that it is righteous.

The English also instituted the norm that 'the Umpire is always right'. The umpire's word is law; there is no appeal; umpire is God. This dotty law was carried to the outposts of the Empire and evolved into another syllogism: 'the white man is the umpire; the umpire is right; therefore the white man is right'.

Today, as we become more familiar with 'actual' history, we have to come to know that this creed was 'for export only'. They were only expected to administer the code, not live by it. You see, it wasn't really necessary for the Englishman to behave like a gentleman because he already was one! It was only necessary for the natives to behave like gentlemen.

* * * * * * * *

"Well, John," said I; "now, what have you got to tell me about our own era of cricket?"

"We must start the 20th century with the prince and the scholar Ranjitsinghji, even though he played cricket in England during the last decade of the 19th. What do you know about him?" asked John.

"Well… He was born in September 1872 in the province of Kathiawad. There are two theories as to his antecedents. He was a Rajput aristocrat, but not of royal blood, merely adopted by the Jam Bibhaji of Nawanagar, who was heir to the throne. He was the illegitimate son of the Jam Bibhaji, who had access to other bedchambers

115

besides the royal one. Whatever the case may be, Ranji found himself to be an embarrassment to the Jam thanks to the intrigues of the royal household and the inhabitants of the seraglio, and his rights of succession were abruptly abrogated. What is to be done with poor Ranji, asked the Jam. Pack him off to England, came the answer.

"But we are skipping over events. Ranji was sent to a preparatory school, the Rajkumar College, run on the conventions of its English counterpart. The college had a pavilion donated by the Maharaja of Bhownagar and a cricket pitch. It was here that Ranji came under the influence of a Cambridge graduate, Chester Macnaughton, an expatriate pedagogue with a passion for cricket. Ranji participated in house matches. His counterparts in England, adorned in chromatic striped blazers and tasselled caps, would have laughed, for Ranji played in native costume. They would have dismissed him as just another brown-skinned native trying to imitate his betters.

"He arrived in England in 1888, attended a London crammer course and went on to Trinity. He soon found that he could not play cricket for the establishment; so he changed his name to the highly innovative 'Smith' and played for the Cassandra Club on Parker's Piece, a plebeian plain, performing feats with the bat the likes of which the locals had not witnessed."

"You take it from there John."

"He was in love with an Englishwoman, you know."

"I didn't know," I said.

"Well, she was the daughter of the Reverend Louis Borissow, the chaplain of Trinity College, Cambridge. It had to be a clandestine affair as anything else would have been a scandal."

"And it would have put a stop to his ambition of becoming an Indian ruler."

"Yes, I suppose it would have put the stoppers on that. Anyway, let us get back to cricket. The captain of the Cambridge team was F S Jackson. One afternoon he strolled along to Parker's Piece and saw a brown boy going down on his knees to play the hook shot – a rare spectacle indeed. But, of course, he didn't pick Ranji for his side; after all, he was a native! It was not until 1893 that he was picked to play against Oxford at Lord's. In 1895 he represented Sussex. In 1896, he played his first Test Match against Australia, when he scored 62 and 154 not out. He was in the England side that toured Australia in 1897-98, when he made a century in his first overseas Test. In 1899 and 1900 he blasted more than 3,000 runs per season. In 1901 he made 265 not out against Somerset. He was captain of Sussex from 1899 to 1903; in 1904 he topped the national batting averages. Then he went back to India when the chances of his succession seemed better. The old Jam died in 1907 and bejewelled Ranji, riding on an elephant, was crowned Jam Sahib of Nawanagar.

"In his acceptance speech he said, 'I shall endeavour to play the game so as not to lose whatever credit I have gained in another field.' What better proof is there of a cricketing man?"

"Therein lay his humility and greatness."

"Yes. He returned to England in 1912 on political business to struggle for the rights of his native state...but still played his game. He scored over 1,000 runs, including a dazzling 176 against Lancashire in such brilliant style that the London evening press informed its eager inhabitants, who had never forgotten him. At the end of the season he was given a banquet at Cambridge. He left again for India. Four seasons later he was back and played for Sussex.

"During the Great War he served on the Western Front. While on leave he lost his left eye in a shooting accident. In 1920, he batted at number eight, scored a single, was out lbw, and retired from cricket."

"James Joyce, an ardent follower of cricket, loved Ranji and incorporated his character in his novel *Finnegan's Wake*. So did John Masters in *The Ravi Lancers*; Krishna Ram is a patent imitation of Ranji. J B Priestley was another one who admired Ranji. But tell me about Fry."

"I was wondering if you had heard about Fry. When Ranji played for Cambridge against Oxford at Lord's in 1893, Charles Burgess Fry was a member of the opposition. He was one handsome fellow; looked like an actor, with a profile like Basil Rathbone or John Barrymore. He was the most glamorous all-rounder around, captained Oxford at both football and cricket, scored six successive centuries for Sussex, never lost a test as England's captain, and held the world long jump record of 23 feet 6½ inches for 21 years. He was the most graceful dancer on the floor and a fine horseman. In later years he took up journalism and wrote a couple of novels.

"He and Ranji became great friends. When Ranji was crowned prince and attended the assemblies of the League of Nations in Geneva, Fry was his sort of secretary/briefer. Ranji was a great success at Geneva and was elected chairman of one of the committees. Everyone, including the Japanese, knew both Ranji and Fry; such was their fame as cricketers. Among the less important at these diplomatic jamborees was little Albania. It was ruled by the Germans. After World War I, Albania found itself kingless. The head of the Albanian delegation was a bishop who decided that the best thing for his country would be to get an Englishman to govern it at a salary of £10,000 a year. Ranji pushed Fry as a candidate, and indeed he was seriously considered, but for some reason the entire thing petered out. In spite of all his erudition, Fry was a naive duffer. He was all praise for Hitler and his discipline in the 1930s. So it was just as well that he did not become King of Albania."

"A Hollywood titbit, if I may. David O Selznick was filming *The Prisoner of Zenda* with Smith and Colman. Fry and his captain of the tour, G O Allen, were invited to the studio sets."

"Ranji, despite his achievements, suffered from the effects of crass racism," continued John. "His contemporaries laughed at him when he landed in England. He had to adopt an acceptable pseudonym to play cricket. It took nearly four years for him to represent Cambridge. F S Jackson, who finally selected Ranji to play against Oxford, went on to become governor of Bengal and then confessed to the blatant racism inflicted by his fellow countrymen on the Indians.

Lord Harris, one time under-secretary of state for India and governor of Bombay and later president at Lord's, objected to Ranji representing England because of colour prejudice – though he put it about that his objection was because of Ranji being born in India. Yet Harris captained England in 1878-79 even though *he* was born in Trinidad.

"In 1906 Ranji, now renowned and respected by fellow players and the public, was given a farewell dinner by his friends at the Cambridge Guildhall. Lord Hawke declined the invitation, saying that he had prior engagements in Scotland. Lord Curzon of Kedleston, described by the *Oxford History of England* as 'one of nature's rats', also declined to attend – stating that he would be visiting Scotland! Others who made similar fictitious excuses were the Vice-Chancellor of the University, the Master of Trinity and Mr Buckmaster, MP.

"Sir Home Gordon testified later that, 'there was so much prejudice against a nigger showing us how to play cricket,' and was himself accused of his 'disgusting degeneracy to praise a dirty black'. Ranji was unmoved by all this loutishness; he simply smiled and got on with the game."

"Let me fill in," said I. "Clement Scott of *The Daily Telegraph* watched the Parsees defeat Lord Hawke's touring side in Bombay. He noted that the Parsee captain, a Cambridge graduate, was not allowed to break bread with the Englishmen in the cricket field and could not enter an English club. One wealthy Parsee had built and furnished an English club and donated it to the conquerors, but he was not allowed to enter its grounds. Scott ends his report with emotion, saying, 'We have India, we have Anglicized India; let us live with India.'"

"Ranji would have admitted to a wry smile at the sentiment," said John. "Whilst we are on the subject of racial prejudice, let me mention Ranji's nephew K S Duleepsinghji. England selected him for the first Test against South Africa in 1929. The South Africans objected. Duleep was not picked again for any of England's matches against SA. The South Africans refused to pick any black players...including T Hendricks, who was an outstanding black cricketer. Basil d'Oliveira was born in South Africa and he was coloured. He was playing for Worcestershire when he was selected in 1968 to tour South Africa. The SA Prime Minister, a devious beggar, accused England of bringing politics into cricket...when it was he was doing so. After weeks of agonizing the tour was called off, and SA has been treated liked a pariah...until recently when they came – at least halfway – to their senses."

"Note that, whilst Ranji and Hendricks were snubbed by their own people, Duleep and d'Oliveira were objected to by the opponents."

* * * * * * * *

"Who invented spin bowling?" asked John.

"Bosanquet, was it?"

"That's right. He too spilled over into the 20th century ...like Ranji. Bernard James Tindall Bosanquet – B J T for short – spent his time playing cards, billiards or cricket. He represented Eton, Oxford, Middlesex and England. B J T was initially a fast bowler and a hard-hitting batsman, once slamming 120 in 120 minutes. But B J T disliked the hard work involved in fast bowling. He was thinking of ways of making bowling easier. He started bouncing tennis balls off a table after giving them a bit of spin. He found that his opponent at the other side of the table could not catch his balls as he could not predict the turn. He started to practise with the cricket ball. How do you spin the ball?"

"Well, if the bowler places his fingers across the seam and turns his wrist from right to left at the time of release, the ball will spin in an anti-clockwise direction and move away from the batsman...the leg spin. The reverse is off spin when the ball rotates clockwise and moves into the batsman. Which is why the batsman has to read the bowler's arm and watch the seam."

"Correct. B J T called his invention the 'Twisti-Twosti'. He continued to experiment for three years, increasing his control and consistency. July 1900: Lord's: Middlesex versus Leicestershire. Left-handed Samuel Coe was on 98. B J T came in and, for the first time in a match, decided to try out the Twisti-Twosti. The ball went into a lazy arc, landed halfway down the pitch and spluttered towards Coe, who – completely befuddled – stepped out to belt it, missed it and was ignominiously stumped.

"B J T had stumbled onto something. He worked on this new ball by dropping the wrist and delaying the release of the ball; though the wrist action was that of a leg-break the ball would spin in a diametrically opposed direction...in other words, the googly. Then he went on to control the ball a bit more and produced a straight

delivery even though the wrist action signalled a spin –
the topspinner.

"Now, this is where the comedy comes in. After
getting batsmen out with his freak delivery, he would act
as if he were himself baffled by it all! He would go up to
the bewildered batsman, tap him on the shoulder and tell
him that it was just a lucky accident of which he was
completely innocent."

"It was almost a pantomime."

"You bet it was. He baited the trap and caught
his rabbits. He would bowl two conventional leg-breaks.
Then he would bowl the googly and uproot the stumps.
In 1904, at the Oval, a chap called Dick Lilley boasted
that he could read every one of B J T's balls. His team
mates laid a bet. When Dick came on, B J T bowled a
googly and pretended that it was a total mystery to him.
Dick is now expecting another freak ball. B J T bowls a
conventional leg-break; Dick executes a glance to fine-
leg…and finds that his off-stump has been mysteriously
knocked over.

"Unfortunately, B J T came in for a lot of stick
from both players and the media. They accused him of
slowing down the game, befuddling the batsmen, who
could not plunge forward, make their strokes and
entertain the crowd. He wondered what all the fuss was
about, for – after all – it was ordinary spin produced by
an extraordinary action. B J T played his last match in
1908 and died in 1936, when his invention became part
of the repertoire of every spin bowler."

"India had and still has some of the best
spinners."

"Oh, yes. Gupte, the quartet of Bedi-Chandra-Prasanna-Venkat. And now Kumble and Harbhajan Singh. But let me tell you about two other cricketers who set the grounds on fire in those early days of the 20th century.

"One was the Yorkshireman Wilfred Rhodes, the only bowler in history to take 4,187 wickets and score nearly 40,000 runs. He played against W G Grace, Trumper, Ranji, Hobbs and Bradman. I'll tell you a story. Lord's – Gentlemen versus Players. Haigh, a Yorkshire player, asked W G permission to leave early to get back home. W G assented. During the match, Rhodes bowled to W G, who hit the ball to Haigh. It would have been an easy catch. The good doctor shouted, 'Take the catch and you miss the train.' Haigh missed the catch but caught the train.

"Rhodes was recalled in 1926 at the age of 48 to rescue England against the walloping they were suffering at the hands of the Australians. He responded with figures of four for 44 on the final day at the Oval, clinching the rubber.

"At the end of his days, when he was coach, he said, 'Tha knows one thing I learned about cricket; tha can't put in what God left out. Tha sees two kind of cricketers – them that uses a bat as if they are shovelling muck and them that plays proper – and, like as not, God showed both of them how to play.'

"The other was Gilbert Jessop, who had amongst his admirers W G Grace himself. Jessop was called 'The Croucher' because of his eccentric stance and was one of the fastest scorers. Let me clarify. Bradman and Compton scored at 47 runs per hour, Ranji at 50, Duleep

(Ranji's nephew) at 52, Maurice Tate at 60; Jessop at an unprecedented 79 runs per hour.

"Neville Cardus, the cricket writer, was a schoolboy in 1899 when he attended a match at Old Trafford. He says that he went to buy himself a bottle of ginger beer when there was a terrible noise and a crash of broken bottles everywhere. He thought that the end of the world had come. A man at the bar soothed his fears by saying, 'It's all reight, sonny – it's only Jessop just coom in to bat.'

"Jessop was also a great fielder. He once finished a match and came to see W G playing at another venue. Just then the ball went over the boundary. And before any fielder could get to it, it came out of the crowd, fast and low like a bolt of lightning, thudding straight into the wicketkeeper's gloves, upon which W G exclaimed to the astonished people on the ground that Jessop must have finished his match early!"

* * * * * * * *

CHAPTER 15
Interlude – Indian Cooking; Unusual Cricket Facts

I went to my room, had a couple of sandwiches and coffee, and boarded the bus to Hartington, some 20 miles north of Melbridge. As I travelled, I thought to myself, how easy, decent and civilized travel is here compared to India. No pulling and pushing. But then these people do not have our population. Take this bus. It has only four passengers. In India it would have about a 100 clinging on. They have to push and pull and scramble to get seats if they do not wish to travel hanging out of the doors and windows. I looked around. No stray animals. In India we would have dogs, cats, buffaloes, donkeys, pigs, even camels and elephants on the roads. Here all animals are domesticated. There they are wild. But surely we can sterilize or put to kind sleep our stray, unowned animals? No people easing themselves beside the roads. Here they have social security. India doesn't. Here people earn decent wages. There they don't. The priority there is food for survival, and then perhaps a metal roof over a little mud-walled room, not building toilets. If we were in their position would we build fancy toilets? No dirty people here. But would they be clean if they had to walk a mile to fetch water? The environment is clean. Yes, we in India could be made to be civic-minded. If Singapore can fine people for littering the place, why cannot India? Surely it would be a deterrent. Courtesy here. No courtesy there – in public or private life. Surely that doesn't need a law or money? No it doesn't. It just needs realization of the importance of etiquette. Why do we lack it? Well... On the other hand, when the Indian ventures abroad, he does not splash secretions, excretions and litter in public, refrains from arrogance and rodomontade, observes traffic rules meticulously, patiently joins queues, desists from bribing officials, is eager to fulfil his obligations courteously and generally deports himself rather decently. So, do rules, laws and environment influence people?

* * * * * * * *

On the main street I found several Indian shops. I stepped into one, took a wire basket and walked down the aisles. Cumin powder, coriander powder, chilli powder, ginger, garlic, desiccated coconut, packet of poppadoms, a couple of limes, a packet of naan bread, a kilo of rice, half a kilo of red dhal, a dozen vegetable samosas, a carton of thick-set yogurt and a small tray of coloured Indian sweets. I returned to Melbridge and bought 12 chicken drumsticks and four slices of filleted trout. I went to the Landrums.

"Hello, there! I've got some goodies," I said.

"Well, well. Indian food, eh!" said John.

"Chicken and fish. I'll need some potatoes, tomatoes, onions," I said.

"We have those," said Shirley. "What would you like me to do?"

"First we fill a saucepan with water and heat it up. While it is heating we wash the potatoes, cut them into inch bits and plop them in. Do you like your potatoes with or without skin?"

"With skin," said Shirley.

"So do I...besides, it is healthier. All the vitamins and fibre are in the skin; the rest is just starch.

While I'm dealing with the potatoes, Shirley, could you chop up the onions? Tinned tomatoes are better. Have you got some tinned tomatoes? Good. If you have another knife I will chop up the ginger and garlic. Now, it is going to smell a bit. Let's put that exhaust fan on and open the windows."

"Connie likes Indian food. Why don't you teach me how to do some Indian cooking?" said Shirley.

"Fine. The only way to learn is to do it. It's quite easy, really. You see, the difference between Indian and English cooking is that the former involves a lot of preliminary preparation. That's what gives it the aroma and taste. That's why Indian food is the most popular foreign cuisine in Britain, and the Brits do like Indian food because there are more Indian restaurants here than all of Europe. Indians rarely go to Indian restaurants because they are not really authentic, the taste being modified to cater to the English palate."

"The bloke thinks he is on television!" said John.

I laughed. "Well – I do have an audience here. So let's pretend."

I plonked the potatoes into the hot water, covered it with a lid and lifted them out 20 minutes later. Meanwhile, I was instructing Shirley. She placed a large frying pan on the gas, poured some oil and then threw in the chopped onions. When they were a golden brown, she threw in the garlic, ginger and two tins of plum tomatoes. Then she added the cumin, coriander, salt and chilli powder. I assured her that a little bit of chilli would not set her mouth on fire; it would add to the taste. She played awhile with the concoction. In a few minutes the 'base curry' was done. We set it aside.

"Now, you have your pototoes either boiled, roasted or mashed...or, of course, in the form of chips. You add salt and pepper and vinegar or mint sauce or whatever on the table. Now, with Indian cooking, all the adding is done while cooking. Nothing on the table. So let us take another frying pan, pour some oil, then some of the spices. You can put all the four basic spices, ginger, garlic, coriander and cumin, or any mixture you fancy. Let us use just cumin and coriander...put some salt in, Shirley, please, and a teensy-weensy bit of chilli powder. Now stir it all up...only for a minute. Now add the potatoes. Stir it about so that they are all coated with the spice mixture. Ah! Nice smell, isn't it?"

"It certainly smells lovely."

"Now, let it fry for five or ten minutes...let the spices get into the potatoes...doesn't matter if they stick to the pan a bit. They taste better for it... Now, see! It's done... Now transfer it into a serving dish and set aside."

"What next?"

"You noticed that I scooped the potatoes out of the hot water. Now we put the dhal into it. I have already washed it out a few times. That takes about ten to 15 minutes. Once that is cooked, I add a couple of chopped tomatoes or plum tomatoes, a bit of salt, and only a bit of cumin and coriander. We must not use a lot of spice when doing dhal. It spoils it."

"So, now we have two dishes ready. What are we going to do with all this tomato-onion mixture we have here?"

"We divide that into two equal halves. One half we put into a frying pan and add the chicken drumsticks that I have de-skinned and scored deeply with the knife. Let's put a lid on and let it cook. It probably takes anything between 30 and 40 minutes. While that is being done, we put the other half of the tomato-onion mixture into another frying pan. To this we add some desiccated coconut."

"I was beginning to wonder when we would use that."

"This is to give it a different flavour. See how wonderful it smells. Just keep stirring it about…see how it thickens up the gravy…nice reddish-brown. If we add turmeric to it it will give it a yellowish hue. But I didn't want to confuse you too much. Similarly, if we add paprika, it will give it a reddish hue. Now, that's enough. The coconut has been cooked. Now add the filleted trout to the gravy, cover it with a lid and let it cook. Fish takes less time…about 15 to 20 minutes."

"So now we have four dishes."

"That's right. Do you know how to make rice?"

"No. You have to have a rice cooker for that, don't you?"

"How did people cook rice before that was invented? I'll show you how to cook rice. First, measure out two mugs of rice into that vessel. Now wash it…see how the starch comes out… Wash it four of five times till the water is more or less clear. Now you add four mugs of water to it…that's right, ratio of 1:2. Add a bit of salt. Now, there is no need to cook the rice now. Rice tastes better when it is freshly cooked. So we leave this aside. We shall put it on the gas 30 minutes before we start to eat."

"Is that it? Have we finished?"

"Yes. The naan bread we grill for a few minutes. The samosas we stick in the microwave for a couple of minutes. Now, that didn't take long, did it?"

"You certainly make it look easy, and it certainly took less time than I thought. The trick is to know how much of spices to put in, I suppose."

"Yes, Shirley. You saw how much we used. That is a guideline."

"What are the limes for?"

"Just to squeeze on the chicken and fish on the table. You could garnish everything with curry or coriander leaves…or parsley or mustard leaves."

"What do we do with the poppadoms?"

"Shove them under the grill."

"What about the yogurt?"

"In India every meal must end with yogurt. Cools down the system; helps digestion. You can have it throughout the meal as a sort of dip to take the fire out of Indian food."

* * * * * * * *

I returned to my room, had a hot shower and was back at the Landrums at half past seven.

Connie opened the door.

"I could smell the food from the gate," she said; "smells delicious."

"I hope your parents like it."

"They have already sneaked a taste of the chicken. They liked it."

"Here's a bottle of wine…though I must say that wine does not go well with Indian food."

"You like Jamieson's, doc. I've got a bottle," said John.

" Thank you, John. I prefer it to scotch."

I showed Shirley how to grill the poppadoms and microwave the samosas. We had them along with our drinks. John and I had Irish whiskey, Shirley and Connie white wine. Half an hour before we sat down to dinner, Shirley put the rice on and simmered it for 15 minutes once it had boiled. The water had disappeared and the rice rose into a fluffy white. When we were ready to eat, we heated up the chicken and fish on the gas rings, the potatoes and dhal in the microwave, and the naan under the grill. For dessert we had the Indian milk sweets.

They enjoyed it tremendously. And so did I, as I had not any Indian food for a few days.

"That was lovely," said Shirley, "thank you very much."

"The pleasure is mine," I said. "Hope you don't have a tummy upset tomorrow."

"What of it? We have a doctor in the house!"

"Ha, ha. Well, I must return to work."

"How's it coming along?" asked John.

"All right, I think."

"Do you know about the great cricket writers of the past?"

"I know some of them... By the way, did you meet any of them?

"I met the greatest – Neville Cardus. Do you know of him?"

"Who doesn't? He was from Manchester, the illegal offspring of a prostitute. He had a tough life and educated himself. He played a bit of cricket. Though he wasn't great at it, he was asked to coach at a school. Later on he worked for the Manchester Guardian where, one day, he was asked to write on a cricket match as the regular correspondent was ill. He stuck with it for 20 years. He died in 1975."

"He gave to cricket the personal touch. Anyone can write about cricket, but only a few can write to create atmosphere. The reader should feel that he is at the ground. Cardus was an expert at romancing the game. He would tell you about the distinctive character of the players, the pitches, the weather, the behind-the-scenes bonhomie and rivalry. He would describe the bowling, batting and fielding actions of the players...and even what they were thinking."

"Yes," I said, "there were other good writers of the game – Robertson-Glasgow, Alan Gibson, Alan Ross, John Arlott, the Australians Ray Robinson and J H Fingleton, the Trinidadian C L R James..."

"We do not have that kind today. Look at the papers. Drab, superficial...even boring..."

"I have seen tremendous matches. But reading about them the next morning...makes insipid the glorious memories... The romance, the colour, the literary flourish, the reconstruction and expression have disappeared."

"You are right. That is because the writers today do not really love the game. They are just doing a job. One has to love, live and breathe cricket to write about it. Why? Even the photographs which the phalanx of highly-paid expert photographers take today are very mundane compared to the ones of yesteryear."

"Do you want to know about unusual cricket matches?" asked John.

"What do you mean by 'unusual'?"

"Well, matches between one-legged men and one-armed men, casualties of war. There was such a one between the Greenwich Pensioners in 1863 at the Oval. Do you know who won?"

"Let's see...I would back the one-armed men."

"The one-legged men won. What about smokers versus non-smokers? The Graces played in one of these matches in Australia and won the game for the non-smokers. Have you heard about the match Cambridge Town played against Cambridge Gowns on ice? The Fens were frozen over. Cambridge Town won."

John rummaged about in his desk and brought out a paper.

"What about this one? 1887, Yatton versus 50 farmers. The farmers won. The pensioners' match in 1906 between Mr Papworth's team and Mr Brasnett's team; the players were between 55 and 75 and both the umpires were 86 years old. They played with top hats and dress coats. The rule was, if any batsman made 20 runs, he had to use his other hand! Papworth won."

"I know an unusual match," I said; "actors versus authors."

"You would know that, wouldn't you?"

"Major Philip Trevor, cricket correspondent of *The Daily Telegraph*, was captain of the authors and your lookalike C Aubrey Smith captained the actors in a match at Lord's in 1907. Who do you think won?"

"I would go for the authors."

"You would have lost, John. B S Foster hit a century for the actors."

"1907, did you say?" said John. "Well, I have something here about that year. The Nottinghamshire Ladies versus Notts. Crimea & Indian Mutiny Veterans at Trent Bridge. Who won?"

"I'll go for the men."

"Wrong. The girls won by 24 runs."

"And then there was another match between the politicians and the actors in 1955. Who won?"

"I would go for the actors."

"The politicians won. One of my favourite actors, Rex Harrison, was out for a duck."

"I've got a peculiar story here. A chap called Ralph Lindsay. He dismissed the same three batsmen in the same order in 1957 and 1963 with hat-tricks. Here's an even more peculiar story. What is the lowest score in an innings?"

"Ten?"

"1964, Elgin, 145 for five declared. Ross County answered with a resounding nought!"

"All out for nought?"

"Yes. How many wickets can one take in an over?"

"Six."

"Wrong. A 14-year old Stephen Fleming of Marlborough College, Blenheim, New Zealand, took eight Bohally Intermediate School wickets in an eight-ball over in the second innings. He bowled one ball in the first innings and took a wicket. So his figures are 1.1-1-0-9."

"Incredible!"

"How many runs can you make in one over?"

"Thirty-six."

"Let me put it another way. How many runs can a bowler give away in an over?"

"Ah – an endless number of runs…if he keeps bowling wides and no-balls."

"That's right. In 1988, Cheshire were set a total of 201 to win but it seemed impossible. So, to liven up the game, the Dorset captain, Reverend Andrew Digby, instructed his bowler, Graeme Calway, to bowl wides. He duly bowled 14 wides, each for four runs. The first ball of the over had already been hit for four. So Calway gave away 60 runs in his over. But Cheshire lost by 18 runs. What is the highest score for last man in?"

"Don't know."

"T P B Smith, 163 for Essex against Derbyshire in 1947."

"John…I don't know what to say!"

"Say 'Thank you'."

I did and took leave.

"I've eaten too much," said Connie, "I'll walk you to the guest house."

We walked through the main street past the church. The night was still.

"The church looks lovely in the dark," I said.

"It does."

"I like cemeteries. Do you want to walk in the churchyard?" I asked.

"Why not?"

So we made our way through the wicket-gate into the churchyard and amongst the graves.

Clouds were scudding across the half-moon. A bit of chill in the air. We climbed a few steps to an upper level closer to the church. Connie slipped and caught my hand. I steadied her up. She leaned against me. I held her close. We stayed thus a few moments.

She looked up at me and said, "Let's go to your room, doc."

"Do you know what you are saying, Connie?" I asked.

"It's just a need, doc. So let's not analyse it."

"If that's what you wish." I said.

We went up to my room and made love.

If the reader does not wish to read about how we made love, he or she can skip the following description.

"Let's take it slow and easy, doc. It's been a long time," said Connie.

I laughed.

"Why do you laugh?"

"You calling me 'doc'."

"That's what we...I call you."

"Well...what's in a name?"

We embraced and stood against each other for what seemed ages. I slowly brushed her hair down with my fingers and palms and kissed her on her head, forehead, eyes, nose, ears and mouth. I fed on her lips, sucking each in turn. I kissed her on the side and front of her neck. She moaned softly.

I sat her down in front of the dressing table mirror and stood behind her. Her eyes were half closed. I kissed the back of her neck, nibbling her white skin.

She was wearing a skirt and blouse. I lifted the blouse over her head. She had on a black bra that accentuated her milky complexion. Her breasts were full, heavy and intensely provocative. I did not undo the bra. I put my hand down her front and pushed the bra beneath her breasts so that they popped up like moons; her pink nipples stood out, pointing to the mirror. I took them between my fingers and rolled them until they were erect and hard. I felt, kneaded and squeezed her breasts. Then I undid the bra clasp behind and let her lovely breasts loose. I stood behind her and took her right breast in both hands and kneaded and pushed it forward. She was looking into the mirror and moaned and caught my hands and wanted to pull me forward.

"You said to take it slowly; keep still." I said, and pushed her hands away from me.

Now I took her left breast and massaged it between the palms of my hands, pushing it forward. Connie was squirming and moaning. I stood her up in front of the mirror and unzipped her skirt and took down her black panties. She stood in front of the mirror and I went all over her body with my hands. When she couldn't stand it any longer, she turned round and undid my clothes.

We were both naked and we held each other as though we were a pair of octopuses. She led me to the bed and lay down. I sat on her thighs, bent down and ate her breasts and sucked at her nipples till she almost screamed. By this time I was full to bursting. Connie spread her legs, I entered, she moaned loudly and gasped.

I squeezed her gorgeous breasts and sucked as if to empty them, groaned loudly with ecstasy, and jerked my pelvis until I was spent.

I lay on top of her. Both of us were sweating. I kissed her neck and nibbled dreamily at her beautiful breasts.

We lay in each other's arms silently. She had a slight smile on her face. I kissed her smile.

* * * * * * * *

CHAPTER 16
Jack Hobbs; World War I Casualties;
Victor Trumper

"Did I tell you that the six-ball over came into force in 1900?" asked John.

"No."

"Australia played an eight-ball over."

"Whom do we talk about today?" I asked.

"A father took his son to see Ranji bat. The son was more interested in the hot pork pie stands in the pavilion. He sang in the church choir and, when one of the choirmasters invited his young singing birds home to tea, our friend would devour the bread, butter and jam. When he was old enough to help his father at Jesus College ground, he would consume more than his share of plum pie and custard. Our friend had a prodigious appetite for comestibles...that was only overshadowed later by his appetite for runs. His mentor was the great Tom Hayward, who was the first to emulate W G in scoring 100 hundreds. And it was in the same Parker's Piece where Ranji played that our hero learnt to lay willow on leather. When Tom and his protégé opened for Surrey against the Gentlemen of England led by W G at the Oval in 1906, Tom scored 39 and 82, the tyro 29 and 85. In the next 28 years he was to accumulate nearly 60,000 runs. He scored more centuries than any other batsman before or since – 197 – and, until Denis Compton in 1947, more centuries in a season than any other player. Of his 15 centuries for England, 12 were against Australia – a record that is in no immediate danger of being eclipsed.

"It was during his time that spin arrived. The gauntlet of the googly was flung at his feet. He promptly used those feet to counter the freak delivery; he played well forward to smother the spin or played well back and watched the ball right onto his bat. There we have it. The greatest batting technician on how to play the cunning ball.

"Yet he was a true gentleman. He walked when he was convinced of his dismissal, absolving umpires from making awkward and difficult decisions. In the 30 seasons he played not once did he raise his voice against anyone, not once did he brush with authority, utter an uncharitable word about a fellow player, not once did he show dissent. I'll tell you how humble he was. 1926; Old Trafford; England versus Australia. A W Carr, the captain, was laid low with tonsillitis. Our man was 43 years old and had played for England on 29 occasions. He was asked to captain the side. He demurred politely, recommending the 25-year-old amateur, G T S Stevens, who was playing his first Test.

"Despite his gastronomic excesses, he was a completely fit man, proven by the fact that he scored more than half his centuries after the age of 40, his last at the age of 53.

"He was born in December 1882, knighted when he was 73 when he had a sports shop in Fleet Street."

"You are talking of John Berry Hobbs, later Sir Jack Hobbs, the first cricketer to be knighted."

" Of course I was. Who did you think I was speaking of?"

"Well, you never mentioned his name."

"Didn't I? I'm sorry."

"You were testing me, weren't you?"

"Not really. I just forgot," jested John. "Who was the second cricketer to be knighted?"

"Sir Leonard Hutton." I said.

"Right."

"I have a poem about Hobbs. Would you like to hear it?"

"Sure."

"I like it because it has to do with the medical profession. I know only the first verse, I'm afraid."

Can nothing be done for J B Hobbs
To make him sometimes get out for blobs?
Or is he doomed for some dreadful crime
To make centuries till the end of time?
An eminent Harley Street specialist
Says that a nervous action of wrist
Combined with a lesion of eyes and feet,
Which is rapidly growing more complete
Through long indulgence without restraint,
Has at last become an organic complaint,
And only a rest in a nursing home
And elbow baths with electric foam,
Or using a bat of exiguous size
And wearing a bandage over the eyes
And batting left-handed after tea
Can uproot this obstinate malady.

John laughed.

* * * * * * *

"Tell me about the war. Did many cricketers die on the battlefields?"

"When I was talking about W G, I told you that he wrote an article to the press asking for the cessation of cricket for the duration of the war, urging able-bodied men to take up arms on behalf of the nation instead of entertaining themselves and platoons of beer-drinkers by laying willow to leather. During the war years *Wisden* was reduced to less than half its usual size due to the cessation of games. In the annals of sporting literature those editions were the most poignant, for they recorded the deaths of cricketers all over the world. It mentions 77 cricketers in its pages – an incomplete list, I suspect.

"Someone killed in action near Ypres was in the Eton eleven; a member of the Lancashire side died in action at Mons; the opening bat of Middlesex succumbed to war wounds in the desolate fields of Flanders.

"I'll tell you about a few cricketers I remember. They will be good for your book.

"Tibby Cotter had a premonition of his imminent death. At Beersheba, he tossed up a ball of mud and said to his fellow soldier, 'That's my last bowl, Blue. Something's going to happen.' He was killed soon after.

"Lieutenant Arthur Collins, who as a Clifton schoolboy in June 1899 scored 628 not out over five days for his house eleven – killed in action.

"The 22nd of July 1916, Percy Jeeves of the Royal Warwickshire regiment, killed in action during the Battle of the Somme. Jeeves was a Yorkshireman who migrated to Warwickshire when his own county did not recognize his bowling skills. One of those scanning the casualty lists was a certain P G Wodehouse, who opened the bowling for Dulwich College and who was now groping for a suitable name for one of his characters, a gentleman's gentleman. He remembered playing with Jeeves, the cricketer. Thus did Percy Jeeves achieve immortality well beyond his wildest dreams.

"I know something about Jeeves as I grew up on Wodehouse," I chipped in.

"OK, clever clogs."

"Percy Jeeves was a young bowler all-rounder who ambled up to the crease with effortless grace. In 1910 he was signed up for Warwickshire but, because there was a two-year waiting period, he did not play until 1912. In a match against the visiting Australians he failed with his bat but took two wickets for 35. 1913 was a rich year. 106 victims, one of those being the great Hobbs. He topped the county bowling averages. 1914, against Surrey, he clean bowled Tom Hayward and Jack Hobbs, and in a match against Yorkshire hit the ball out of the ground into Edgbaston Road. He married Annie, the sister of the Warwickshire scorer, and when the unpleasantness broke out joined the Warwickshire Regiment. And, as you said, he was killed on the Somme in 1916. It was in 1913 that P G Wodehouse saw Jeeves playing against Gloucestershire in Cheltenham and was impressed with his fluid bowling action, though he took only one wicket in the match. Wodehouse read about his death when he was in America in 1916 when he was about to start his immortal Bertie-Jeeves saga. The name must have clicked. Rowland Ryder, a cricket correspondent and Wodehouse fan, sent Wodehouse a Warwickshire tie that he wore for the rest of his life. I'll tell you something else about

Wodehouse.   Wodehouse also noted the death of Lieutenant K L Hutchings in September 1916 – killed in action. P G had dismissed Hutchings and his brother and run through the rest of the opposition on a June day in 1899. Hutchings was famous for establishing a record that has stood ever since.   In the 1907-08 tour of Australia, he scored a century in boundaries out of a total score of 126 at Melbourne."

"Very good...very good.   Another famous cricketer who gave up his life in France during this military obscenity was the Kentish star Colin Blythe, slow left-arm bowler who had 2,509 scalps to his credit. He took 13 or more wickets in a match 15 times, including 17 in a day once; for England he claimed exactly 100 wickets for 18 apiece.

"*Wisden* also records the deaths of Lieutenant Henry Webber and Brigadier-General Roland Boys Bradford, both of whom were very modest cricketers. What can we learn from the deaths of these two obscure gentlemen? Only life's irony that the Brigadier-General was a young sprig of 25 and the Lieutenant a venerable 68.

"One great cricketer who died during the war but not on the battlefields was an Australian whom many regard as the greatest cricketer that that continent has ever produced – including Bradman. You could bowl six balls on the same spot and he would hit them in six different directions. England's captains tried their best to trap him, but he would hit them out of the ground. He could play on any kind of wicket against any kind of bowling...such instant mastery over unfamiliar conditions was beyond even Bradman. Like Hobbs he was the embodiment of modesty and fair play...liked and esteemed by his peers. At the age of 30 he had an attack of scarlet fever. Seven years later, while playing for a full day in the Australian 1914-15 season, his ankles swelled up. He dismissed the doctor's advice as nothing. Six months later he was on holiday with his family when he became ill again. This time he was in bed for three months. When he was recovering he caught a chill and within two days he was dead. The death certificate said that the cause of his demise was Bright's disease.

"There are many ways of gauging a person's worth. Let me tell you how greatly he was regarded by the public. In 1902 the Cricketers' Benevolent Fund Society held a public auction of 44 cricket bats donated by their famous owners. The bat of Tom Hayward fetched £4. C B Fry for five guineas. Ranji went for 13 guineas. Our man's reached the record of £42 before the gavel was banged down. What of W G's bat, you may ask? Well, England's honour was saved when, after a flurry of telephone calls, someone bid 50 quid for it."

"Now you are up to your tricks again, aren't you, John?"

"What do you mean?"

"The cricketer's name."

"Don't tell me you don't know who I am talking about."

"No. I don't."

"Victor Thomas Trumper."

"Thank you very much."

"One of his greatest innings was at Melbourne in 1904, on a wet pitch with the two greatest left-handed bowlers of the day – the Yorkshiremen Rhodes and Hirst bowling in tandem. Trumper carried his bat, making 74 out of a total of 122. Charles Fry in London raised his glass and toasted Trumper and Mrs Fry, also a Trumper fan, demanded that his portrait be hung in the National gallery. You can see how he was loved by all...though he was an Aussie. I have not read a single derogatory word written about Victor Trumper the cricketer or Victor Trumper the man. He owned a sports shop in Sydney and once lost count of time as he was working. He suddenly realized that it was the morning of a Test, grabbed his bat and made 185 not out. After the match, an admirer came to the shop and asked to buy any used bat of his. Trumper showed him the bat he had just used. The admirer asked him the price and Trumper said, 'Well, my son, I bought it for 45 shillings but, since it is now second-hand, I'll give it to you for a pound." Can you imagine such a thing happening today? Another time, a young stranger in the bat-making business requested Trumper to use his bat. It was a blunderbuss weighing 3lb 6oz. But Trumper, to the astonishment and consternation of his colleagues, went out with it and made 87 and autographed it for the young man. I'll tell you another thing about Trumper that I have heard. He could have made many more runs but would look around for a deserving youngster down on his luck and give away his wicket unostentatiously to him. People who were lucky enough to see him, Ranji and Bradman maintained that he was the best. The story goes that Warner once asked Hirst where he would like the field placed and Hirst ruefully replied, 'It doesnt matter where we put 'em, sir; Victor will still do as 'e likes.' When Trumper visited South Africa, the Springboks thought he could not play on matting. Trumper scored a double century and teased the rival captain with his cuts, hooks and drives, placing the shots at exactly the point where the fielder was shifted from. Even amidst the mayhem, whilst helplessly seeing his team torn to shreds, the rival captain, Percy Sherwell, magnanimously said, 'Ah, we have seen batting today!' The great Bosanquet once bowled Trumper with his first ball – a googly – but subsequently Trumper used to massacre him to all parts of the ground displaying his lithe grace, quickness of foot and astonishing power. Arthur Mailey, the incomparable Australian spin bowler once clean bowled Trumper. In his autobiography, Mailey wrote, 'I was ashamed. It was as though I had killed a dove.' Neville Cardus paid him one of the greatest tributes when he wrote, 'The art of Trumper is like the art in a bird's flight, an art that knows not how wonderful it is…'."

"Great!"

"How is it that you don't know about the great Victor Trumper?"

"I know about him…I just couldn't place him initially. I read somewhere that there are eight thoroughfares named after Victor Trumper in Australia. Bradman has twenty-two."

"I didn't know that."

"Well, I'll forgive you!"

* * * * * * * *

CHAPTER 17
Barnes; Albert Trott; Woolley

After the miserable and probably the most ludicrous war in all human history came to an end the public were once again ready for games. The county game, for some inexplicable reason, was reduced from three to two days, resulting in innumerable drawn games that understandably angered the public. The authorities soon saw the folly of their idiotic policy, however, and discarded it...never to be resumed again. Some comical notions were not implemented – disqualifying left-handed bowlers; penalizing the batting side when a maiden was bowled.

The professionals who were fobbed off with miserly salaries and no retirement security were now tempted by the Leagues, but luckily the cricket-loving public showed up in unprecedented numbers after the war to watch the games – it almost seemed that they were starving for cricket – thus ensuring a better deal for them.

"Now, no name games. Have you heard about Barnes?" asked John.

"Yes. He was a fast bowler. Did he develop the fast leg-break, pitching on leg and middle and knocking down the off-stump?"

"Yes; that's right. Mr Sydney Francis Barnes was a queer bird. Players nowadays think they are past their sell-by date at the age of 35. During his 20 years with Staffordshire, Barnes took 1,432 wickets at eight runs apiece; in 38 summers in the Leagues he bagged another 3,471 at under seven apiece. In 1934, when he was 62 years old, he took 86 wickets at around ten runs each. Remember, Rhodes was recalled at the age of 48 and acquitted himself well. What the hell are today's cricketers compared to the likes of Barnes and Rhodes?"

"Today they play more cricket, John. And the game is different. Especially for one-dayers, you need to be and keep fit."

"Well, anyway, Barnes played for Warwickshire between 1894 and 1896. Then he turned his back on first-class cricket and vanished into the Birmingham District League. The next year he was signed up by Burnley Club and the following year by Lancashire where he was spotted by Maclaren, the captain of England, when he was scouting for bowlers to take along to Australia in 1901. Barnes took 13 wickets in the second Test and injured his knee. In 1902 he took 82 wickets and, in 1903, 131. He then played for a gallimaufry of clubs all over England, refusing to rejoin Lancashire County. He took 49 wickets during the first four Tests on his South African tour and then declined to play the fifth, claiming that it was not worth the effort to bowl against such meagre opposition.

"The fast leg break you described was known as 'the Barnes ball'. He worked hard at his game and made it look simple; so people tended to consider him a natural, effortless bowler. He was considered by many to the finest bowler of all time. After years in the wilderness, Barnes was recalled to the England side in 1921 at the age of 49. The West Indian tourists of 1928 unequivocally stated that Barnes at the age of 56 was the best bowler they had faced all season.

But he was not pleasant company. He was dour, arrogant, proud, aloof and short-tempered, and he rarely smiled. When asked to bowl at the wrong end he would scowl and sulk and fret. If the umpire disallowed his appeal, he would show his disgust and contempt for minutes before turning back to his starting point. If he was given out he would glower at the umpire for what seemed like ages, to the utter consternation of everyone except himself, before slowly trudging back to the pavilion. His team mates hated him to such an extent that, when they were travelling to Australia and the seas turned rough, Maclaren himself murmured, with some degree of consolation, 'If we go down, that bugger Barnes will go down with us.' He was an expert at gamesmanship – like Grace. Barnes had to bowl the last over of the day in a match. After bowling five balls and just before delivering the last ball, he stopped and instructed Bernard Hollowood to move to a particular spot and Hollowood, not fully understanding Barnes, moved to silly mid-off. Barnes came charging in, stopped again just before delivering the ball, marched up to Hollowood, his face like the darkest of rain clouds, caught hold of his arm and led him to the precise spot. The crowd laughed hollowly to ease the tension. The batsman was in a state of jitters. Barnes bowled, the batsman prodded. The ball fell gently into the waiting hands of Hollowood."

"Why did he behave so?"

"Well, I think that he had a huge chip on his shoulder. He thought that he wasn't recognized for his true worth by the other players and his country, and he thought that he was poorly paid... Everyone was poorly paid. In those days, the players had no union. They were treated like servants by the autocratic men in charge and paid poorly for their art, which they practised for six hours a day in all conditions. Most of the professional cricketers right up to the end of the Second World War died in utter penury. They had no pension funds. If they were lucky they had benefit matches but even that did not give them much. If they were famous, they picked up decent sums from coaching, lecturing or advertising. He was asking for rights that did not materialize until sixty years after him. He was ahead of his times."

"I feel sorry for the old codger... Who is next?"

"Someone you may not have heard of. Mr Albert Trott."

"Hold on, there. Hold on," I said. "I've heard that name. Wait...wait... Yes! Was he an Australian who played for England?"

"My God! I would have bet anything that you had not heard of him."

"But that's all that I know of him."

"Well, I would have won half the bet."

"What do you mean?"

"He was an Australian but he didn't play for England. I am telling you this story because you want the human angle...besides facts and figures. Piqued at not being picked for the Australian tour of England, he landed in England in 1898 and signed up for Middlesex. He made cricket history by becoming the only player to hit a ball over the pavilion at Lord's. He was really a bowler, medium-paced off-breaks. He used to practise his bowling by putting a huge fruit crate in front of the stumps and trying to bowl around it. For two consecutive seasons he took 200 wickets. Then he slumped. He was a dipsomaniac. Realizing that his days were over, they decided to give him a benefit match. It is the most unforgettable benefit match swansong in the history of cricket.

"1907. Whitsun fixture. Middlesex versus Somerset. Trott didn't have a great match with the bat; he scored 1 and 35. In the first innings he bowled five overs for ten runs with no wickets. On Whit Monday, Somerset was posted 264 to win. Trott came on to bowl. In four balls he took four wickets. He followed this up by taking three wickets in three balls and thus performed the most amazing freakish feat – a double hat-trick in an innings – in cricket history. He ended up with figures of seven for 20. He became an umpire in 1910, but by 1913 his health had deteriorated to such an extent (due to the contents of several bottles) that he retired. He was now a dropsical wreck. He was admitted to St Mary's hospital but he couldn't live without a regular imbibition of spirits. He discharged himself, wrote out a will leaving his only possession – a wardrobe – to his landlady and shot himself. The MCC paid the funeral expenses. *The Daily Telegraph* commented, 'A more pathetic figure of a man in later days it would be difficult to imagine'."

* * * * * * * *

"Were there any other great players of the era?" I asked.

"Yes. But I don't know any stories about them. There was the incomparable man from Kent, Frank Woolley, who could make a legitimate claim to being one of the greatest all-rounders of the game – who can surpass 59,000 runs, more than 2,000 wickets and more than 1,000 catches? What about 'Patsy' Hendren, Middlesex run machine who scored 170 centuries and four double centuries on his West Indies tour of 1929-30? Walter Hammond, who topped the first-class batting averages for eight consecutive seasons? 'Tich' Freeman, who mesmerized 3,776 batsmen into giving up their stances at the crease; who took 100 wickets in a season 17 times, 200 wickets eight times, and 300 once?"

* * * * * * * *

CHAPTER 18
Interlude with Connie

I returned to my room at lunchtime. I had a lot of catching-up to do. Two days' work. So I got on with it. It takes time to sift all the dialogue, make notes and then put it on the screen. A writer cannot sit continuously at his work. He has to get up, move about and tune in to ideas and thoughts in the ether. Industry is futile if it is not preceded by inspiration – an entity that cannot be precisely described. He gets mentally tired; a cumulus of hebetude envelops him. It is pointless trying to force oneself to sit in front of the screen and carry on regardless of the stultifying writer's block. The quality of work invariably suffers. So, when I am tired or fretful, I set aside my work and go for a walk, or simply sit, waiting for a propitious moment when ideas come to me out of the blue.

That evening I went for a brisk three-mile walk in the country roads near Melbridge. The fields were waving their green wheat and yellow oilseed rape as if in greeting. A farmer was on his way with his flock of woolly sheep. The sea gulls were cross with me and made raucous conversation. A magnificent weeping willow dozed in the distance. A spectacular laburnum tree with its incredible yellow blossoms swayed languorously. The clouds made kaleidoscopic patterns. The air was still and warm. The little stream flowed silently around the weeds. A family of ducks cruised by with the majesty of a Viking flotilla. A few swans looked disdainfully at their cousins, puffed up their snowy white feathers, straightened their artistic necks and seemed to tell me, look at us, doc; we are more beautiful than all that you see. I nodded in agreement.

The weather is capricious in England. One moment, bright, happy sunshine; the next, dark, angry clouds; the next, a warning burst of rain – then a vengeful shower of hail. In the winter months that could be followed by snow and then once again sunshine. The cycle goes on. Such is the cycle of life. Effulgence alternating with tenebrosity; delectation with infelicity; prosperity with impecuniosity.

I returned refreshed in an hour. My mind had cleared. I sat down and finished my work at about 7:00 p.m. I tidied up and undressed to take a shower.

Knock, knock, knock.

"Who is it, please?"

"It's me," said Connie's voice.

I swished a towel around me and opened the door.

"I'm disappointed," I said.

"Why?"

"Grammatical error. 'It is I', school-ma'am."

She laughed.

"I'm sorry; I was about to take a shower. Would you like some white wine? I got a bottle today...seeing that you like it."

"Thanks."

"Would you like to help yourself while I take a shower?"

"OK."

And then we made love.

If the reader wishes titillation...read on.

I was in the shower. The door opened. Connie came in, stark naked. She joined me in the shower. I held her with her back towards me and we let the spray of water hit us all over, slowly turning round and round. She became pinky-white. I supported her breasts with my palms and slowly massaged them and pinched her nipples. I took each breast in turn in both my hands and massaged them slowly at first and with vigour later. I turned her around and crushed her towards me. She put her hand on my erection and massaged it, pulling and pushing to and fro. I kissed her face and sucked her lips and chewed on her tongue. Both of us were making love sounds. I bent down and kissed her neck. I pushed both her breasts together and buried my face in the deep, soft valley and filled my mouth with her pink-white flesh. Then I paid attention to each of her breasts, kissing, biting, sucking, licking. I bit and sucked her nipples until she screamed. She once again put her hand on my erection. I took it away and bent down lower and kissed and sucked her stomach and navel.

The water was cascading on us, warm, stimulating. I knelt before her and parted her vulva and gently massaged her clitoris. I put my lips to it and started to suck gently. I nibbled at it. Connie crushed my face to her and burst inside with a loud moan. I continued to suck her clitoris and inserted my finger into her vagina and massaged her vigorously inside. She screamed and came again.

I stood up and started to suck her breasts again. Gently I pushed her down. She knelt before me and took my flesh in her mouth. I closed my eyes in ecstasy. I let the water rain on me. Connie flicked her tongue across

the head and sucked and moved her head back and forth.
I screamed as I burst in her like fireworks on Guy
Fawkes' night.

We clung to each other like a pair of sea
anemones under the water. When we recovered, we
soaped and bathed each other. Her body was slippery
and enticing. I washed her all over with soap, taking my
time massaging every inch of her. I played with her
breasts again...massaging, sucking her delicious, ripe
pink nipples. She soaped and washed me. We were
excited once again. She rubbed my erect penis. I
slipped a finger into her vagina and a thumb onto her
clitoris while she pumped me. We both came together
once again.

It was a longish shower.

"I could go for you," she said.

"Don't," I said.

"Why not?"

"What do you mean, 'Why not?' My home is
6,000 miles away. I am here only for a few days. And –
as you said the other night – this is only a need...like
food."

We agreed that there was nothing wrong about
passion with mutual consent.

* * * * * * *

CHAPTER 19
The Don and the Black Bradman

"We come to the years between the two bloody wars," said John.

"Another bloody war was in the offing...this time on the playing fields of England and Australia," I said.

"That's right. Remember, England won the 1926 series against Australia, winning the Fifth Test due to the exploits of 48-year-old Rhodes after four frustrating draws. England then went on to win the 1928-29 tour of Australia by four matches to one, this time thanks to Walter Hammond. The Australian tourists now arrived in England in 1930. They were about to deliver a devastating counterstroke.

"On the 27th of August 1908, in Adam Street in an insignificant town with an Aborigine name – Cootmundra, New South Wales, Australia – there was born a prodigy. When he was not yet three the family moved to Bowral, some 80 miles south of Sydney. He had no neighbours. He had to devise his own games. At the back of the house was an 800-gallon water tank set on a brick stand. He would throw a golf ball at it and hit the unpredictable fast ricochets with a stump. He would compose two teams in his head and play, taking the place of Grace, Ranji, Collins, etc. You know who we are talking about?"

"Easy. Donald Bradman."

"His name first appeared in the *Smith's Weekly* when he was 13 years old. Don Bradman sent a ball over the boundary fence. It struck half a brick, rebounded onto a fence post, poised there for an appreciable time, and ran along the top of the palings the whole length of a panel of fencing before descending outside the boundary. At the age of 17 he scored 300 runs opening for the Bowral Team against the Wingello Team in 1925. When the lad was 19 years old he was inducted into the State side. The next year he was selected for Australia. He was relegated to twelfth man in the first two Tests and introduced to the world in the third Test against England. He made 79 and 112 against the likes of Tate, Freeman and Larwood. It was evident even to the uninitiated that he was witnessing a legend. The technique was flawless, the concentration olamic, the temperament consummate. In the fourth Test he partnered Archie Jackson, who, at the age of 19 (one year younger than Bradman), became the youngest player in history to slog a Test century. Four years later he was dead...tuberculosis. Australia lost the first four Tests. It won the fifth Test at Melbourne, Bradman making 123 and 37 not out.

"In the next Sheffield Shield cricket season, January 1930, our Don made a world record – 452 not out in 415 minutes against Queensland.

"He came to England. Warm-up matches. Worcester – 236, beating H H Massie's record of 1882. Leicester – 185 not out. Oval – 252 not out. He seemed to like English conditions; they suited him, as he preferred to play off the back foot.

"First Test Match – Trent Bridge; Bradman scored 131 in the second innings. Australia lost the Test.

"Second Test Match – Lord's; Duleepshighji (Ranji's nephew) made a princely 173. Don matched it with 254, which he regards as technically the best innings of his life. Australia won.

"Third Test Match – Leeds; our man accumulated 334 – century before lunch, another before tea, and the third before close. Leonard Hutton later excelled this record score. Test drawn.

"Fourth Test Match – Old Trafford; match disrupted due to typical Manchester weather. Draw.

"Fifth Test Match – Oval; Bradman made another double century, 232, and Australia won emphatically by an innings.

"Australia had won the series two to one.

"To the English players and public it was unbelievable. It was shocking. It was atrocious. It was shameful. The descendants of convicts had bested them; they who had invented the game! They must regain the sacred Ashes.

"The English rightly deduced that the difference between the teams was Bradman. He had an awesome aggregate of 974 runs at an average of an incredible 139.14. The English were faced with an adversary who was seemingly immune. Pelham Warner encapsulated everyone's feelings when he said that one trembles to think what lies in store for bowlers. He constituted a factor so novel that only a novel strategy could neutralize him. They must either stoically admit defeat – which was unthinkable – or conspire, if necessary illegally, to bring down the enemy. Bradman was the cheekiest, grinningest and most confident thing in cricket. England had to wipe that grin off his face. The question was, to what extent were they willing to go? How low were they willing to stoop? The gentlemen in charge held a conventicle. The gentlemen decided to break the rules. They thus flung themselves headlong onto the path of self-deception...which, if questioned, can only be met with righteous indignation, the kind of indignation that cannot be pacified or rectified. They bent the rules of play."

"What exactly is bodyline, John?" I asked.

"Well, the term 'bodyline' was invented by either the father of Chester Wilmot or by Jack Worrall, copied by Hugh Buggy of *The Melbourne Herald*, and made famous by the sub-editor, Ray Robinson, who later became a well-known cricket writer. A lot of people have written about it. Jardine, Pelham Warner, Larwood, Bradman, Kippax, Hammond, Fingleton, Lawrence Le Quesne, etc. Let me describe to you the tactics of bodyline.

"One – it is a fast ball.

"Two – it is a short-pitched ball.

"Three – it is aimed at the batsman's head and shoulders.

"Four – it is bounced on the leg side.

"Five – it is bowled to a stacked leg-side field of six to eight men: four to six close in at short-leg, and one to two deep at long-on."

"So, if the batsman defends, he is liable to be caught by the near fielders at short-leg or, if he hooks, he is liable to be caught on the boundary at long-leg," I said.

"Exactly."

"But that is precisely what we call 'bouncers' today."

"Ah – but there are differences.

"One – now we are not allowed to bowl more than one per over. Then all six deliveries could be bouncers.

"Two – today it is deemed 'unsportsmanship' to bowl such balls at tail-enders. In that series all the eleven were hammered.

"Three – today we have all sorts of protective wear to guard against mortality and morbidity. Then they had none. They just got out of the way, or got out, or got hit. Many were badly bruised, physically and psychologically.

"Four – most importantly, such a sort of bowling was 'not cricket'. Excepting for Jardine and his two principal fast bowlers – Larwood and Voce – none of the players in the England camp approved of the tactics. The public was disgusted."

"But when does a ball cease to be legitimate?" I asked. "When is one to decide whether a beach is land or sea? No law can define the precise moment when a delivery becomes deadly assault. No law can plug all loopholes."

"That's it. Cricket, as any game, must be played according to the spirit of the sport. The players must decide according to their sensibilities. Bowling that intimidates by sheer speed is legitimate. Bowling that is aimed to maim is illegitimate."

"How did it all start?"

"Well, according to Larwood, bodyline was born at the Oval in August 1930 – the last Test between England and Australia – when he noted that Jackson and Bradman seemed a bit diffident against what he calls 'fast-leg theory'. But remember Bradman scored 232 there. So we can discount that for a start.

"Next we come to the Surrey versus Yorkshire match at the Oval when Bill Bowes started such intimidatory bowling against Jack Hobbs, who walked down the pitch and remonstrated. Pelham Warner wrote off to the press condemning such bowling. The irony is that the same Pelham Warner was manager of the team that left the shores of England for Australia in 1932.

"According to Hammond, the obstetrical ward for bodyline was at the grill room of the Piccadilly Hotel, London, where the logistics were worked out over convivial beverages by Jardine, Carr, Voce and Larwood. This was apparently after Jardine discussed the notion with F R Foster, who later disassociated himself from the entire plan.

"Bradman is of the opinion that it all started on the sea voyage between England and Australia."

"Tell us about Jardine. He seems a character. I know that he was of Scottish extraction, born in 1900 in Bombay."

"He sure was a queer bird. Douglas Robert Jardine. His father was also born in India – Simla. Jardine later went on to be Advocate-General of Bombay. Douglas was sent to Winchester school, where he became captain. He played for Oxford and then for Surrey. He made his Test debut at Lord's against the West Indies in 1928. He was a decent enough batsman but he also saw himself as an aristocrat. He displayed his hauteur openly. Maybe his upbringing in the highfalutin circles of Bombay contributed to his sense of superiority that made him behave with unveiled arrogance towards lesser mortals. He lacked imagination and humour and saw himself as a sort of Messiah for the rebirth of English cricket. He was just not going to let the barbaric Aussies win in a game that was English. He behaved like an aristocrat and gave an impression of supercilious contempt to one and all around him. But he had one thing going. He was intrepid, stood by his decisions, backed his team and ignored officialdom. Those were the qualities that inspired his team.

"To such a man was entrusted the job of captaincy by the revered gentlemen of the MCC. How the strategy was finally distilled is immaterial. It was Jardine's brainchild and he implemented it with unprecedented zeal in the face of all opposition. He gave precedents to his plan of action by stating that his 'leg-theory' had been invented by an Australian, Warwick Armstrong, some 25 years ago, and that the Yorkshireman George Hirst used to bowl to a packed leg-side field, as did W B Burns of Worcestershire. More recently he quoted the Australian, Jack Scott, who bowled bodyline against Percy Chapman's tour of 1928-29 – as did Bill Voce against Nottinghamshire."

"So it was nothing new."

"No; but what made it controversial were the cannon-ball speed, the deadly accuracy and remorseless leg-stump line, the packed leg-side field and its sole purpose – to maim the batsmen. It was made worse by Larwood, who took on a personal vendetta against the Don, for he deemed that the Don had showed him up."

"In other words, to get the opposition out through sheer intimidation…"

"That's correct. Jardine had with him the perfect bowler to fulfil his requirements – Harold Larwood, a miner who could bowl his rockets with uncommon precision. He also had Bowes and Voce, a left-armer. The fourth fast bowler, G O Allen, refused point-blank to have anything to do with bodyline…though he was a key fielder in the leg-trap for the other bowlers. The other members in the team, players like Hammond and the Nawab of Pataudi, were cowed by the maniacal ruthlessness of Jardine. Jardine actually asked the nawab to buttress the already overcrowded leg trap but His Highness refused."

"Conscientious objector."

"The stage was set. But Jardine was a shrewd and cunning cove. In the preliminary matches he under-bowled Larwood and rarely played his two henchmen, Larwood and Voce, together. He loosened the reins now and then, as against Western Australia, when Larwood and Bowes thudded several of their bumpers against the batsmen. Jardine noted that Bradman was dismissed five times by pace in his six innings, and that too cheaply; Bradman made only a measly 62 in all the pre-Test matches. Jardine licked his lips. Bradman was shrewd enough to know what was going to happen even before the Tests began. He reported his suspicions to the administration. No one paid heed.

"First Test. It was something of an anticlimax, for Bradman did not play as he was laid up with influenza. Jardine set his field. Four close-in catchers forming a ring on the leg side with three sweepers in the deep. For Larwood, there was no fielder on the offside. From 87 for four Australia rallied to score 360, due to a superb innings of 187 not out from Stan McCabe. Larwood, five for 96; Voce, four for 110. England replied handsomely with 524 – magnificent centuries from Sutcliffe, Hammond and the Nawab of Pataudi. Australia made precisely the difference of 162, Larwood taking another five wickets for 28. Sutcliffe and Wyatt strode out to make the one run required for a win."

"Ah, but no Bradman."

"Second Test at Melbourne. The Don came in with the score 67 for two. Bowes came in to bowl. Bradman had decided to go on the offensive and hooked the first ball. The ball got the bottom edge and knocked into his leg stump. The whole of Australia was silent with stunned disbelief. Their God had failed! Thanks to Fingleton's obdurate 83, Australia reached 228. England replied with 169. The second time around, Bradman came and played what many consider to be one of his greatest innings in the face of inexorable hostility. You will see what I mean when I state that his 103 was of a total of 191. England had to make 251. They were bowled out for 139."

"One Test apiece."

"After the win, Bradman again brought to the notice of the administrators the possibility of grievous bodily harm resulting to the Australians from the English bodyline tactics. Still no one heeded him. He thought it was best to protest when they had won the match, and not later as it would seem like whining."

"He was right."

"Third Test at Adelaide. England made a creditable 341, when they were at one stage languishing at 37 for four. Jardine opened his battery with Larwood and Allen. Allen got out Fingleton for a blob and Bradman walked in. Larwood staggered Woodfull with a hit to the chest. Jardine called out, 'Well bowled, Harold.' Later, as Larwood was running in to bowl, Jardine waved his men into the familiar sinister leg-side trap. The crowd jeered. Jardine disdainfully dismissed the tumult. Larwood, who drew inspiration from adversity, bowled his fastest ball of the tour and blasted Woodfull's bat out of his hand. The crowd exploded in vociferous fury. If any one spectator had stepped onto the field in anger, there would have been a murderous invasion and the England team would have been annihilated. Larwood was unfazed. He got Bradman to dolly a catch to Allen, who then got Woodfull. When Woodfull returned to the pavilion, Pelham Warner, the MCC manager, came to enquire and was given the famous remark, 'There are two teams out there, but only one is playing cricket.' The end of play saw three Australians badly hurt and mounted police had to quell a riot. On the fifth day of play, 18 January, the Australian Board of Control cabled the MCC. The MCC deplored the cable and stuck with Jardine and his men. Telegrams and telephone calls whizzed across the lands and seas. Australia, at one point, even threatened to secede from the Commonwealth. The MCC, outraged at the insouciance of the upstart Australians, threatened to recall its team. Through it all, Jardine was icy cool, supremely poised, sartorially elegant, seemingly unaware of the commotion he had caused. Finally, the Australians could not make the financial sacrifice of cancelling the match and called, 'Play.' In the final innings, the Australians were set an impossible 532 to win. Woodfull made a heroic 73 and the Don a dogged 66, improvising by moving to the leg side and cutting to the off. England won by 338 runs."

"Two to one for England."

"England won the fourth and fifth Tests. Due to the adversity whipped up by the press the grounds were packed. They came like a pack of dogs to see blood spilt...even though it was their own. It was macabre. They scented the contest between Bradman and Larwood. So far Bradman had not been hit by Larwood. In the final Test, Larwood managed to give the Don a blow on his right arm. But Larwood too suffered. His feet ached badly. But Jardine would not let him rest. It was only after Verity bowled Bradman that he gestured to Larwood to leave the field. The two great protagonists left the field together with not a word exchanged.

"So, Jardine's ploy worked!"

"It did in the sense that he was able to contain Bradman. His average was 56 – an insult judged by his standards. But the ruthless victory was pyrrhic, the triumph tarnished with the brush of vindictive unsportsmanship, and relations between the two nations severely wounded.

"When the flak ended and the debris cleared and the post-mortem finished, the Australian Board formed a committee and sent its findings to the MCC. The MCC – let us give them their due – once they had the evidence in front of them, roundly condemned the tactics of bodyline."

"So, we are left with the possibility that the MCC was not totally aware of Jardine's measures and the effects they had on Australia and cricket in general."

"That's right."

"What happened next?"

"The MCC demanded an apology from Voce and Larwood for their bodyline bowling. Voce apologized, was forgiven and continued to play for England. Larwood refused, for he was only following the orders of his captain. He disappeared under a cloud and never played for England again. He became a bitter man..."

"Justifiably..?"

"Yes. He refused to associate himself with cricket in any way. He melted into obscurity in a little side street in Blackpool, where he had a small shop. He refused to even have his name on it. He could have cashed in in a million ways with his name...but did not."

"I read somewhere that he took snuff..."

"Yes, he used to take it on the field. And he liked his beer after a game."

"Did you know that Larwood was invited by the Maharaja of Patiala to coach his team? In the finals of the Quadrangular Tournament, the Hindus beat the Europeans by a comfortable 257 runs. Larwood's heart was not in it. His mind was with the England team then touring Australia. Disappointed and disillusioned, Larwood excused himself from Patiala and caught the boat back home to England."

"Well, I didn't know that little episode."

"What happened to Jardine?"

"Jardine stoutly defended his position and refused to hide behind words of hypocrisy. He bravely faced the

West Indians – Constantine and Martindale, who bowled bouncers and beamers – and then took Clark and Nichols to India and employed the bodyline field and split Merchant's chin, cut Naomal's eye and Hussain's head."

"A case of not just eagles against sparrows, but demons against minnows…"

"Quite right. When an umpire told Jardine that he would stop Clark bowling his thunderbolts, Jardine retorted that he would stop him from umpiring…and did. Witnessing the mayhem meted out by the second-string bowlers on the Indians, Australia was hesitant to visit England. The MCC, having stood by Jardine, could not sack him. Jardine, however, announced that he would not play and everyone heaved a sigh of relief. The MCC reassured the Aussies about bodyline. The tourists arrived. Voce gave vent to his injured feelings and bowled bodyline in a preliminary match. The Aussies told the MCC that they would sail back if Voce played. The MCC came out with a report that outlawed bodyline. The Australians won back the Ashes.

"A grim chapter in the history of cricket had come to an end."

"I have often wondered about the manager of the England side, Pelham Warner. What was he doing during these shenanigans?"

"Good question. But no answers. There is complete secrecy about his part in the affair. Did he object? Did he condone? No one knows. He was later knighted for his services to cricket. We do not know what he did. Maybe he helped to calm the troubled waters, kept Australia within the Commonwealth and encouraged the 1934 Australian tour to England to materialize. Who knows..? England had two managers on that fateful tour – Warner and Palairet. Palairet was the junior and did not involve himself. Warner, it is believed, denounced Jardine's tactics but felt that he must be loyal to the MCC and his country...and to victory. So he came out as a rather pathetic figure."

"I know something about Bradman," I said; "check me out."

"OK, clever clogs," said John.

	Innings	Aggregate	Average	Centuries
All Matches	669	50,731	90.27	211
Test Cricket	80	6,996	99.90	29

Methods of dismissal	
Innings	669
Caught	340
Bowled	148
LBW	37
Stumped	22
Run out	14
Hit wicket	1

"Good for you. I didn't know about the 'methods of dismissal'," said John.

"Well, you are not the only clever clogs around, you know. There is something else you don't know about Bradman. He went to Hollywood."

"You are the movie buff. Go on, then. Tell us about it."

"1932. Australian tour of Fiji islands, Honolulu, Canada and America. Los Angeles – Hollywood. Don and his team met the stars Mary Astor, Jean Harlow, Myrna Loy, Boris Karloff, Leslie Howard, Maureen O'Sullivan, Norma Shearer and our friend C Aubrey Smith. They spent a memorable day at MGM studios. The English expatriates of Hollywood organized a cricket match. Smith was captain of the Hollywood team (remember that Smith captained the England team to Australia in 1887?). The match itself wasn't much. The Australians were too good. But everyone enjoyed the camaraderie.

"In ten weeks the team had travelled 6,000 miles, Don played 51 innings, scored 3,779 runs at an average of 102."

"What do you know!" exclaimed John.

"I have a little ditty about Bradman too.

Sing a song of Woodfull,
Wiping England's eye;
Thirty-thousand people
'Neath a baking sky;
When 'Boy' Bradman opened
The ball began to sing;
Wasn't that a dainty dish
To set before the King?

"That was written at Lord's by some bloke," I said.

* * * * * * * *

"What is the story about the Ashes, John?"

"It is the first defeat of England on home soil. 1882, August the 28th. Australia made 63, England, 101; Australia, 122. England needed 85 to win. But a chap called Freddy Spofforth ran through the England side – that included W G – with figures of nine wickets for 75. The whole of England was stunned. On the 2nd of September an obituary notice appeared in *The Sporting Times*.

In affectionate remembrance of English Cricket which died at the Oval on 29th August 1882. Deeply lamented by a large circle of sorrowing friends and acquaintances.
RIP.
NB – The body will be cremated and the ashes taken to Australia.

On the 14th of September, Ivo Bligh's team set sail for Australia on the *Peshawar*. Ivo fell in love with the beautiful Florence Rose Murphy, companion of Janet, wife of William John Clarke, president of Melbourne Cricket Club, who had been recently knighted. On Christmas Eve, after a social cricket match, Lady Clarke burnt a bail, put it in a wooden urn and presented it to Ivo – well before England had legally won the cricket series, which they did 2-1. A Mrs Anne Fletcher, wife of the secretary of Paddington Cricket Club, presented Ivo with a small crimson velvet bag as a receptacle for the ashes. Ivo Bligh had the bag and the wooden urn with the ashes of the single bail with him at Cobham Hall in Kent. It was presented to the MCC after his death. They are in the Memorial Gallery at Lord's."

I sighed and closed my book.

"We are not finished yet, doc. I am going to tell you about The Black Bradman."

"The Black Bradman?!"

"Yes. George Headley, the West Indian, is considered by many pundits to be greater – in some ways – than the Don. What are the cardinal qualities of a good batsman?"

"A good batsman should see the ball early and read it correctly. He must move his feet, shoulders and arms quickly into position to deal with the oncoming ball. He must keep his head still when hitting the shot. He must be quick with the bat. He must follow through. He must place the ball into the vacant areas, for the job of a batsman is to get runs."

"Well put. The Don was the master in all those qualities. George Headley of the West Indies was another. If the Don had a weakness, it was on a sticky wicket. George thrived on sticky wickets. Someone compiled a few statistics to bear this out. Between 1928 and 1938, the Don played 15 innings on dicey wickets in Australia and England. He passed 50 only once and ended up with an average of 16.66. Between 1933 and 1939, George played 13 innings on uncertain wickets in England. He passed 50 seven times with an average of 39.85. Another point we have to bear in mind is that Bradman had other greats playing with him – Ponsford, Woodfull, McCabe and the others. George had no one. He had to shoulder the burden of his entire team every time – like your Tendulkar. Another point to bear in mind is that Bradman played against the weaker teams like New Zealand, Pakistan and India. George met the onslaught of the two best teams in the world: England and Australia. When he went to Australia at the age of 21 he lambasted the bowling. The Aussies took to bowling to his leg side. By the time of the third Test he had worked out his strategy and he scored 309 runs in three Tests with a couple of centuries. He used to work out his strategy like a general and would not sleep before a match, going through the motions in his head, visualizing the ball coming towards him and the stroke he was going to play. He had every stroke in the book. The only strokes he loathed were the pushes. He believed that a batsman should make runs, not push and stand."

"I had never heard of George Headley," I said.

"One more titbit for your book, doc," said John. "Have you ever heard of a chap called Mr Spedegue?"

"Nope."

"Well, he was a schoolteacher. He had a unique way of practising his bowling. Do you know what he did? He tied a rope between two trees some 50 feet above the ground. He marked out the pitch under it and planted his stumps. Then he practised bowling the ball over the rope and onto the stumps."

"Surely you must be joking!"

"No. The crazy fellow did just that. He was slugged into the England team and he ended up with figures of seven for 31 against the Aussies. That was Sir Arthur Conan Doyle's story."

* * * * * * * *

CHAPTER 20
Charlie Macartney; Stan McCabe

"Have you heard of a chap called Charlie Macartney?" asked John.

"No," I replied.

"Well, listen to this story. Trumper was 25 and Bradman 22 when they exhibited their vintage qualities. Charlie was 40 – an age at which today's players are forgotten. Charlie was nicknamed 'the Governor General', for he was defiant, dogmatic and domineering; he entered the arena with the air of one about to inspect the ranks, unprepared to put up with any nonsense. A strong jutting chin, alert twinkling eyes and thick hairy wrists added to his personality. Charlie came to England in 1912 and was on 99 at Lord's. Foster bowled him a full toss and Charlie went at it as if to hit him into St John's Wood. Only – he didn't connect and was out. 'Damned full toss. Made of a mess of it,' he said. He was not one of those who approaches his century like a cat burglar. If there was a stroke to be played, he played it. 'If the first ball of the Test asks to be hit for six, why – you just hit it for six.' That was his pugnacious policy. Jack Fingleton, the famous cricketer-writer, once opened with Charlie. 'I'll take strike, son,' said Charlie to Jack. 'And keep your eyes open for the first ball.' Jack was nonplussed, not knowing what Charlie meant; maybe be alert for a quick single, he thought. The bowler pitched the first ball of the innings. Jack fell to earth; the bowler fell to earth; the umpire fell to earth as if an air raid was on. Charlie had smashed the first ball straight back at them. It had travelled like a meteorite and crashed into the pickets. Jack shakily got up and went down the pitch to Charlie, who said, 'It's always a good idea to aim the first ball right here at the bowler's head. They don't like it. It rattles 'em.'

"1926. Charlie came along with the Aussies to play England again. They rated England's Macaulay as England's best bowler. Charlie strode up to his captain, Bardsley, and said, 'This bloke could go through us. There's no better bowler in England. I want permission to "murder" him immediately.' Bardsley, slightly perplexed, gave his assent.

"Carr, England's captain, won the toss and put Australia in to bat – a decision he would rue for the rest of his life. Bardsley was out first ball for a duck. In strode Charlie Macartney, his bat aloft and twirling as if to cut down a field of lilies. His brown eyes roved the field to pinpoint the openings. He glided Tate's third ball for two through the slips. He snicked the fifth ball to Carr waiting in the slips. Horror of horrors! Carr floored it. By the end of the day that muffed catch had become the most publicized event in cricket history, for, instead of being two for two, the score at stumps was 235 for one. Macauley opened from the pavilion end. Charlie twirled his bat and took a two. The next ball he socked for six over mid-off. The 'murdering' of Macauley had begun.

"In the next 40 minutes, Charlie had blasted Macauley for 40; Australia was 50 for one. The 100 came in 79 minutes, of which Charlie's contribution was 83. At lunch he was 112. The field had spread out in all directions, but balls rocketed from Charlie's bat before the fielders had time to move. He went on ruthlessly to

151, when he was caught by Hendren off Macauley. The English crowd rose as one and applauded him for the greatest exhibition of controlled hitting they had ever seen.

"He was also a good bowler, who whipped his balls in at high speed. In first-class cricket he made 14,217 runs and took 366 wickets.

* * * * * * * *

"I've got to tell you about another Aussie – Stan McCabe. You may want to know more about English cricketers but I don't think it is wrong if you mention some all-time greats of other countries. They still comprise the history of cricket; besides, they did play in England during the course of their careers."

"I agree. I am interested in any cricketer – as long as there is a story to it."

"Well, this fits the bill. During that bodyline series of 1932, one Aussie stood out undaunted. He was McCabe. Bradman did not play in the first Test due to illness. Australia was 82, battered and bruised by Larwood and co. Stan came it at number five, determined not to die. Without flinching, he stood up to the diabolical bowling. He hooked, drove and cut to all parts of the field. England didn't know how to get rid of him. By the end of the day he had made 127 with 17 boundaries in about three hours. The next day, he carried on where he had left off the previous evening. In 55 minutes he belted another 60 runs before he was out. He had made 187 while his seven partners had managed 90 between them. His magnificent innings against the most fearsome bowling deliberately devised by a team ranks alongside – or even surpasses – the 185 n.o. by Trumper while his seven partners fell for 95, and Ranji's 154 n.o. while his nine partners managed 112.

"1938. Nottingham. England had made a colossal 658 for eight declared. It was Australia's turn to bat. Disaster. Fingleton went for nine, Bradman for 51, Brown for 48. Within 15 minutes of play the next day, two more wickets had fallen; half the side out and still more than 500 runs behind. McCabe was unwell with a fever and cold when he came in to bat. He saw his mates falling at regular intervals. But when the sixth wicket fell, he determined that something had to be done. For the next couple of hours he hammered the English bowling all over the ground. It was not slogging. It was precision. He played all the strokes in the textbook with perfect timing and placing. The English fieldsmen simply didn't know where to stand to prevent the runs. When the last man, Fleetwood-Smith, came and defended admirably the 18 balls he received, McCabe plundered 72 runs in an enthralling 28 minutes. His total of 213 came up in 200 minutes, the last 127 in only 80 minutes. His eight partners had managed to scrape up only 58 runs in that time – an achievement surely without parallel. He had taken the steam out of England, though his side was still 247 behind and had to follow on.

"Bradman, always magnanimous, greeted McCabe in the pavilion with the words, 'If I could play an innings like that I would be a proud man, Stan.' Even the redoubtable S F Barnes stated that that was the best Test innings he had ever witnessed.

"1935. South Africa. Australia needed to score 399 runs to win. They lost the first wicket at 17. Any other team would have doggedly dug in for a draw. But McCabe never believed that the best defence was defence. He refused to give the advantage to the bowlers. He set about them with grim determination. He raced to his 100 in 90 minutes. The sky darkened and rumbled with thunder and forked out lightning. Eventually an appeal was made against light – not by the batsmen but by the South Africans, as they were in danger of being hit by McCabe's thunderbolts. When finally the thunderstorm broke, McCabe had made 189 not out and the match was drawn. Many players have made bigger scores, but none have had to come to their side's rescue so often in desperate situations and score at that rate to stave off defeat."

* * * * * * * *

CHAPTER 21
Interlude; World War II; Shirley and John

The Second World War loomed because some idiot thought he was better than the others and wanted to prove it by getting rid of the others.

"What happened to cricket?" I asked John.

"Well, the 1930s saw the last giants retire. Jack Hobbs in 1935; Patsy Hendren in 1937, Frank Woolley in 1938. Here's another for your book.

"1939. The 1st of September. Hove. Last fixture of the season. Yorkshire vs Sussex. At the end of the day's play the match cards proclaimed the incredible news.

"Six Overs. One Maiden. Nine Runs. Seven Wickets.

"Mr Hedley Verity of Yorkshire had massacred Surrey. Four years later Captain Verity was hit in the chest by a German bullet in Sicily and died in an Italian POW camp. News of his death reached England on the 1st of September 1943 – four years to the day after his devastating achievement."

"Did play stop during the war?"

"The fools had learnt their lesson from the First War. They did not equate sport with malingering. The Minister of Labour confirmed that all cricket and football matches would proceed as usual. But most of the players had volunteered to give their share of blood and guts on behalf of King and Country. So bizarre teams were playing at Lord's – Buccaneers vs British Empire XI; Lord's XI vs Canada; Metropolitan Police vs London Fire Service. Some of the retired players participated in some of these fixtures, to the delight of the spectators – Hendren and Woolley, for instance. One of the gods – Andrew Ducat, now 56 years old, ex-football and cricket international cap – died on the field at Lord's in 1942.

"In the summer of 1942 at Lord's all the players threw themselves to the ground when a German aircraft cruised overhead. The hushed crowd prayed. It flew over and dropped its bombs a mile away. The players dusted themselves off and the Middlesex batsman Jack Robertson belted the first delivery for a six, to the cheer of the crowd.

"Did you know that even prisoners of war played cricket in their POW camps throughout Germany and Italy? At Eichstatt, Germany, the POWs produced their own cricketer's magazine and played matches with bravado to distract the guards while they tunnelled away beneath their very feet."

* * * * * * * *

"Shirley," I said, "tell us about the war years. What did you do? How was it?"

And this is what she told me.

"When the war started we were in Wallingford in Surrey, with our son aged 11 and daughter aged nine. John went off to join up. We were living in a terraced house, three bedrooms. We carried on as usual during 1939 and the beginning of 1940: the 'phoney war' phase. But from then on we took it seriously. We had to take in evacuees from London. The children slept with me in one bedroom. We billeted a cockney family of a grandmother, a mother and her four children in the other two bedrooms. They had run into the nearest underground station on hearing the air raid siren. When the all-clear was sounded they emerged. It seemed as if the world had erupted. Their entire street in London had been razed to the ground by the German bombers. They were very nice people and helped with everything. Their children got on well with ours and played in the rubble.

"By 1941 Wallingford was no longer safe. We had to be evacuated to Somerset. We were separated from the cockney family. We were moved to Chadwick Hall, a great rambling house with gardens and fields. There were ten families in there.

"We kept chickens, goats and cows. We needed the eggs; the chickens we ate when they were too old to lay eggs or if they got sickly. All the animals were frightened of the flying airplanes and exploding bombs...the chickens refused to lay and the animals gave a paltry amount of milk. But, I suppose, after a few months they sort of got conditioned to the noise and carried on as usual. The goats and cows were important to supply milk for the babies and children. Ill animals were taken to the butcher's. In those days, we had no time to tend them. We used their manure for the kitchen garden. We eliminated the flower beds and converted them into vegetable patches. We grew potatoes, cabbage, cauliflower, carrots etc. Those were the days of rationing, you see.

"One lb of meat, 4oz of bacon or ham, 8oz of sugar, 225g of fats, of which 115 was margarine and 55g was butter per week. 30 eggs per year. Nursing mothers and children were allowed three eggs a week and half a litre of milk per day. In 1942, rationing was extended to canned and dried foods, cereals, chocolate, biscuits, groceries and soap.

"If we billeted an officer we were allowed 3 shillings per day – 10oz of meat, 1oz butter, 10oz vegetables. If we had a horse we were given more – 3 shillings 9 pence for 5lb of oats and 10lb of hay.

"I worked in the Church army forces canteen doing shift work...cooking and washing endlessly. I also drove the food supplies van.

"We learnt not to be afraid. After some time, like the animals, we got used to the overhead air battles, the dropping bombs, the screeching vehicles on the roads, the anti-aircraft batteries, the swords of light cutting through the air to find the enemy planes, the emerging from air-raid shelters and finding our neighbourhood reduced to rubble. If we got killed, we got killed. Just bad luck. One of the trench shelters got a direct hit. With our bleeding hands we removed all the rubble. It was a terrible sight. Some 24 people had died in the rubble. Posters were everywhere asking for blood donations. All of us gave our blood regularly. Who knows? One of us or one of our loved ones in battle might be saved by a pint someday.

"But there were good times too. All of us used to sit around a goat or a cow watching it giving birth. The children were fascinated. To them the war was 'free entertainment'. They didn't know fear. They would run out to see the air battles and would scream with delight at exploding bombs. They were always the last to enter the shelters. After screaming at them a few times, we just gave up...as long as they did creep in eventually.

"One young couple decided to get married. He was in for a few days' leave from fighting Rommel in Africa. We trooped to the church, glad for the chance to wear good clothes for a change. After the ceremony we came out of the church and posed for the photograph. Just then the air-raid siren wailed and we heard the Germans.

"'Never mind screaming,' shouted the photographer, 'just *smile*'.

"There was a beautiful girl living with us. She was the life and soul of the place. She could win over anyone with a smile. Even we women liked her...even though she was a prostitute. She didn't make any bones of it. She simply loved her job. All the soldiers went for her. Many fought each other for her favours. She used to tell us wonderful stories about them. I suppose, in some way, we were a bit jealous of her. We arranged sales to raise money for the Russians. I remember an old man trying to sell a print of the Virgin Mary to her. She smiled ever so sweetly at him and said, ' I am not much of a virgin, really'.

"The Americans landed in 1942 and the women went crazy. It is not fiction about the Americans. They didn't know what war was in their country. Once they were here, they were shocked. They concluded that England was poor and dirty...and small. They always seemed to have tins of food and chocolates and cartons of cigarettes with which to barter for anything. And, of course, the English girls fell for them. One day I returned home to find a tall blond American in our sitting room with our children on his knees feeding them bars of chocolate. He was missing his own children of similar age. He was invaluable around the house. A burst pipe; call Jake. Oven not working; call Jake. Chicken pen needs fixing; Jake will fix it. And the black Americans! In those days we called them Negroes. The girls were fascinated with them. They would sleep with them just to see how it was. And, of course, our children had never seen a black man before. They would run to them on the streets and the big burly soldiers would swoop them up onto their shoulders like sacks of flour.

"Then we had the drills and war manoeuvres. They were fun. The roads were chock-a-blocked with troops, guns, lorries, jeeps etc. We had to make hundreds of sandwiches and lay them out on trestle tables under the trees. We laughed at the way they played their phoney war. They used real bullets and sometimes they ricocheted. It is no fun dodging bullets whizzing past your head.

"One day the Germans seemed intent on wiping out our part of the world. Endless sorties. The skies were filled with them like swarms of locusts. The night skies were full of them; we couldn't tell the planes from the stars. The searchlights wove fantastic patterns. The smell of war was in our nostrils. We learnt the next day that a nearby town had been demolished. We drove with food and medicines. The King and Queen were there alongside the mayor, giving their support and sympathy. Our children were encrusted with mud and soot and oil doing their bit in shifting the rubble...bricks, furniture, girders etc. But they stood with the others and smiled and waved. I believe the King saw them and smiled.

"Soon after the King and Queen left, some loonies were out with their placards: 'Behold, the end of the world is nigh', and 'Repent for your sins'. I actually screamed at them for not joining with us and helping the injured and those buried under tons of concrete.

"Churchill was on the radio, telling us about confident, bright and smiling eyes amidst the ruins and the spirit of an unconquerable people. His words did cheer us.

"We had an Italian POW camp some miles from us. One day a prisoner escaped. All of us were frightened. We never went out alone. He had killed one of the guards. They eventually tracked him down to a disused farmhouse and killed him.

"One day I discovered a lump in my breast. I consulted the local doctor, who said that I had to go to London to see a specialist. I caught the train to London. It was packed with white and black American troops. London was a nightmare. Burnt-out buildings everywhere. It was there I had the first taste of the V1 rockets – doodlebugs. They flew overhead and spluttered and went silent. Then they would swoop down and explode. There were so many of them that they stopped sounding the air-raid sirens. We just waited with bated breath to see where they would fall. Then there would be a mad rush to rescue the unfortunate people.

"After nearly three years I had a room to myself, clean sheets and a hot bath in the hospital. I was grateful. The biopsy revealed that it was benign – a fibroma or something. I had it excised and returned to Chadwick.

"The women also formed details to collect sphagnum moss that was used for dressing gangrenous wounds and foxgloves to make digitalis.

"Oh, yes. We did go to the pictures too. Earlier during the war we saw *The Wizard of Oz* and *Gone with the Wind*. Great movies. They show them at least once a year even today on television. Then there were 'recruitment movies' – *Devil Dogs of the Air, Here comes the Navy, Rear Gunner, Dive Bomber, Casablanca, Sahara, A Yank in the RAF, Mortal Storm, The Sea Hawk*, etc.

"One day an American woman was billeted with us. Real glamorous one. Her husband was reported missing in France. One of the husbands fell for her and we could hear the rows from their room. Her husband ended up in a POW camp in Italy. We had a drunk on our hands once – the dangerous type. He used to run amok with a knife. One day, Jake had to sock him unconscious. We shifted him to a hospital.

"Many women worked as field hands in the farm lands doing men's work, and many worked in factories manufacturing arms. In those days it was almost impossible for a woman under 40 to avoid 'war work'. We mobilized our resources more thoroughly than any other country, including Russia and America – 55% of the people were involved in the war in some capacity.

"And then there were those terrible days when one of the people received a Home Office telegram. We could do nothing but put our arms around the bereaved and hold them to us. All of us lived in constant dread of that terrible telegram. Though we lived our lives and got on with whatever it is we had to get on with, subconsciously we had fear within us. Fear not for us. If we got killed, we got killed. But fear of someone close to us dying somewhere in a foreign land; we could never cope with that – not being able to see the person or the body; not really knowing how it all was."

* * * * * * * *

This is John's story.

"I was an accountant. And I was 33 years old when the war began. I was deemed 'old'; besides, I was told that I had flat feet. What the hell has flat feet got to do with anything? I was playing cricket for donkey's years with my feet. But they wouldn't listen. So I was assigned to supplies.

"For me the war is divided into three experiences – Dunkirk, Tunisia and Normandy. Of the three Dunkirk was the worst.

"I went over with the British Expeditionary Forces into Europe and we were beaten back by the Germans. The French, the British and the Belgians were deployed like a barrier across France and Belgium against Germany. The French were in the south from Sedan to Gembloux; we occupied a small stretch from Gembloux to Louvain; and the Belgians were to the north of us from Louvain to Antwerp. But it was no use. We were all ill-prepared and were no match for the German army and air force. Beaten, weary and frightened we retreated through Belgium to Dunkirk. On one side of the road was the British Force in trucks, Bren gun carriers, service corps, ordnance, Austin 8s, dispatch riders, canteen trucks, supplies trucks; on the other side were the stream of refugees. People of all ages in every kind of vehicle imaginable, piled high with their belongings; everyone one of them haggard with the air of hopelessness. Hundreds of people travelled in horse and donkey carts with a cow or a horse or a donkey in tow; some had chickens piled on top of their possessions; some had pigs and calves; nearly every cart we passed had a grandmother or grandfather with babies or children on top while the more fit trudged along with rifles or bundles of food or clothing; prams contained babies hidden under bedding. Bicycles were used not to ride on but to carry their precious possessions. The Germans were bombarding us with land guns and from the air with relentless regularity. The trains that carried troops and civilians were raked with machine-gun fire and bombs from the air with devastating effect. Whole trainloads of people were killed. We scampered off the roads into ditches when we heard the Messerschmitts and Stukas; yet thousands died all around me. Bits of bodies flying through the air, bodies sliced in two due to flying debris, groups of people transformed into minced meat by direct hits.

"As some of the troops were fighting desperate rearguard battles the bulk of the army was heading towards the English Channel to be rescued. When we reached Dunkirk it was already smouldering from the airborne bombing; fires were raging in pockets all over the town, and our ears reverberated to the sound of explosions. We were thirsty, footsore and frightened out of our wits. As we passed through the towns we were not able to get any water. People in hotels refused to give us water; we had to buy wine or soda water. The irony of it all, as we saw the death and destruction, heard the cries of pain and grief, smelt the cordite and burning flesh and tasted the ashes of defeat – the sun was shining down on us gloriously, oblivious of the hell it was witnessing. The countryside that had not been pock-marked with bomb craters was more beautiful than England.

"When we reached Dunkirk we were billeted in a house that must have belonged to a wealthy Belgian – antique furniture, costly curtains and crockery. I went upstairs and opened the door of the bathroom. I nearly fell 20 feet onto the street; that side of the house was blown to bits. We rummaged for food and went down into the cellar, where we found hundreds of bottles of wine. We filled ourselves with it and managed to sleep through the night despite the consternation all around. We had not slept for 48 hours and we just didn't care. The next day we went down to the beaches through the town. The town hall was burning. As we were crossing the town square the Stukas swooped down and riddled us. Nine soldiers were mowed down in their tracks hardly six feet from where I stood; one of them was almost cut in half at his waist, another had a clean hole through his skull.

"The harbour basin was full of little boats and fishing craft. Troops in their thousands were waiting like us, praying for the boats from England; and while we were waiting, we were being strafed by the Germans. Thousands died on the beaches. There was nowhere to go. The town was being continuously bombed. The houses along the seafront were ablaze and we could hear the German artillery a few miles from Dunkirk breathing down on us. We spent the night on the beaches of

Dunkirk. No one can describe how we spent it or how we felt. After a time, I suppose, we were all in a state of shock and carried on like zombies. At last a British destroyer appeared in the distance; a little later, a string of three Thames barges; then 14 drifters, each towing two boats, appeared. The great evacuation had begun.

"It was painfully slow work. Each boat could take on only 50. As we scrambled from the beach through the waters we were sitting targets for the German planes that came on every ten minutes – always from west to east. We had dug little holes for ourselves in the sands with our rifles for whatever protection they could offer. As we moved down towards the boats, another wave of troops moved in from the town to take our places. I jettisoned my kit and scrambled to the pier. Two men staggered along with a stretcher. I helped them load him into a boat. Another stretcher. His insides were hanging out. He was a goner. A medic took one look at him, shook his head and gave him an intravenous shot; we left him by the water's edge. In the midst of all this we also had some German prisoners...if you can believe that. We had to take them along; but they would be occupying places that could otherwise be filled by our own men. There was a terrible row. Some of the soldiers wanted to kill them. The officer in charge fired his machine-gun into the air and said that he would shoot the first one to lay hands on the prisoners.

"Cold, wet, weary, hungry and shocked, we cowered in the boats as they returned, maddeningly slowly, back to England.

"Some 350,000 people were saved by Operation Dynamo, which lasted for nine days commencing the

26th of May 1940. This was made possible by Hitler, who stopped firing – for some inexplicable reason – on the retreating soldiers for a vital 24 hours on the 24th/25th of May.

"I had a few days' leave pending, which I spent with my family in Hallingford just before they had to evacuate to Somerset.

"My next foray into the war was in Tunisia.

"We were taken to Liverpool and boarded the *USS Coamo*; 1,600 of us. We didn't know where we were going. We sailed up to the Kyles of Bute in Scotland, where we were stunned to see a huge array of sea craft – battleships, troopships, cruisers, submarines etc. Someone told us that we were going to North Africa.

"French North Africa – Morocco, Algeria and Tunisia – were not occupied by Germany. They remained under the Vichy government of Pétain. Rommel had lost the battle of El Alamein in Egypt and was beating a retreat to Tunisia with Montgomery's 8th Army in pursuit. The Allies planned to trap him by sending troops by sea and air from Algiers. *Operation Torch* was set up under Eisenhower in London on the 14th of August. The Allied Western Task Force under Patton, who had landed directly from the USA, landed on the 8th of November 1942. He met with the fiercest resistance. The Centre Task Force under Fredenhall landed at Oran and the Eastern Task Force under Ryder landed at Algiers on the same date, but did not meet with much resistance. An armistice was concluded on the 10th of November and Ryder set off towards Tunis to meet

Rommel. The battle in Tunisia raged until May 1943. About 275,000 German prisoners were taken.

"So, there we were in the deserts, sweating in the day and freezing in the night. The Arabs were all around and I suspect they didn't know what was going on. They mingled with the hares and the hounds. I remember one day when we had buried our dead in the sands. The next day we found the graves robbed. The Arabs had come during the night and taken the woollen blankets from the bodies. Another time, they ran off with our food and helmets – after we had bought goats and chickens off them.

"The funny times in the midst of all this nonsense was the digging of trenches for easing ourselves. One of the lads got stuck in and dug so deep that he couldn't climb out. When he didn't turn up for his daily food ration, we found him collapsed due to heat exhaustion in the bloody toilet trench. Another time, the soldiers were playing a game of football when suddenly two of them disappeared underground; they had fallen into a toilet trench dug by someone else – the French or the Italians.

"Once, our platoon commander told us a tale. He and his men were stuck in a trench with the Germans on a sort of mound. The Germans couldn't see them and they couldn't scramble out without the Germans seeing them. They held on, not daring to smoke or speak, eating boiled sweets. In the night they heard German voices. The commander threw a hand grenade at them. A while later they heard an English-speaking German asking if they could come down and retrieve their fallen comrade. The commander assented. They came out of the trenches, chatted and exchanged cigarettes with the

Germans. The wounded man was their commander. The Germans gave him a helmet as a souvenir and acceded to the request that they could get back to their positions in the rear without danger of being fired upon.

"I cannot say anything much about the war. It was tough. I was injured in March 1943. A German bullet made a neat hole through my thigh. Luckily it was a clean flesh wound. Just look at the irony of it all! At Dunkirk I could have been killed a thousand times every minute. Yet I survived two days with not a scratch when all were dying around me. And in Tunisia, when I was happily going along in a convoy, a German fighter came down from the skies and aimed for me when I was scrambling into a ditch by the side of the road.

"I returned to England and spent my leave with the family in Somerset. There was a big camp of Americans nearby. Their food was cooked using Sawyer boilers. During one of the air raids all ten boilers were blown to pieces. You should have seen the mess: bits of food and burnt and twisted pots and pans all over the place. We had to cook for the Americans at the Church canteen. They lived on potatoes and dumplings till the boilers were replaced. Two German planes were shot down in the surrounding countryside when I was there. I went along with the local troops and constabulary. As we approached one of them took out his gun and shot himself in the head. The other surrendered. He was a handsome bloke. He was full of camaraderie and, in spite of the fact that he had 14 kills to his credit, the American and British soldiers took to him. He spent the remainder of the war in a POW camp in Wales, where he took up farming in a big way. After the war, he returned, married a Welsh girl and settled around Bangor.

"The third outing was on D-Day, the 6th of June 1944.

"Plans for the invasion of Europe via France were discussed as early as 1942. But it was not until the Quebec Conference in August 1943 that serious plans were laid. Eisenhower was made Supreme Allied Commander and Montgomery was directed to prepare the plans for the invasion. The operational radius of the Spitfire was a crucial factor. Everyone expected the port of entry to be Calais. So Normandy was chosen. Monty decided to land five seaborne and three airborne divisions. The beaches were given names.

Seaborne
3rd British	–	Sword
3rd Canadian		Juno
50th British	–	Gold
1st US Division		Omaha
4th US Division		Utah

Airborne
6th British, 82nd and 101st US Airborne Divisions landed east of Sword and west of Utah.

"Two Mulberry floating harbours, one British at Arromanches, another American at St Laurent. The latter was unfortunately wrecked by a gale but the former remained, supplying up to 11,000 tons of vital supplies daily.

"The total host comprised 50,000 men, with a further 2,000,000 to follow in 39 divisions, 138 warships, 1,000 minesweepers and auxiliary vessels and 4,000 landing craft supported by 12,000 aircraft. It was the greatest seaborne armada in human history.

"Against this Hitler gave Rommel the 7th and 15th Armies and Rundstedt the 1st and 19th Armies. But the trouble was he didn't know where to deploy them; consequently, they were thinly dispersed all along the coast. The worst casualties for the Allies were at Omaha, where some 3,000 died. At Utah they strolled through casually.

"The Germans suffered greatly – during the Battle of Normandy they had half a million casualties, including 210,000 prisoners, and lost 2,000 tanks and self-propelled guns.

"Despite all this, the whole of *Operation Overlord* was a shambles; all the reasons ascribed to 'human error'. How much of the blame should be laid at Monty's door has since become an endless debate in military circles. Nevertheless, all agree that we should have ended the war in 1944 – if everything had been planned and proceeded with rightly.

"Some have said that the endless days of waiting in the cold, wet weather, either aboard the ships or in ground camps, was worse than the beaches of France. Rubbish. We were at least safe in England. On the beaches it was murder. We couldn't see the enemy. They were hidden in their bunkers, taking pot-shots at us as we were struggling through the water and scrambling onto the beaches with our equipment and trying to get some sort of shelter. Being a supply man I was in the second wave to alight on the beach. Shells were exploding everywhere. People were shot as they were leaving their crafts. Even after they had fallen into the water, the bullets continued to spray them. I made a mad dash up the beach. A soldier fell to the sand. He was shot through the shoulder. I pulled him along with me. I had dropped by rifle. My platoon commander ordered me to retrieve it. I ran back for the rifle. I was with about 20 men in a hole. Maybe the Germans couldn't see us. But we saw many of our men shot to bits and we couldn't do a damned thing. It was terrible. It was like a turkey shoot. Towards the evening we were exhausted. We tried to get across the barbed wire and stakes under cover of darkness. A couple of men wormed their way through and managed to cut holes in the fencing. One by one we crept through.

"Some of the soldiers went on ahead to demolish the concrete bunkers from which the Germans were hammering us. We waited for the silence of the guns. One of the men was bleeding badly from a wound. We had no medic with us. I bandaged his wound. We heard a terrific explosion…the German bunker. We stood up to run. I fell to the ground in agony. A sniper had got me through the thigh. The bone was shattered. Someone patched me up and gave me a shot of morphine. The next day, I was shipped back to England.

"So I didn't get to see Berlin.

"I spent the rest of the war in England."

"If it weren't for a few mistakes, Hitler would be ruling the world now," I said. "Can I tell you my theories?"

"Go ahead," said John.

"One: he should have finished off the retreating British as they trudged through Belgium and waited for days at Dunkirk in the early days of the war. If he had, he would have had that many fewer soldiers thrown back at him later.

"Two: he should have started the Battle of Britain soon after Dunkirk, and concentrated on the military targets when Britain was just starting to manufacture airplanes, ships and the weapons of war, instead of wasting his bombs on civilian targets.

"Three: he should not have turned on Russia. I know his timing was wrong – Russian winter and all that – but he needn't have wanted Russia at all.

"Four: similarly, he needn't have had ambitions in North Africa. Once again he diverted his troops and war machinery that could have been used to conquer the whole of Europe, including the outposts of the British and French Empires."

"You are probably right," said John. "But he needn't have started all this caboodle in the first place. He could have been happy with annexing what he claimed to be Germany by annexing Austria, the Rhineland and Sudetenland. After all, we agreed to give them to him."

"Greed and power always bring one to a sticky end."

* * * * * * * *

CHAPTER 22
Compton; Sobers; The Tie –
Australia versus West Indies;
Cowdrey; Boycott; Botham

"Soon after the War you Indians came over and lost," said John. "England then went to Australia for the 1946-47 series. England lost miserably by an innings and 332 runs in the First Test, Bradman scoring a century. In the Second Test, Bradman and Barnes slammed double centuries and England lost again by an innings. The Third Test was drawn. The Fourth Test was saved by a new fellow called Denis Compton, who scored a century in each innings. Australia won the final Test easily. So, England returned a leaderless rabble, for Hammond was a total failure as a captain and as a player. A sorry end to a scintillating career – over 50,000 runs, 167 centuries, 700 wickets, and over 800 catches.

"In 1947 the South Africans paid us a visit and got slaughtered by Compton, who appeared in front of his home crowd like an Olympian god, resplendent in white armour and willow, hitting them all over the perimeter for six hundreds and a 97.

"Between July and September of that year he scored 2,074 runs, including 12 centuries at an average of 109.01. At the end of the season he had amassed 3,816 runs, including 18 centuries, surpassing Tom Hayward's 3,518 and Edrich's 3,539, and Hobbs' 16 centuries.

"Compton was also a brilliant Association footballer – a left-winger with Arsenal, and an England cap on 11 occasions. Once the twin talents clashed, in

1938-39; Compton chose to be a winger rather than a batsman. In the end, playing two strenuous games, both at international level, took their toll. His cartilages wore out. He retired at 40 and immediately became the first brand image; he was anointed by the Brylcreem firm, and his handsome countenance smiled down upon millions of people from gigantic posters.

"The following season, the English crowds had their first taste of Garfield Sobers. He was a 21-year-old lad, and scored his first double century at Nottingham. Speaking of the West Indies, we have to mention a certain C L R James, who had campaigned for a black captain for the West Indies all his life. His efforts finally bore fruit in the 1960s when the amiable Frank Worrell was crowned captain. His tour of Australia is now history. One of two Test Matches that ended in a tie. The other was…"

"Between India and Australia."

"The Brisbane Test has become a historic set piece. Australia needed 27 to win with half an hour to play. Last over of the day and the match. Six runs needed for a win. Three wickets left.

"1st ball – one leg-bye.

"2nd ball – Benaud caught.

"3rd ball – no run.

"4th ball – one bye.

"5th ball – a single run.

"6th ball – Meckiff hit it high to leg. Hunte fielded on the boundary. The batsmen completed two runs. Hunte threw in low and fast. Grout was run out by a foot taking the third run.

"7th ball – scores level. Kline came in. He played to square leg and ran. Solomon fielded. He had only one stump to aim at. He threw. The ball hit the wickets and Mekiff was run out.

"History was made – and witnessed by a privileged crowd on that day.

"The Australian people feted the West Indian tourists like loved royalty.

"Worrell, who brought dignity and pride to the game of cricket and to his countrymen, was knighted for his services to cricket in 1964 and became a senator in parliament. He died in 1967 of leukaemia at the age of only 42. At Radcliffe Town Hall, where he played while studying economics at Manchester University, the flag flew at half mast in his remembrance. Did you know that he was the first cricketer to be given a memorial service in Westminster Abbey?"

"No. Talking about the West Indies, don't you think that we should mention Sobers?" I asked.

"There is no cricket if you do not mention him. He was one of the true greats. What do you know about him?"

"Well, Sir Garfield St Aubrun Sobers was born on July 28th 1936 at Bridgetown, Barbados, educated at Bay St. School, and played first-class cricket when he was 16. He made his debut against England in 1953-54 as a bowler. After Sir Frank Worrell, he captained the West Indies from 1965 to 1972 for 39 Tests, and retired in 1974. He made a colossal 28,315 runs with 86 centuries and 1,043 wickets in first-class matches. In Test Matches he made 8,032 runs at an average of 57.78, slamming 26 centuries, and took 235 wickets at an average of 34.03. He made over 500 runs in Test series on six occasions. His two famous records are the six consecutive sixes against poor Malcolm Nash of Glamorgan in 1968, and the 365 not out at the age of only 21 in 1958, which has only been bettered by a fellow I do not like – Brian Lara – in 1994. Sir Garfield was knighted by the Queen in 1975 and declared a national hero in his country when he was 61."

"Not bad…what else do you know about him?"

"What else is there to know?"

"Ah! You are not as clever as you think…he also represented Barbados in table tennis, golf and football."

"Football!"

"As a goalkeeper!"

"I didn't know that…"

* * * * * * * *

"Do you think Compton was the last of the 'greats' of England?"

"Well…we have had Cowdrey, Dexter, May, Barrington, Statham. They were good. I wouldn't say they were great."

"Let me tell you about Cowdrey since he comes from my part of the world," I said. "Michael Colin Cowdrey was born on Christmas Eve 1932 at Putumala, Ootacamund – which is only 17km from Coonoor, where I have settled in the lush Nilgiri hills of south India. He represented his school at the age of 13, played for Kent for 26 years starting from 1950, made his Test debut in 1954-55 against Australia, captained England in 1959, and retired from Test cricket 20 years later in 1974-75 when he was sent out as an emergency replacement to

Melbourne for the last Test against the Australians, who had won four of their six Test Matches with sheer power cricket that not only injured but demoralized the England team. Unfortunately, he made only five runs in the first innings. But England won the match by an innings and four runs. He made 7,624 runs with a highest score of 182 at a creditable average of 44.01; 22 centuries, 38 fifties, 120 catches. He also made one run in the only tamasha match he played against the Australians at Melbourne in 1970-71."

"What match did you say?"

"'Tamasha'… Sorry; it is an Indian word for fun, celebration, joy. That's what I call the one-dayers."

"Apt description; tamasha…"

"In first-class cricket he made 42,719 runs at 42.89, including 107 centuries. Cowdrey and Peter May hold the world record for the 4th-wicket partnership of 411, against Australia. He was *Wisden* 'Cricketer of the Year' in 1956, knighted in 1992, and appointed to the House of Lords in 1997 – only the second one to be so honoured after the Bishop of Liverpool, the Rev David Sheppard. He died of a stroke at the age of 67 in 2000."

"You know about Colin only because he comes from your part of the world," said John with a snigger, "but let me tell you about one person who had a sensational individual statistic.

"Overs: 46. Maidens: 18. Runs: 88. Wickets: ten.

"Overs: 51.2. Maidens: 23. Runs: 53. Wickets: ten.

"Let me see if you can crack that…"

"Jim Laker, 1956," I said.

"Correct. The first was in a county game against Australia at the Oval. The second was at Old Trafford; the Fourth Test. England made 459. Laker took nine for 37. Australia followed on and this time Laker scalped all ten tourists."

"Anil Kumble did the same trick for us against Pakistan in 1999."

"Oh, yes. That must have been quite a day there."

"It sure was. In his home town of Bangalore, they have named a road junction as 'Anil Kumble Junction', and he was given a car and loads of money."

* * * * * * * *

"What about Geoffrey Boycott?" I asked John. "You haven't mentioned him."

"Well, he was a good cricketer. But he had no charisma. And I suspect that he had few friends – even in the circuit – for he was one of those who was interested only in staying at the crease for as long as was possible. Nothing wrong in that, for the longer one stays the more runs one is apt to get...and sometimes individual glory buttresses team glory. But there are other times when such a player can become a pain in the you-know-where. Let me give you some figures about Boycott. He scored 1,000 runs for Yorkshire a record 19 times. He averaged more than 50 for 11 consecutive seasons, which is another record. He was also the only English player to average more than 100 twice – in 1971 and 1979. He topped the English averages six times. He played 193 Test innings, scored 8,114 runs at an average of 47.72, with a highest score of 246. He's got 22 hundreds and 42 fifties. He also played a few ODIs (one-day internationals). In 36 matches he scored 1,082 runs at an average of 36.06, with a highest score of 105. Oh yes! He did score a century in a one-day match. If you combine all his first-class batting he scored a massive 48,426 runs in 1,014 innings, at an average of 56.83, with a highest score of 261."

"How the hell do you remember these things?!"

"You've got to have big brains, my lad."

"Geoffrey wasn't a dashing cricketer – but he is certainly a dashing commentator. He is now famous, especially in India, as a ruthless but fair commentator. I suspect that he has a soft spot for India...I know not why. His predictions are rarely wrong. Some Indians wish that he be made one of the national selectors or expert coach to the Indian team!"

"Yes. He is forthright with his comments and reading of the game."

"What about your friend Botham? You have mentioned him a couple of times."

"Mr I T Botham. Due to the defections of the players to play in Kerry Packer's Circus in Australia, England found themselves with a large hole in their team when the Aussies came to England in 1977. They decided to gamble on a 21-year-old from Somerset in the third Test at Trent Bridge. Botham celebrated his entry into the international Test arena by taking five wickets in the first innings. In the fourth Test at Leeds he decimated the opposition with figures of five for 21. He was then an automatic choice for the next ten years. When there was a national paucity of heroes, Botham appeared like a medieval knight – or a pasteboard hero from the comic books. Nothing more typified the man than his achievement in the summer of 1981 at Leeds, when his apotheosis arrived during the Australian tour.

"The series began sedately enough, with no hint of the hurricane to come. Australia won the first Test at Nottingham. The second Test was washed out by rain. The third Test at Leeds witnessed something unprecedented. The Aussies declared at 401 for nine. Botham took six for 95. England was humbled for 174, Botham making 50. England followed on. The entire country thought that the game was over when England stumbled to 135 for seven. Some of the England side – including Botham – had already checked out of their hotels.

"Enter I T Botham. He started quietly enough, taking his time. He made 39 in 90 minutes. It was teatime. Graham Dilley joined him. Botham took him aside and asked him if he was going to hang around for a day or more. Dilley replied that he didn't really fancy it. And Botham said, 'Come on, let's give it some humpty!'

"*Wisden* says that, 'He stretched the bounds of logic and belief.' His captain, Mike Brearley, later wrote, 'That was the stuff of which heroes are made when victory is snatched out of thin air.' Botham squared his shoulders, rolled his beefy arms and decimated the Aussie attack with an unbeaten 149 that included 27 fours and a six, challenging Australia to make 130 to win. The tourists were in a state of shock after having witnessed the most brutal annihilation of their supposedly feared bowlers. Botham opened the bowling, but it was Willis with the unbelievable statistics of eight for 43 who hammered in the last nail of the

Aussie coffin. Australia collapsed and England rode the high seas again.

"The circus moved to Birmingham. The Aussies needed 151 for victory. They were 105 for four. Captain Brearley, acting on an impulse, threw the ball to Botham, who had not performed well with the ball and who was not very keen to bowl.

"Enter Botham. He bowled ten overs for nine runs and stemmed the rot. And then he swept all before him, taking five wickets for one run in 28 deliveries. Once again Botham had snatched victory from the jaws of death. It was the most prodigious exhibition of all-round cricket in the annals of cricketing history. Every citizen in Britain, even those who did not know anything about cricket, were laughing with exultation and embracing strangers in the streets. Botham was now known throughout half the world.

"Fifth Test at Manchester. England dismissed for 231. Botham out for nought. Australia floundered for 130. England collapsed like the proverbial pack of cards, for 104 for five. Enter Botham again. He took Lillee and Alderman apart as if they were schoolboys, with such effortless brilliance that *Wisden* compared him to the legendary Jessop. He plundered 118 runs in 123 minutes, which included six sixes (a record against Australia) and 13 fours. His first 28 runs came in 53 balls in 70 minutes. Then he erupted like Vesuvius and smashed 66 off 48 balls.

"In 1935 another Somerset man, Arthur Wellard, had smashed 66 sixes in a season. 50 years later Botham exerted his muscular self with 80 glorious sixes. In 1986, he created another record by hitting 13 sixes in an innings against Northants. He was the first player to score a century and take eight wickets in a Test and the fastest in achieving the double of 1,000 runs and 100 wickets in Tests. He holds the English record of playing in 65 consecutive Tests, and during his phenomenal Test career he kept the scorers busy by bludgeoning 5,200 runs from 161 innings with 14 hundreds and 22 fifties and capturing 383 wickets at an average of 28.40, taking five wickets 28 times and ten wickets three times. In the county games he accumulated 11,154 runs and took 618 wickets. In ODIs he scored 2,113 runs in 106 matches, with a highest score of 79 at 23.21, and took 145 wickets."

"He acknowledged greatness in fellow cricketers even if they were in the opposite camp," I said. "In the great 1979 Test at the Oval, when India finished desperately for 429 – just nine runs short of victory – and Gavaskar made the memorable double century, it was Botham who picked up the stumps as souvenirs for Gavaskar – who later said of him that it was, 'The gesture of a person who has always treated the game as a sport.' In one of his books Gavaskar mentions the comic side of Botham. Gavaskar was frightened of dogs. Botham locked him inside a telephone booth and placed a dog outside and laid siege to the Indian."

"I didn't know that."

"Oh yes. What about the quick-fire 99 before lunch at Leeds in the 1979 tour of India, when he hooked Kapil Dev and Ghavri into the car park several times? And I remember the 122 he scored at Indore, India, in 50 minutes off 55 balls with seven sixes and 16 fours. At the end of the innings the entire stadium stood up and paid homage to the god of the day."

John went on, "Besides all this he was a professional footballer – like Denis Compton – and played for Scunthorpe United. In 1981, in Los Angeles, he was invited to a game of baseball where he far outstripped the striking rate of the stars and complained that the ball was not pitched fast enough! He is a moderate golfer, too. In 1985 he walked from John O'Groats to Land's End, in 1987 he walked across Ireland, and in 1988 he emulated Hannibal; all that self-inflicted torture to raise millions on behalf of leukaemia sufferers. A man's body can only take so much. He wore his back out and had to have several operations. I believe he still goes on his walking binges for some cause or another.

"So, for a chap who has achieved all this in a single lifetime, does it matter if he has a few sniffs of cocaine or a few illegitimate romps in beds, I ask you?"

"It doesn't matter at all."

"Thank you very much."

"Would you care to mention any other contemporary England cricketers?" I asked.

"Well, not in the same breath... Botham was one cricketer who both entertained and played crucial innings. You know that he single-handedly won many matches for England. The fourth Test at Christchurch in New Zealand, the Lord's Test against Pakistan, the Headingley and Edgbaston Tests against Australia in 1981; and what about the Golden Jubilee Test in Mumbai in 1980, when he demolished you lot with a whirlwind 114 and 13 wickets for 106?"

"What about Gower and Gooch?"

"Gooch: 8,900 runs, 20 centuries, highest of 333 against you, average 45.58. Gower: 8,231 runs, 18 centuries, highest of 215, average 44.25. Nothing much to write home about."

"But they have better averages than your pet, Botham!"

"Ah! But they were only batsmen, though Gooch rolled his arm over a few times. My boy was brilliant in all aspects of the game. And he made things happen. How many wickets did he get from bad balls because he had prepared the hapless batsman for the trap? He was a character."

"Can't win when you go on about him!"

Botham is a phenomenon. It is no exaggeration. He is not a normal man. He is the true *extraordinare*. He is a genius. He is a law unto himself. He is a fearless buccaneer. He is a giant with prodigious talents. He is impulsive and maddening. He cannot conform. We have to take him as he is. We cannot expect him to be a saint one day and go out and whack the opposition on the cricket field the next.

He is the only one to have had his portrait commissioned by the National Portrait Gallery.

People who probe into the private lives of athletes with the intention of marring their public achievements are little people.

* * * * * * *

CHAPTER 23
Alletson

"Have you finished, then?" asked Shirley.

"We have to ask John," I said.

"I think we have. It seems that I have told you more about 19th-century cricket than the 20^{th,} and even in the 20th we have spoken more about the pre-1950 era. I hope that is OK with you. The only reason I can think of is that the post-war era didn't produce many brilliant English cricketers."

"That's alright. It is true with regard to many things. Art, music, literature etc. were all better in those days. Take films, for instance. Who could match the golden stars of Hollywood – Bogart, Cagney, Gable, Flynn, the Barrymores, Chaplin, Garbo, Bette Davis, Greer Garson, Colman, Granger, etc. They conveyed love, passion, hate, anger, seduction, violence, evil with just their eyes or by an inflection in their speech. They had talent. They had charisma. After the 1960s the screens were filled by ugly and untalented people."

"What have you two decided to do about cricket? Bring in the timeless matches?" asked Shirley.

"We would if we could," said John.

"What do you say, Shirley?" I asked.

"I have no time for the Test Matches – I have to cook and clean and wash and mend; I enjoy the one-dayers."

John said, "I would make it even more difficult by making all the fielders stay within the 30-yard circle for the first 25 overs and then move them all back for the next 25 overs."

"Or, first 15 overs, all in the circle; second 15 overs, all outside the circle; and 20 overs anywhere..." I added.

"Why don't you get the players to tie one hand behind their backs and make them wear clogs?" asked Shirley. "That would make things a bit more exciting."

"Well, there's an idea," said John.

"Let's not get carried away," I said. "Well, John, I must thank you for your time and information and hospitality. I must get you something – a token of my appreciation. What would you like?"

"A copy of your book," he said.

"If and when it gets published, you will get the first copy."

"Let's hope I will still be around."

"Nonsense," I said. "What about a meal out at 'The Hare and Hounds' – or would you like another Indian meal?"

"Let's go out for a change, eh?" said Shirley. "I have picked up a few tips about Indian cooking. I know the base spices of garlic, ginger, cumin and coriander. I can experiment with those. Did I tell you that I cooked a dish with chickpeas yesterday. It was good. John has come to having spicy roast potatoes instead of just boiled potatoes since that day, you know. Connie likes to cook but she is so busy. She has evening meetings at school for the next two days. But over the weekend she likes to do some cooking."

"When shall we go out for dinner?"

"Sunday will be fine, "said Shirley.

"Sunday it is then. Shall I meet you there at 7:00?"

"Yes. Thank you."

* * * * * * * *

I spent the next two days in front of the computer. On Saturday evening I went to the Landrums', used their printer and gave a copy to John and Shirley for their criticism.

Of course, I left out the sexy bits.

* * * * * * * *

Sunday evening, 7:00 p.m. I went to 'The Hare and Hounds' pub, which also did good meals.

It was an early 19th-century structure, low exposed wooden beams, mahogany tables and cushioned chairs. The walls were decorated with old prints of fox-hunting and angling, an array of horse shoes, and pewter tankards; the open fireplace had its compliment of brass tongs. It was a cosy place. There were two couples at the bar.

John, Shirley and Connie walked in almost as soon as I entered.

The usual greetings: "Hello" and shake hands with John; chaste cheek kiss for Shirley and Connie.

"Well, what can I get you?" I asked.

"Pint of bitter for me," said John.

"Medium dry white wine for me, please," said Shirley.

"A dry Martini and lemonade, please," said Connie.

I ordered a double Jamieson.

"Have you had time to read through the manuscript, John?" I asked.

"Yes. But I wish you wouldn't put all those big words in my mouth. Hell, I had to have the blinking dictionary next to me."

I laughed.

"I like to be bombastic sometimes. People read books for entertainment and to get information. Why not read books to improve vocabulary?"

"I've read it too," said Shirley; "I think it has come out well. It certainly is not like the usual cricket book. More of a human angle to it, which makes it interesting...like a novel."

"Don't look at me," said Connie, "I haven't had time to read it. But I promise to read it and send you my comments."

"Thanks a lot. Being an erudite school teacher, your comments will be valued."

"See what I mean? Big words again," said John with a smile.

"Sorry!" I said, and laughed.

"But I did read a few pages of *Interview with Jesus*," said Connie. "I am intrigued. Do you mind if I showed it to the local priest, who is a good friend?"

"Not at all...provided it is not going to wound his sensibilities."

"I wouldn't think so. He is not an evangelical Christian. I'll see what he has to say."

"Maybe he can give me some more information about the lost years of Christ...though I haven't been able to find any books on the subject so far."

We had another round of drinks and gave our orders.

Suddenly John said, "Doc, do you believe that your star can shine for a certain time and then fade?"

"What do you mean, John?" I asked, amazed at the question.

"Don't tell me you have at last gone gaga," said Connie, looking at John.

"Who's gone gaga? I was just asking a simple question."

"Simple question, indeed! Star shining and fading?"

"What do you mean, John?" I asked again.

"Let me put it this way. Talking about cricket, do you agree that, at certain times, a particular player plays exceptionally well? Sometimes even ordinary players play exceptionally well. How do you account for that?"

"I see what you mean now," I said. "What immediately comes to mind is Botham at Headingley against the Australians."

"That's right. On that particular day, Botham played exceptional cricket; his star was shining. Remember that 175 your Kapil Dev made against Zimbabwe in the 1983 World Cup? *His* star was shining then."

"It certainly was."

"I have an extraordinary story to tell you to illustrate that point of the star."

"Hold on, John. I have no tape recorder with me. Let me get a piece of paper."

I went up to the bar and got a piece of paper from the bartender.

"Right. Go on," I said.

"An obscure old man crippled with arthritis died at the age of 79 in an obscure Nottinghamshire village. One of the better newspapers reported his death. For a couple of hours, long time ago in his life, his star shone so brightly that its effulgence lasts even today in the breasts of the few thousand cricket-loving public who were blessed enough to be present on that particular day at that particular match.

"He was a professional cricketer but he was a complete nonentity compared to the players around at the time – Fry, Hobbs, Rhodes, Blythe. Our man was a bit player, a tail-end batsman who drifted in and out of Notts. between 1906 and 1914. He worked hard to deliver the fast to medium leg-break – the only reason he was in the team.

"Notts. was playing Sussex at Hove. Our man was drafted in at the last minute only because another bowler was injured. Notts. were all out for 238. Sussex compiled a respectable 414. Notts. were heading for certain defeat and the local newspaper did not even bother to send a reporter to the ground the following day, the 20th of May 1911."

"John; tell us the name, will you?" I said, unable to contain myself.

"He has this exasperating habit of keeping you guessing, doesn't he?" said Connie.

"He certainly does," I said.

"I thought you knew, clever clogs," said John.

"No, John, I do not know."

"Edwin Boaler Alletson. Are you happy now? Let's get on with the story. Alletson went for a swim that morning at Hove beach. Why? Because he had an injured wrist and thought that perhaps contact with sea water might help.

"An hour before lunch on that fateful day, Notts. were seven men down and only seven runs ahead. The players in the Notts. dressing room resigned themselves to a defeat. The captain, Arthur Jones, didn't even bother to brief his batsmen.

"Enter Alletson. He asked his captain, "Mr Jones, does it matter what I do?"

"Jones replied, a bit bewildered, "No, Alletson, I don't think it matters what you do."

"Oh," said Alletson, "then I'm not half going to give Tom Killick some stick."

"Tom Killick was the Sussex bowler who had uprooted the Notts. batsmen.

"Alletson was just over six feet tall, broad-shouldered, deep-chested, 15 stone; a perfect physical specimen. His 2lb 3oz bat seemed absurdly flimsy in his massive hands as he strode forth from Hove pavilion. In the 50 minutes before lunch he scored 47 runs, including two sixes, while he lost two batsmen. One wicket to fall and all would be over. Notts. had a lead of only 84. The spectators went through the gates for their lunch. Only a few returned for the formalities. Only one reporter out of four bothered to return, making him the only official observer of the afternoon's events – the most extraordinary batting episode in the history of cricket.

"No one knows to this day what transpired in the pavilion during the lunch hour. Did the gods visit Alletson? Did they give him a secret potion? For he strode forth like a god with a nimbus hovering about him. He was in a mood of 'inspired dementia'. He set about the bowling like one possessed. Fours ricocheted from his bat like cannon balls. One ball flew out of the grounds, hurtling into the pavilion bar, breaking bottles and cascading beer and whisky all over the place. Another straight drive soared over the entrance gates into the streets and was lost. It was found by a boy, who was later found playing with it on the beach.

"Another ball travelled 160 yards and landed on the roof of the skating rink. He smashed his second 50 in 13 minutes. By this time he had struck five balls out of the grounds, never to be retrieved. Play was stopped; bemused officials wandered about the streets trying to find the balls. Killick was now reduced to a whimpering idiot; he was too frightened to bowl. He was worried that Alletson might hit one back at him. All the other fielders dared not put their hands to the ball. The ball fizzed and hummed through the fielders as though they were ghosts. No place was safe.

"Alletson had his hundred. Now he got down to business in earnest. It was half past two. He demolished the pavilion clock face. He appeared to the opposition like a mythical giant and everyone about him cowered in dismay. The fieldsmen and the umpires were in real danger of serious bodily injury, or indeed death, if they had the misfortune to establish contact with the ball flying from that puny piece of willow. Relph, a Sussex player, later said, 'It cost us a match we were winning, but I don't think anyone minded about that. It was such an experience to watch it.'

"The audience were hysterical, unable to make sense of what their eyes were witnessing.

"2:55 p.m. Alletson had amassed 189 runs. A Notts. rout had been transformed into a Sussex massacre. Another huge hit. C Smith caught it with one foot over the boundary line with his head resting on the grandstand. It was a six. But Alletson walked to the pavilion. He was informed that he was not out. 'It's all reet,' he replied. He had had enough. In 90 minutes he had scored 189 runs, the last 142 in only 40 minutes!

"He never accomplished anything of the sort in his later years. He was just a mediocre player. He was fouled for his bowling action when he tried his fast leg-breaks. He retired at the age of 30, went to live at Worksop and worked at the Manton colliery. In 1950, he was confined to a wheelchair, crippled with arthritis."

Absolute silence. We were enthralled. We were actually there witnessing Alletson's miracle.

"Now, how do you account for that?" asked John.

"His star was shining – as you said, John – just for those brilliant 90 minutes of his life. A sort of metamorphosis. Luck. Karma. It was his destiny that he had to make cricket history on that particular day. Who knows?" I said.

We had a quiet dinner. I was still at Hove. I am sure we all were.

Goodbyes. Thank-yous. Handshakes. Hugs. Kisses. 'Keep in touches'.

I was leaving the unspoilt, delectable village of Melbridge the next day.

* * * * * * *

221

CHAPTER 24
Interlude – Goodbye to Connie

Connie said she'd walk me home.

"That was a brilliant story, wasn't it?" I said.

"Oh yes. He can tell a tale."

"Well – this has been an interlude for us. I have enjoyed every moment of my stay here Connie. Your grandparents have been marvellous. What are you going to do?"

"Just carry on as usual, I suppose."

"Why haven't you remarried?"

"Haven't met the right person, I suppose."

"I'm sure if you are so minded you could get anyone. Attractive, intelligent girl like you."

"Don't get me wrong. I have met a few men. Some were good. Some were not. But always something happens and I back out."

"Are you sure that it is not concern for John and Shirley that is keeping you back."

"It may be. They have been good to me all these years…when my own parents shut me out. I would like to stay with them till the end. I will never put them in one of those horrible nursing homes."

"In India it is very difficult for a divorcee or a widow to remarry. Social stigma. But here you could at any time. You could marry and still continue to live with your grandparents."

"Ah. But will my husband be willing to live with us? He may for some time. Then the usual things will crop up. He not being the focus of attention and all that sort of rubbish."

"I see what you mean. In India, if you were to marry, the husband is conditioned to make way for the elderly. It makes things easier if one accepts these things. The trouble starts if the elders start to monopolize the situation – or if the new member starts to ask for special privileges. Resentment. Anger. Frustration."

"I don't mind being as I am. I have a good job. My daughter is working and happy. If I am attracted to someone and if that someone is equally attracted, we have a nice time – as we are now. So all is really well. If something comes out of something, I'll take it."

"Yes. You must take it. Don't be afraid to take it. That is the advantage of living here. You could even live together without marrying. In India one cannot. In India a widow would not be accepted socially and would not be a candidate for remarriage. In some societies, widows are not presented to strangers at all; they live their lives out as slaves, shunned by all. They have a terrible life. Your counterpart in India will simply not casually walk out with a complete male stranger."

"Lucky I am born here, eh?"

"You bet you are. In India the same social stigma attaches to a divorcee as to a widow. Terrible. Whereas divorce is so easy here. So, if things don't work out, you can always show him the door. So don't be afraid…if you come to really like a person."

"I suppose you are right."

We went up to my room and I made love with Connie for the last time.

Cricket-lovers looking for sensual stimulation may read on.

I closed the door and turned around. Connie came to me. We stood in silent embrace for a few minutes, knowing that we might never see each other again. We had a mutual attraction to each other. It was sensual passion. It was not anything deeper. As we agreed before, it was simply fulfilling a mutual physiological need.

I removed her clothes and then removed mine. I lay her on the bed.

"Don't move," I said.

I placed her hands over her head and, without touching her with my hands, I kissed every inch of her. I turned her over and kissed her all over. I turned her again on her back and filled my mouth with her breasts and sucked deeply at her nipples. I tickled and nibbled and bit at them. Connie started to moan. She brought her hands forward to embrace me. I made her put her hands back over her head. I continued to kiss and suck and bite at her heavy, big, white luscious breasts and tasty pink nipples until she moaned and groaned and had an orgasm.

Then I lay on my back and asked Connie to kiss and suck my nipples. My nipples are very sensitive. It is as though there is some sort of an electrical circuit between them and my penis. My entire body gets aroused and inflamed. I asked her to be rough and bite my nipples. While she was sucking my nipples I twisted her nipples between my fingers and squeezed her breasts till they hurt. Then we alternately sucked each other's nipples until I could stand it no longer. I gently eased her on top and astride of me. I eased my throbbing flesh into her and both of us moaned loudly. I asked her to lie still to delay my ejaculation. When my preliminary throbbing had subsided I moved her above me, back and forth.

"Pinch my nipples – harder...harder," I said hoarsely.

I squeezed and pinched her nipples.

A few moments later we screamed and came together. She fell on top of me.

* * * * * * * *

I visited my friends in Liverpool. All my doctor friends were unhappy in their respective jobs in the hospital side or as general practitioners, because of the idiotic policies and the general incompetence of the health system in Britain.

I introduced my guest house – 'The Tryst' – to them, inviting them over.

All of them have since visited me and enjoyed their holiday.

I also met some travel agents, but they weren't of much help. My enterprise was either too 'exclusive' or too small for their requirements.

I caught the Air India flight from Manchester to Madras.

I had to meet a certain Mr Rangachari, who was an expert on the history of Indian cricket – a sort of Indian version of John Landrum.

* * * * * * * *

PART TWO –
INDO-BRITISH HISTORY

CHAPTER 25
Indo-British political History

Well before the Christian era, the Chinese, the Egyptians, the Greeks and the Romans were trading with India.

The Portuguese were the first European blighters to come to India in modern times. And they came with a crucifix in one hand and a sword in the other. On the viceroy's arch in Goa is sculptured a saint whose foot is on the neck of a prostrate Indian. Vasco da Gama sailed into Calicut on the 27th of May 1498 and the local Hindu king, Zamorin, allowed him to open a trading centre. The first Portuguese viceroy was Almedia (1505 – 1509). The second fellow, Albuquerque (1509 – 1518), captured Goa (in 1510) and Malacca (in 1511), built fortresses and encouraged intermarriage with the Indians. He also killed Zamorin for allowing the Arabs the right to trade as well.

The Portuguese did not enter into the interior parts, being quite happy on the coastal areas. They eventually lost their hold because of their corrupt rule, avarice, religious intolerance, the rise of the Marathas, a militant community in north-west India, and the advent of the Dutch and the English.

The Dutch took over. The United East India Company of the Netherlands was founded in 1602. They lost their footholds at Calicut, Madras and Bengal to the English, and were finally routed by the latter in 1759 at the Battle of Niderra. In Europe, meanwhile, war broke out between England and France and also between England and Holland, resulting – in 1791 – in the annexation of all Dutch territories in India by the English.

The French descended on India after the English, but let us deal with them now. The Bourbon monarchy was in power. In 1611 Louis XII granted a company of merchants the right to trade in the East. Louis XIV authorized a new company to trade with India – La Campagnie des Indies. In 1667 the first French factory was established at Surat by Francis Caron. During the following years they established themselves at Masulipatam, Pondicherry, Calicut, Mahé, Karikal and Chandanagar – all due to a chappie called François Martin, director-general. In the course of time they, too, got embroiled in political intrigue, and eventually lost out to the English.

Within a century of the death of their prophet, the Arabs extended Islamic rule from Spain to Sind – in 712 AD. In the 11th century, Mahmud of Ghazni, an Afghan, plundered north-western India. Another fellow Afghan plunderer was Muhammad of Ghur. He left behind his former slave, now general, Qutb-ud-din-Aibak, who later declared himself an independent ruler of the sultanate of Delhi. Between 1206 and 1526 it was ruled by five Islamic dynasties, either Afghan or Turkish in origin. They expanded their territories, and soon local governors grew restless and crowned themselves petty kings of all that they surveyed.

1526. Enter Babur. He was not an Afghan. He came from east of the Caspian Sea, in southern Russia. On his mother's side he descended from the famous – or infamous – Genghis Khan, a Mongol; 'Mughal' is a derivative of 'Mongol'. On his father's side he descended from the equally (in)famous Timur or Tamerlane, who in the last decades of the 14th century sacked Samarkand and Delhi and left them to the Sayyids to govern. But now the Sayyids had died out and the Lodis were in place. Babur, a king of the minor kingdom of Ferghana, now decided to reclaim his heritage – in spite of the fact that the Lodis too had an impeccable pedigree. But what the Lodis did not have was gunpowder. Babur had it and defeated Sultan Ibrahim Lodi at the Battle of Panipat in April 1526 and installed himself on the throne of Delhi. But he was not allowed to rest. He was challenged by the great Rajput, Rana Sanga of Chitor, whom Babur defeated in the spectacular battle of Khanau in March 1527. Now Babur was secure.

Thus started the Mughal rule of India.

The Mughals ruled over India from 1526 to 1856 (though for the last half-century power effectively resided with the British-owned East India Company). The next year saw the Great Indian Mutiny against the English, after which India came under the direct administration of Queen Victoria. Shah Alam II was the first Mughal emperor to come under the tutelage of the East India Company, after the Second Anglo-Maratha War of 1803-1805.

Bahadur Shah II was the 19th and last Mughal emperor, albeit a pensioner of the East India Company. He was 82 in 1857 when the mutineers prematurely proclaimed him emperor. He was packed off by the victorious English to Rangoon, where he died at the age of 87.

Besides the above bunch, another fellow, Nadir Shah of Persia, came charging into India in 1738. He pillaged and raped what was left over from the previous maladministrations. It is said that he killed 30,000 people in Delhi in one day and walked off with 300 million rupees in cash as well as jewels, diamonds, the peacock throne, horses, carpenters and a bevy of girls. His booty was so fantastic that he suspended taxes in Persia for three years! Anyway, he was assassinated.

Akbar is the only Mughal who has the suffix 'the Great', a title he richly and rightly deserved; a title that was bestowed with love and respect, by both his peoples and his historians, for it was he who actively sought to bring equality and peace amongst his Hindu and Muslim subjects. Akbar's son was Jehangir, the fourth scion of the Mughals. He ruled over 70 million people and was the richest and most powerful monarch in the world in 1600 when Queen Elizabeth I ruled over England.

We shall leave the magnificent Mughal court for a moment and see what was happening 6,000 miles away. The Dutch controlled the spice trade from the East; they sold spices to the countries of Europe. They decided to raise the price of a pound of pepper by five shillings. The English were incensed. "Five shillings! Damned if we are going to pay that to the bloody Dutch; who do they think they are?" On the 24th of September 1599, 24 merchants of the City of London held a conclave, their whiskers positively bristling with righteous indignation at the effrontery, and decided to short-circuit the flaming Dutch by forming their own company – their only concern being the age-old love of lucre. Some 125 shareholders subscribed to a capital of

£72,000 and, on the last day of the year 1599, Queen Elizabeth signed a royal charter giving it exclusive trading rights to all countries beyond the Cape of Good Hope. Thus was a company born that was eventually to conquer India and create the British Raj – the East India Company.

If only the Dutch had not been avaricious – who knows? India would probably have been a Muslim country.

August 24th 1600; the *Hector*, a 500-ton galleon, captained by William Hawkins, dropped anchor at Surat, on the west coast of northern India. Hawkins set off with a group of Pathans as warrior bodyguards to seek out Jehangir at Agra. Jehangir welcomed dour old Hawkins in a way that must have titillated the hardened sea-faring barnacle. Jehangir gave to him, to do with as he wished, a beautiful Armenian Christian girl from his seraglio. Hawkins hung around for a couple of years and left empty-handed; the Portuguese were whispering malicious consequences into the Emperor's ear if the British were allowed to trade. Sir Henry Middleton turned up later and was met with similar indifference, but he met it with a different tactic. He anchored off the seashore and held to ransom the Indian vessels. Another chap, Thomas Best, went a step further; he sunk a few Portuguese vessels. This display of sea power finally had the desired effect. An imperial order was issued in 1612 allowing the East India Company the right to open depots north of Bombay at Surat.

If only Jehangir had booted out the English, India might have remained a Muslim country – or would the Hindus have found their long-lost pride and installed themselves on the thrones dotted about the vast peninsula, when the Mughal strain had degenerated in the post-Shah-Jehan era to spawn an interminable line of oafs?

Never mind the 'ifs' – and 'buts' and 'perhaps'.

Let us get on.

What was happening in London? The East India Company was raking in the profits; dividends were exceeding 200 percent. Two shiploads of goodies were unloaded at the Thames docks every month. Slowly the company's galleons were being seen silhouetted off the coasts of Madras and Bengal. A chap called Job Charnock set up a trading counter – supposedly under a banyan tree – in the delta of the river Ganges (Ganga). Did he know that he was to spawn the conurbation of Calcutta – the second biggest city, after London, in the British Commonwealth of Nations?

'Trade, not territory' was the constant refrain of the English; Mammon, not land. But all that changed soon to eventually leave the English as undisputed masters of India.

If we delve into the entire logistics of the mayhem in India, aided and abetted by the foreign powers, we will be hopelessly bogged down with unpronounceable names, crass nepotism, fratricide galore, greed for lucre and land, stunning betrayals and affiliations, a legion of dates, and innumerable battles. Whenever the French and the English fought each other in Europe their counterparts in India fell on each other with sabres and cannon. It was utter nonsense. Suffice it to say that, if the local rulers had been strong, had behaved well and ruled their subjects with justice and benevolence, none of these foreigners would have been able to establish a military foothold in India; they would have just got on with the business for which they initially came – trade.

* * * * * * *

CHAPTER 26
Enter the British

There were never more than 100,000 Britishers in India at any one time. Yet they were able to rule over more than 300 million people. How did they do it? With the active connivance of the people, of course.

I shall enunciate my theories.

1.   Just as an individual experiences the normal ups and downs of life, entire peoples, cultures and nations go through similar cycles of material and intellectual prosperity and penury. Look what happened to the great ancient civilizations – Egyptian, Greek, Roman, Mayan, Inca, Aztec, Chinese and Indian. They disappeared well before the dawn of the Christian era. The first 1,500 years of the present age produced nothing of consequence except intolerance and bloodshed. The last 500 years belongs to the European civilizations, either in their home countries or in their colonies – e.g. America. Perhaps time will see the degeneration of these modern nations and a resurgence of some other culture.

2.   Just as an individual has certain aptitudes, certain peoples or nations are known for certain qualities. The Jews and Jains are imbued with business acumen; the Germans are famous for regimental discipline; the Swiss for watches and chocolates; the Japanese for their warlike approach to modern technology; the British for reticence and probity; the Americans for violence and double standards; the French for their cuisine; the Italians for their vendettas etc. I am an Indian in the sense that I happen to have been born in India. Nevertheless, I must state that Indians are noted for their

discourtesy, uncleanliness, sloth, intolerance, cowardice, treachery, envy and corruption. These must be some of the factors that have enabled foreigners to rule us comparatively easily for centuries. Many of my compatriots will no doubt vehemently deny my general condemnation. They will go into platitudes of the greatness of India in the past. Oh yes, I concede that we were great in the past. We have archaeological evidence of that; we even have above-ground evidence of great engineering feats that have somehow withstood the vicissitudes of history. But what about now? We are the pits of the earth. They will tell you about the magnificence of the Hindu religion. Yes, in essence, Hinduism is truly great; but look at the way we actually practise it. It is an abomination. The Hindu suspicion of the Muslim equals the Muslim's subconscious fear of the Hindu. The Hindu of one caste is intolerant of another. Some idiots will hark back to a mythological time and kingdom called *Rama Rajya*, when life on earth was paradise – conveniently forgetting that even in this mythological context there was a chap called Ravana, who was the embodiment of evil, and that Rama had to banish his wife Sita because of the calumny of his dear subjects.

I only ask fellow Indians to look around. Can they deny the existence of the evils I have stated in almost every private and public exchange?

3.   Rulers of past kingdoms or present democracies are evil, tyrannical, despots – unless otherwise proved. And there have been very few who have been thus proved in the history of the world. India was ruled by many such personalities. The rot was

existent in our culture all the time, as we have rarely had benevolent rulers. Indian history can only throw up Asoka, Chandragupta and Harsha. Even they were marauders and existed more than 2,000 years ago. The rot worsened when the Mughals conquered India in the 16th century. Except for Akbar, they were a rotten lot. All that they were interested in was acquiring more real estate, more precious stones, more concubines and more tiger skins – besides indulging in a bit of fratricide for light relief. For the past 500 years the Indians have been systematically sapped of their self-respect. They became an enfeebled people – physically, intellectually and morally – due to the rapacious exploitation of their rulers. When the British took over, India was a land of starvation and apathy, fear and insecurity, superstition and sickness. The Muslims treated the Hindus with contempt. The Hindu had to pay a poll tax simply because he was a Hindu. No one knew who owned the land. The land was not mapped. There were no documents. If a piece of land was mortgaged the local rich Hindu lent money to his fellow poor Hindu and gleefully swallowed it later when the exorbitant payments were not remitted. Agriculture was not promoted. Education was virtually non-existent. No effort was made to search for and use the lands's resources. The common man lived a wretched existence, humiliated and exploited at every turn by the ruling Muslims and Hindu henchmen. The spirit of the people had virtually vanished. This was the state of affairs when the British came to India. Now you can see how they so easily conquered India. They were infinitely better, despite all the rascality, than the Muslims.

Nonetheless, after more than 300 years of British rule (or misrule), our condition worsened. Only one man could re-infuse the spirit of self-respect and potential for accomplishment – Mahatma Gandhi. But even that was but a fleeting episode in the psychological history of the peoples of India.

4.   Given that scenario, can you expect integrity? Is it just to ask such a people to uphold the principles of honesty, compassion etc. when even the richest people of the world, who are secure for generations, cannot follow such precepts? It would be unfair. If someone comes along and flashes a few rupees, the impoverished peasant will greedily and gratefully accept the purse irrespective of the nature of the job, be it manual or intellectual labour – or even treachery towards a fellow citizen. What is most important to him is the security of the next meal for him and his family – not the means to it. Let me give you an illustration. Even as late as the middle of the 18th century, the manager of a British factory received £40 a year, a writer (clerk) £5 – paltry sums even for those times. But compare it with a total wage bill of £100 for 80 Indian employees of a city district council. The Indians were not forced to accept such pay packets. They accepted only because the British scenario was infinitely better than their then circumstances. Imagine their truly pathetic plight. If I were in a similar situation, I would kill for a meal for my family.

5.   The British were foreigners. They spoke an alien language called English. But even the British spoke it with inflections that were indecipherable to inhabitants of different parts of Britain. They came to

India to trade. To trade one must know the local language. To their consternation they found that people a few miles apart in this vast country spoke in completely different tongues. They had to employ the locals – the *banias* – who would act as interpreters and general organizers. Now, we know how pedantic the Indian is; a simple transaction can snowball into a major politico-military exercise; an epic can be spun with no plot; clouds of smoke can be generated without even a spark. How often do we take the easy way out and prefer to pay and shut up the blighter – be he trader, technician, taxi-driver, professional or bureaucrat – rather than get involved in a convoluted haggle? We also know the Indian's penchant for nepotism and corruption. For a fee, anything can be accomplished. Even today, a miserable creature who cannot afford a single meal a day or a single pair of clothes has to raise the equivalent of several months' wages to bribe a municipal official for a job as a street-sweeper. So, you can see the scene is set for the Indian drama. Corruption did not originate with the British. It was existent within the psyche of Indian society long before their advent. The British, perhaps overwhelmed by the heat, dust, sounds, smell, languages, dialects, poverty, misery and the 'Indian mentality', simply succumbed to the order of things; they shut their eyes as the easy way out – very much as foreign visitors shut out the poverty and bureaucracy when touring India. One learns to accept or ignore situations when they cannot be overcome or rectified. Some attempt to apply logic; but, to the Indian, logic is an absurd idea.

6.   The British exploited India. Of course they did. They didn't come here for the benefit of the Indian people. They were purely commercial traders and Mammon was their God – as it is to every trader. Why should they not exercise their professional rights and take as much as they want for as little as possible? Have you met a benevolent and just trader? In 1693, a parliamentary enquiry exposed that bribes were being paid to various personages to the tune of £1,200. This sum became £90,000 after William III of Orange came to power. The Duke of Leeds was impeached for taking a bribe of £5,000. At every renewal of its charter, the East India Company had to bribe the government and the Bank of England.

7.   The British inadvertently stumbled onto their empire in India after the Seven Years War (1756-63). It was only after they realized that they had come into an awful lot of real estate that they set about documenting their assets. They did this purely for the love of lucre. They built railways, roads, irrigation canals, schools, law courts, post and telegraph systems, clubs, cricket fields, military barracks and magnificent buildings, surveyed the land meticulously, and recruited millions of Indians solely for their own benefit – to further their trading opportunities and thus their profits. *The advantages to the locals were incidental.* I cannot see anything wrong in that. If I were a conqueror, I would do all in my power to milk the conquered people. The majority of the British were rotters; some of them raised the taxes on an already impoverished, starving people simply to organize an orgy of pig-sticking. They were bullies; they threatened people and their rulers,

Mafia-style, collecting protection money. They were fanatical racists, looking down on Indians as a degenerate race of no-gooders and no-hopers – an assessment not totally without foundation. They were thieves; how else would they build their magnificent houses, gardens, bridges and factories back in Britain? (Before someone rises up in ire, let me also state that many of their beautiful structures were built well before their Indian connection with loot from elsewhere.)

Let us consider good old Robert Clive, son of a poor country gentleman, who came out to India in 1744 to try his luck as a writer (clerk). He was a manic-depressive kid of 18, noted for ebullient exploits such as steeple-climbing. Within a few weeks of his arrival, he was so bored that he twice tried to blow his brains out. Within 16 years, however, he had accumulated more than £400,000 – a staggering sum even by today's standards. He became a Member of Parliament for one of the notorious boroughs by buying his votes; was given an Irish peerage, purchased an Irish estate, repaired Styche Hall (the family home), and bought another one a few miles down the road *and* a house in Berkeley Square, London. He later held a parliamentary seat at Shrewsbury, where he slit his throat and died.

Eyre Coote bought estates in Ireland, Wiltshire, Hampshire and London after his stint in India. John Holwell, a timber merchant's son, returned with £96,000 and purchased Chilton Lodge, near Hungerford. Richard Barwell, well known as a rogue, bought Stanstead and had it landscaped by 'Capability' Brown. William Watts acquired properties in Berkshire and London. Bisham Abbey in Maidenhead, Caversham Park at Reading, and

Somerford Hall in Hampshire are some of the real estates snapped up by sons returning from India. Seeing the craze for property, a lottery in Calcutta offered as first prize an estate on the Hertfordshire-Middlesex border.

Let me give you another example of the English shenanigans. When Siraj-ud-daula was defeated and Mir Jafar was installed as nawab in Calcutta, he had to give the following sums to his benefactors: Robert Clive – £211,500; Governor Drake – £31,500; Mr Watts – £117,000; Major Kilpatrick – £60,750; Mr Walsh – £56,250; Mr Manningham – £27,000; Mr Scrafton – £22,5000; Messrs Boddam, Frankland, Mackett and Collett – £11,367 apiece; Mr Lushingham – £5,625; besides the aforementioned, poor Jafar had to cough up £187,000 to pay the select committee of the Bengal Council and £275,000 to the army – from both of which transactions Clive got a piece of the action. Eighteen months later, Clive obtained a grant of £27,000 a year for the rest of his life. An investigation committee of the House of Commons concluded that, in the one year 1757, Britons were paid 'presents' worth a total of £1,238,575, and that between 1757 and 1765 a sum exceeding £2 million had been disbursed – which would mushroom in 1781 to the colossal sum of £4,750,000. That was the extent of the corruption amongst the British – known for their discipline and probity. Can you imagine the plight of the people of Bengal, who had to suffer prodigious taxes levied on them by the nawab to raise the money demanded by the British?

Thus it can be seen that a hitherto impecunious employee of the East India Company had much brighter prospects of making good during his stint in India.

Several thousand pounds changed hands if a director nominated so-and-so for a post as a writer (a clerk or accountant) in India. Henry Dundas, a Scottish lawyer, was notorious for accepting such bribes from fathers of sons he recommended to the company. Sometimes new posts were created to accommodate a favourite – a special paymastership was created in Oudh for a relative of Sir George Wombwell, company chairman. The Lord Chief Justice and the Archbishop of York urged Hastings to find positions for their clients.

Another craze of the rich booty-hunters returning from their stint in India was politics. Thirty people between 1760 and 1784 sat at Westminster, several of them virtually buying their constituencies – such as Major Scott, who bought West Looe for £4,000 from the nephew of Lord Bathurst; General Richard Smith, a cheesemonger's son, who gave five guineas to everyone who voted for him; or Francis Sykes, who bought Basildon Park with his loot of diamonds.

Before the English came, people owned the land they tilled. By creating the zemindari system (whereby a British loyalist was awarded the title of zemindar, given land, and told to grow specific crops), the English invented the landless labourer and the despot zemindar. I have read several books in which is stated a truly satanic hobby of the English: the thumbs of Indian artisans and weavers were cut off to promote British-made products and the Lancashire cotton mills.

8.   People talk about the great 'discipline' of the British – a facet that has completely disappeared from the Indian scene today. Firstly, it must be stated that there was little of it during the infancy and

adolescence of the East India Company, when its sole purpose was Mammon, not territory. Discipline played a more active part only after the Crown took over in 1858. Initially the sort of Brits who came over to India were adventurers in the mould of slave-traders and mercenaries – people of the lower classes, uneducated, desperately poor and systematically oppressed by the upper classes of Britain. But once these people returned to Britain with their fabulous treasures and set themselves up in style as the new class of gentry, sons of the upper classes stepped in for a slice of the action. They were educated in the proper schools and had discipline instilled in the classrooms and the playing fields. They marched into India like schoolmasters. They were disciplined, and they implemented discipline. They had to know how best to exploit the country. The British are, after all, tradesmen. Without discipline in all professional spheres, how could they have acquired an empire? They had to instil discipline throughout the ranks, amongst both British and Indian personnel. But once they left, discipline left along with them – for discipline is a fuzzy concept to the Indian.

9.   The major difference between the British and the other invaders is that the former saw themselves as alien conquerors whose only concern was lining their pockets. No one bothers to invade, conquer and subjugate another people for nothing. They do it for profit of some kind. They came because India was a land of fabulous riches of all sorts. They also came, attracted like iron filings to a magnet, because they had heard of the esoteric wisdom of the holy men of India. The other difference between the British and the others

was they chose not to identify with the Indian people and always saw Britain as their home – even if they happened to be born in India and had never glimpsed the white cliffs of Dover. This detached quality is present even today amongst the Brits who have 'settled' in India. The other conquerors simply left their own lands, conquered India and made it their home. If only the British had treated India as their home, they would never have been asked to quit.

I cannot condemn them completely for this superior attitude and general disgust. Their loathing and contempt for the Indian came only after they arrived, mingled with and lived amongst the people. They were flabbergasted by the contradictions of Indian life – chastity and sensuality, renunciation and avarice, humility and arrogance, animal worship and animal cruelty, philosophical loftiness and silliness, megalomania with obsecration, xenophobia with xenolatry, violence and pacifism, intelligence with stupidity.

The Muslims were an intolerant lot. They despised everything about Hindu culture and went about killing Hindus and demolishing their temples. At the same time, they needed the Hindus to run the country. The upper-class, enterprising Hindu had to adapt to help in governance and to live; some of them thrived. The lower-class Hindu simply survived. Both classes in their own ways were forcibly humiliated and had their spirits broken, as they could see no end to their misery. The only period of peace between Hindu and Muslim was during the reign of Akbar. Since the Muslims had broken away from their roots in the Middle East, they treated India as their home.

The British were a different lot. They were not fanatical about their religion, until very much later, and that, too, in an insidious, harmless manner compared to the Muslims. Reading various commentaries (as I was born after India's independence), the most blinding truths that comes through are: a. their almost fanatical loathing and contempt of the Indian and anything Indian (both Hindu and Muslim); b. their insufferable racial pride and arrogance through being the supreme power then in the world; c. their irrational fear of a mass uprising to slaughter them (which was worsened by the Indian Mutiny of 1857); and d. their abhorrence of any Anglicization in the Indian.

The first I can not only understand but also forgive. The second trait I never can. The third was simply poltroonery, for such an uprising was totally impossible in the given milieu and given the utter incompetence of the Indian to organize or head anything, let alone a revolt of such staggering proportions. I have read that the Indian soldier acquitted himself admirably when under British command, but was a spiritless coward when under Indian. The fourth is totally incomprehensible, as it is against all that history teaches us. Any conquering power imposes its brand of civilization on the conquered. Whereas the Muslims went about it ruthlessly, the British couldn't have cared less. The slightest Anglicization of the Indian angered them to the point of fulminating apoplexy, though they too needed the Indian to deal with administration and for which a degree of English knowledge was necessary.

But if the native showed any cleverness at it, he was immediately ridiculed and chastised.

Some of the literate amongst the British did learn about Indian culture, but most of them did so only to decry it with authority. They practised a ruthless system of apartheid until the very end – and they had the cheek to denounce the South African government of yore. Their treatment of the subordinate Indian was akin to the American's treatment of the African slave – a subhuman nonentity who, when he showed signs of intelligence, was likened to a performing monkey. The subhuman, nevertheless, noticed the uncouth behaviour of his master and mistress, and this, coupled with the new political ideas of the late 19th and 20th centuries, fuelled the Indian. The upper classes, with their newfound knowledge of their own culture offered by the European, dug in and became fanatical or even militant Hindus – the swing of the pendulum. The lower classes simply survived. And both classes sharpened their innate cunning and toadyism, their innate xenophobia and militancy. They played to the audience by bringing to the fore their expert act of self-abasement before a ruling power while simultaneously plotting villainy.

Finally, the stupidity of the British, the short-sightedness of the Hindu, and the intransigence of the Muslim wrested away the most glorious part of the British Empire.

And thus was gone a truly God-given opportunity for the British to Anglicize India and maintain their proverbial 'jewel in the crown' – even unto the end of time. They should have either implemented wholeheartedly the magnanimous words of Queen

Victoria when she exhorted them to cultivate, encourage and respect the Indian, or they should have said, "The old girl's gone soft!" ignored her, and imposed their own culture ruthlessly. Instead they vacillated and fell rather miserably between the two proverbial stools, to their utter ignominy. This was their greatest folly; a folly compounded with their fixed psyche of not treating India as their home, of not treating Indians as intelligent human beings, of not recognizing the awe, respect, *acknowledgement and need* the Indian had for British rule, despite everything, for – all said and done – British rule was better than the foregoing. For this blighted short-sightedness, for this unforgivable sin, I hold the British solely responsible.

Needless to say that not all the British were as described above. But that only proves that the exception makes the rule.

I have observed that people of other countries are decent in their own countries but become monsters once they gad about. We have mentioned the Brits. They are exemplary within the British Isles. I can bear personal testimony to that. But once they leave their chill shores, they become insufferable – and that holds good even now in India. I can bear personal testimony to that too.

Take the Americans. However crazy they are, they are still fairly decent in the United States. But send them abroad, say to Vietnam, and they became demons. The Dutch are an amiable lot in the Netherlands, but transport them to Africa and they go berserk. The French are a sophisticated lot in France, but let them out and they create horrendous penal colonies.

I have also observed that this Jekyll and Hyde phenomenon is present in the Indian – but only in reverse! The Indian is worse at home. He/she is admired for his/her diligence and principles abroad.

Even until the recent past, the Hindu Indian could and did not spread his tentacles outside India; he had no ambitions to conquer other lands. This was due to the hidebound Hindu belief that one loses caste if one sets foot across the waters. Therefore he has not experienced anything else besides his own hidebound environment. But when he did start to gad about, he was stunned. He started to look around. He saw that the inhabitants were fairly decent people in their own habitat. He started to metamorphose – as he had to live amongst them. Part of the decency rubbed off on him, and he became a better person.

The truly self-respecting man discovers what he is and can
Deserves and dares and understands by travelling in foreign lands

Panchatantra, R W Ryder

I am sure you do not agree with a single word I have said!

Some of you may deliberately misinterpret what I have said above. You may think that I have given the usual droll, conventional Indian excuse of foreign domination for most of the Indian ills. I have not. Firstly, Indians never had it in them to rule. They are not leaders, only followers. Secondly, they were and always will be a blighted lot. Thirdly, Indians have been able to bear their misfortunes, both personal and historical, because of not only their insensitivity to the finer and gross details of life but also their adamant refusal to face facts when they seem to be opposed to their beliefs, superstitions and lopsided interpretation of their great theory of karma.

10.   India was never, in its long history, a united nation. Rulers of tyranny and occasional benevolence ruled over areas as big as Europe or as small as a cricket ground. Even under the British, India was not a single nation. Two-thirds of geographical India was under the viceroy; one-third answered directly to the Crown. This one-third, comprising some 100 million people, a quarter of India's population, was under 565 rulers with fancy names – maharajas, rajas, nawabs, Nizams, etc. The Nizam of Hyderabad ruled over a kingdom bigger than France. The Raja of Bhadwa, an ex-railway guard, ruled over 1,401 subjects. Over 400 of the 565 princes ruled over states smaller than 20 square miles.

Both Indian and British royalty liked this cosy relationship. Treaties were drawn up between individual rulers and the Crown whereby the former acknowledged the viceroy in Delhi as the representative of the Crown and ceded control of the 'twins' – defence and foreign policy; in return they were allowed to exercise their autonomy within their kingdoms. Each of the kingdoms had a British 'political agent' – an English Resident – stationed at court as a sort of watchdog to see that the ruler did not misuse his powers. But this was simply so much window dressing. Would you report a despot if he presented you with wealth and free access to the harem? You would only report him if he were planning something naughty against you – i.e. the British. Otherwise, why would you bother about a few rapes and murders?

11.   Now and then the British did throw up benevolent viceroys and administrators who truly cared for the welfare of the natives. Here and there Britishers came to love the romance of India, intermarried and settled down within its frontiers. Some even actively fought their own government in Britain to get the Indians a good deal.

Some of the more enlightened members of the British Empire were instrumental in putting an end to the horrendous Hindu practices and superstitions rampant then – child marriages, forced marriages, suttee or widow-burning (most of whom were forcibly thrown onto the funeral pyres of their husbands by their own family or clanspeople), thuggee (people who specialized in garotting fellow-travellers to appease the goddess Kali), the human sacrifice of adults and babies to appease some other rotten god or goddess, human slavery or bondage, unscrupulous money-lenders, dacoits (bands of armed robbers), plunderers and rapists. Some of them worked towards communal harmony, brought about a system of government and judiciary that was well ahead of its times even when compared to Britain. Some even learnt Indian languages and customs to be nearer to the people they governed. Some did priceless work in translating ancient Indian literature, preserving artefacts, writing books on the Indian peoples, climate, wildlife and natural resources, and transforming arid land into fertile pastures. In 1910, there were nearly 32,000 miles of railway, compared to 3,000 in China. Some 13,000 miles of primary and secondary canals and 42,000 miles of distributaries irrigated 23 million acres of land – half the acreage of Britain. Thousands of Brits died in and for India; some due to the pestilences of the land, some in battle, and many from pure exhaustion as they gave their lifeblood during the course of their civil duties that carried them through some of the most inhospitable parts of the land to brave the marauders, deal out justice, map a piece of earth and see their pet project come into being.

At one stage the East India Company had to go cap in hand to the Bank of England for a loan of £1 million to bail it out of its difficulties due to the rapacious activities of its employees. Governor General Warren Hastings, through a Regulating Act of Parliament in 1773, stipulated that revenue and justice officials would not be allowed private trade – side business – and that 'presents' (bribes) should not be accepted by civil and military officials. He stabilized trade and made the company a profit of £13 million. He was not a bigot. 'The people of this country do not require our aid to furnish them with a rule of conduct or a standard for their property.' He overhauled the legal system, set up courts with British judges who would adjudicate on the advice of a Hindu *pandit* and a Muslim *maulana*, as the case required. He broke through the self-imposed barrier of language and encouraged people such as Nathaniel Halhed and Charles Wilkins to learn and translate Indian works. Wilkins published his *Grammar of the Bengali Language* on the first vernacular printing press in India. He then translated the *Bhagavadgītā*. Jonathan Duncan learnt Persian. Henry Colebrooke started to learn Sanskrit when he was assistant collector of revenue in Tirhut. William Jones, a High Court judge in Calcutta, and a scholar of Sanskrit, Arabic and Persian, put forward the theory that there was a common and Aryan source of Indo-European languages. He was president of the Asiatic Society of Bengal, founded by Hastings in 1784. Thus was started the famous school of 'Orientalists' that carried out much valuable work in the ensuing centuries.

Lord Cornwallis came to India after surrendering his forces to George Washington at Yorktown. He was a strong-minded zealot, and removed all Indians from high posts and made a mess of revenue collection in Bengal. But he abolished the savage punishments of the Muslims and left behind a criminal code more humane than the one existing in England. No one was above the law; even government officials could be summoned to court by a Briton or a native. Such a thing was unheard-of until then.

Lord Wellesley – along with his brother Arthur, the future Duke of Wellington, who was to gain fame at Waterloo – vanquished Tipu Sultan in the south and the Marathas in the north. Suddenly the humble East India Company, to its genuine consternation, saw that it had taken over a sizeable chunk of India. He noticed that his subordinates didn't have a clue as to the Indian way of life. He therefore created Fort William College for both the Briton and the Indian, staffed with the growing number of British orientalists and scholarly Brahmins, and presented a bill of £140,000 to Leadenhall Street,

London. It became a leading centre for linguistic research and within five years published more than 100 original works in oriental languages. By 1818 Calcutta had 11,335 printed and manuscript sources; Oxford had only 1,561. John Gilchrist, the Urdu teacher, started the Hindoostanee Press; William Hayleybury inspired the Calcutta School Book Society. This has been referred to as the Bengal Renaissance; Rammohan Roy fell under its spell and acquired European notions of equality and fundamental rights. He started the Hindu Sect, which later evolved into the Brahmo Samaj and lobbied for the abolishment of suttee and press censorship. Wellesley also started building Government House in Calcutta, modelling it on Kedleston Hall in Derbyshire.

In 1805, the directors created Haileybury College in Hertfordshire to groom prospective employees aged 15 and over – a refresher course – before packing them off to India.

After Wellesley, the Gurkhas were vanquished and pacified, the Marathas and Pindaris were finally defeated, the Rajputs made peace with the British and the Mughals were fast declining. India was now introduced to some of the most impeccable characters in its history; rulers noted for rectitude, courage, benevolence. And, most importantly, people who were delighted and willing to work amongst the natives: Charles Metcalfe, Mountstuart Elphinstone, John Malcolm and Thomas Munro. A statue of Munro mounted on his horse still stands in the city of Madras – a tribute for saving Madras peasants from Cornwallis' 'Permanent Settlement'.

Lord Bentinck believed that British glory must be based on Indian happiness. He cut down on British allowances, sacked corrupt officials, and abolished flogging – a form of punishment that would not be abolished from England for another 50 years. He built the Grand Trunk Road between Calcutta and Delhi, 1 foot 6 inches above the highest flood level, and planted trees at intervals of 60 feet on both sides of the metalled surface. He started a steamboat service on the river Ganges. He wiped out the infamous sect of the thugees, ritual religious stranglers of travellers, and abolished suttee, the burning of widows on the funeral pyres of their husbands. He proposed to admit Indians to the covenanted ranks of senior civil servants like Britons, but the company obliterated the clause. Bentinck nevertheless quadrupled the salaries of Indian judges, fostered their advance by appointing Indians as honorary magistrates and deputy revenue-collectors, and mixed freely with the natives, hoping that shiploads of fellow Britons would come to India, intermarry with the autochthons and settle down. But this was not to be. Two years after he left India, he had this to say to the Parliament in London:

"In many respects the Mohamedans surpassed our rule; they settled in the countries which they conquered; they intermixed and intermarried with the natives; they admitted them to all privileges; the interests and sympathies of the conquerors and conquered became identified. Our policy has been the reverse of this; cold, selfish and unfeeling; the iron hand of power on the one side, monopoly and exclusion on the other."

Thomas Babington Macaulay battled for the abolition of press censorship and fought for the right of Indians to appeal to higher courts – for which cause he was nearly lynched by a white mob in Calcutta. He promoted English schools; at the Hooghly College, 1,100 students attended the English faculty, 300 the oriental. He also laid the foundations of perhaps the most comprehensive penal code in the land, embracing the best of Roman, Hindu and Muslim law, which was finally enacted in 1860.

* * * * * * * *

1857. The year is written in red in the history books of India. It is the year of the Great Indian Mutiny. It was neither great nor was it an all-India phenomenon. It was confined to a few miserable places in north India; the rest of India couldn't have cared less. And it was waged most incompetently by a minority of the Indian army and other Indian forces. This proves that – even then – India was not a united country, and that the Indians even then could not organize anything, let alone an uprising.

What were the causes of the mutiny?

Let us first learn the astonishing fact that, in 1857, there were only 21,197 British troops in India. The native army totalled 277,000. So India's 200-odd millions were held by bluff. It was a mercenary native army officered by the foreign British. The Indian joined the army because it gave him a somewhat decent livelihood, along with position and honour. He felt a fierce pride in his regimental colours.

Secondly, we must learn that the mutiny was neither wholly political nor military. Mutinies of some sort or another had occurred in Buxar in 1764, Vellore in 1805, Barrackpur in 1824 and in Sind in the 1840s. It had been brewing for many years.

1.   Lord Dalhousie wanted to acquire as much of India as he could – because he felt that it was best for the Indians. So, he annexed states in which the rulers had died without leaving heirs. He must, therefore, have rubbed a lot of people up the wrong way. Oudh was annexed by Dalhousie in 1856. (Records show that, way back in 1830, Lord Palmerston, Foreign Secretary, ordered William Bentinck to nab Oudh, which Bentinck refused to do.) Yet it was the British who raised the most vociferous objections, on moral grounds, when the Russian Emperor confiscated the property of the Polish nobles in 1831, when the Austrian government sequestered the estates of the Lombard noblemen in 1849, and when Louis Napoleon grabbed the real estate of the Orléans family in 1851.

2.   Field or foreign-service allowance was denied the troops serving in the Punjab and Sind, as the British flag flew over them after the raid, not the local ruler's – a typical instance of financial pedantry.

3.   After November 1856, it was ruled that Indian sepoys must serve overseas. To the average Indian this was unthinkable, for he would be deemed an outcast in his village if he crossed the water. How could he eat the ship's biscuits and salt pork or beef and be a Muslim or Hindu? The Bengal army was recruited from Hindus of high caste (Brahmins and Rajputs) who observed all the nuances of their religion and refused to eat with their British officers and preferred to starve if their shadows fell on their cooking pots – but would fight to the death for these same officers. The Bengal army refused to cross the sea and attack Rangoon; the Sikh regiments were drafted in.

4.   Foreign education, science and medicine, and unheard-of technologies such as trains and telegraph, were thought to be dangerous to the ways of the superstitious and hidebound Hindu.

5.   Convicts and soldiers were told to eat in messes rather than separately. Who could be sure what he was eating or whom he sat next to? This might pollute his caste.

6.   Child marriage, suttee and thuggee were outlawed. But, to the Hindu, this seemed an intolerable intrusion into his religious practices.

7.   Both the Hindu and the Muslim felt that his/her religion was in danger.

8.   The English, at this particular period, tended to become racially proud and intolerant and to despise everything Indian.

9.   Whereas, previously, the company commanders spent their evenings in pleasant chit-chat with their Indian subordinates, now the easier routes of travel were bringing to India letters and women from Britain. So the camaraderie, so essential to the soldier, was missing.

10.   Some of the British officers were too old or too complacent or too incompetent to command respect from the Indian army.

11.   When the mutiny broke out, trusted officers were either absent or transferred, and young unknowns were in command of the regiments.

12.   The British had been thought to be invincible in battle. But news came from Kabul and the Crimea that the Brits had suffered reverses. So, they could be beaten, thought the Indian.

13. There was a good deal of Christian evangelism in the air. At that particular time, the Brits were riding high and thought it their duty to convert the heathen Indian to better and more uplifting ways. Maharaja Dulip Singh of Oudh allegedly embraced Christianity.

14. Official Blue Books (documents published by the British Parliament and Foreign Office) of 1856 and 1857 expressly state that some of the British officials in India employed various methods of torture to extort money from the Indian populace. That such allegations were true was admitted by Lord Dalhousie himself in 1855.

15. The infamous Enfield rifle was the final straw. The army was to be re-equipped with this new rifle. The cartridges of the rifle had to be heavily greased with tallow, which was made from animals of all kinds – including the pig and the cow. The cartridge had to be bitten to open the end and release the powder. The muzzle of the rifle was also greased with it after loading. To handle such a concoction, let alone apply it to the lips, was anathema to both the Hindu and the Muslim. They thought that the British were out to break their caste and convert them to Christianity. (Malicious rumours were abroad that the ground bones of bullocks were being mixed with the flour and sugar.) The cartridges were in the ordnance depots, ready to be issued. The rumblings of the soldiers were heard by the officers on the 24th of January, 1857. It was reported to the government. The 25th was a Sunday. On the 27th of January, orders went out that the greased cartridges were to be used only by the British; the Indians would use

grease made from beeswax and vegetable oil. The rifle drill was also altered; the greased cartridges could now be broken with fingers, not bitten off.

But it was too late.

Bengal (Berhempur and Barrackpur) mutinied, but there was no attack on the officers. In March Ambala mutinied. In April, Lucknow followed suit and 85 soldiers at Meerut refused cartridges of whatever type. They were imprisoned; worse, they were disgraced. On the parade ground they were publicly stripped of their uniforms and fastened into irons by smiths. This must have taken hours – hours of humiliation and a sense of gross injustice. On a Sunday evening, they broke out of their jails, murdered the British officers, their wives and children, and set off for Delhi, where the mutineers had murdered the English commissioner, chaplain and officers. Ferozepur, Lahore and Peshawar joined the carnage.

By May the rebellion had spread throughout northern India; Agra, Bareilly, Moradabad, Sindhia, Patiala, Mainpuri, Kanpur.

Suffice it to say that both sides behaved in a manner quite appropriate and singular to the human species – with mindless, dastardly ferocity. The person who was responsible for healing the wounds, Lord Canning, who insisted on mercy, understanding, reforms and reconciliation instead of the bloodthirsty cry of the lynch mob, was vilified by his own people.

Much is made of the heroism of the Brits. Let me state that their task was made easier by the Indian sepoys. True to their nature, either they were ill-equipped or they did not know how to make the best use of their arms; they had no leader; they were divided amongst themselves by religion and caste; they had no plan of regrouping and attacking at the opportune moment their enemy's vulnerable points; they were cowardly and fled from the ferocious redcoats; a good many of the sepoys were more interested in robbing the dead and looting those they suspected of being in league with the Brits than fighting. There was hardly any hand-to-fight fighting during the mutiny; the mutineers were either bombarded with long-range guns, or fled in fear. The mutiny happened during the height of the summer season – a season that also heralds the onset of torrential rains. Some of the British regiments – especially those that had been rushed to India from England and thus had no chance to acclimatize – lost half their men through sunstroke, cholera and other delectable diseases. Lucknow could have been taken in May; but a number of idiotic orders, compounded by the pusillanimity of the Brits, postponed the inevitable until September. Kanpur could have been taken in July, but, due to the dispersal of troops, this could only be achieved in December 1857. Delhi could have been taken in June, but that was achieved only in September. And every place captured was systematically ransacked by the British soldiers, who found themselves overnight with enough money to buy estates and seats in Parliament when they returned home. It is said that some 150 officers, their backs heavy with swag, sent in their resignations to Sir Colin Campbell after the fall of Kanpur and Lucknow. If, instead of looting the palaces, they had pursued the motley crew of fleeing sepoys, the rebellion could have been quashed earlier.

The one Indian who is constantly mentioned when the mutiny is discussed is the infamous Nana Sahib, who on June 26th 1857 offered a safe passage of retreat for the beleaguered British forces and their families at Kanpur. Some 400 people embarked in the boats to proceed down the river Ganga (Ganges). When the boats were midstream, Nana Sahib opened fire. There were only four survivors. On July 16th, Nana Sahib butchered British men, women and children at Kanpur. Tantia Tope, cousin of Nana Sahib, was another screwball.

On September 20th 1857, the Moghul Emperor, Bahadur Shah II, and the Empress, Zinat Mahal, were captured and thrown into prison. On January 27th 1858, the death sentence was commuted and Bahadur was transported for life to Rangoon.

* * * * * * * *

Even whilst the mutiny was raging the Great Memsahib, Queen Victoria, informed Canning: "The Indian should know that there is no hatred to a brown skin, none; but the greatest wish on their Queen's part to see them happy, contented and flourishing." When the East India Company was disbanded and Victoria took over India she was outraged by some of the paragraphs in the proclamation drawn up by her ministers. She personally amended the offending stanzas: "We do strictly charge and enjoin all those who may be in authority under us that they abstain from all interference with the religious belief or worship of any of our subjects on pain of our highest displeasure." She let it be known that she wanted Indians participating in the governance of their own country. "In their prosperity will be our strength; in their contentment our security." Noting some of the abominable failings of some of her countrymen, she wrote to her Prime Minister, "The Viceroy must not be guided by the snobbish and vulgar, overbearing and offensive behaviour of many of our Civil and Political Agents..."

On the 1st of November 1858, the Queen's proclamation was made at every British station throughout India, to the accompaniment of appropriate church services and fireworks. India would now be governed directly from Whitehall. Ten years later, Mr Disraeli opened India House, in which sat a full Secretary of State – no other country of the Empire was so favoured. The post of Governor General was no more; the man who ruled India would be known henceforward as Viceroy, second only to the Queen; even the Prime Minister of Britain had to defer to India's Viceroy. The only local 'checks' on his authority was the Executive Council (wholly British) and the Legislative Council (made up of Britons, princes and respectable Indians).

When Victoria became Empress of India in 1877, she took an even more enthusiastic interest in Indian affairs – an interest she did not show to other parts of her vast empire. She once made Lord Salisbury, the Prime Minister, apologize for referring to Indians as 'black men'; she complained bitterly that not enough Indians had received awards in her 1898 Birthday Honours; she campaigned to reduce perinatal mortality amongst Indian women and gave five Kaiser-I-Hind medals to women doctors in 1900. And then there is her peculiar relationship with a certain Abdul Karim, which started in 1887. The son of a hospital attendant, he had been a clerk at Agra jail till the age of 24, when he was somehow drafted into the Queen's service. He was appointed a groom of the chamber, cooked Victoria Indian curries, was given the title of *munshi* for teaching her Indian languages, accompanied her to the Braemar Highland Gathering and to the theatre, and was privy to all the confidential correspondence pertaining to India. She refused to believe a single word said against him. Being an Indian, he did lie; being a Muslim, he did side with the Muslims; Hindus, being Hindus, were quite indignant that such a person should have the personal ear of the monarch. After Victoria died, Karim's papers were burnt at Frogmore Cottage, one of his several homes. He returned to Agra and died there in 1909.

Osborne House, set in 2,000 acres of verdant scenery overlooking the Solent, a mile from East Cowes in the Isle of Wight, represents the personality of Queen Victoria. It was her favourite hideout. It was designed by Thomas Cubitt and the Prince Consort, Albert, in 1845-48. The most majestic part of the house is the famous Durbar Room, with its plumed exoticism and Indian plaster decoration by John Lockwood Kipling, father of Rudyard. It is now open to the public, and an oil painting of Abdul Karim adorns one of its walls.

To date no one is able to offer a satisfactory explanation for this peculiar relationship between a virtual nobody such as Abdul Karim and Victoria, Empress of India.

* * * * * * * *

India had its caste system. The British in India had their class system elaborately codified in the Warrant of Precedence, an infallible guide to hierarchy and protocol. By the end of the Raj, there were 61 different levels of social status.

1 – The Viceroy, of course.
17 – The British residents of Hyderabad and Mysore.
27 – Vice-chancellors of Indian universities.
33 – The director of intelligence.
39 – Presidency senior chaplain of the Church of Scotland.
45 – The assay master, Bombay.
56 – The managing director of the opium factory at Ghazipur.
61 – The director of the vaccine institute at Belgaum.

The class system for the 565 princes was marked by the number of field gun salutes.

21-gun – Five.
19-gun – Six.
17-gun – 13.
15-gun – 17.
13-gun – 16.
11-gun – 31.
9-gun – 30.

For the great majority the guns never tolled.
* * * * * * * *

Lord Dalhousie created the Public Works Department, laid 4,000 miles of telegraph wires, completed Bentinck's Grand Trunk Road from Calcutta to Delhi and introduced to flabbergasted Indians the steam railways, the first being a 21-mile run between Bombay and Thana on the 16th of April 1853, with 14 carriages and 400 guests. By the end of the century 10,000 miles of track had been laid; by 1920, 700,000 people were employed by the railways. Then, as now, the railways were used by the Indians to visit places of pilgrimage. The princes got in on the act, the Gaekwar of Baroda being the first to have railways installed in his kingdom; of course, he had a special carriage, with a throne. With the opening of the Suez Canal in 1869 and the network of railways criss-crossing the country, the total value of imports and exports rose from £39.75 million in 1856 to a staggering £155 million in 1887.

Lord Ripon sought to introduce the Ilbert Bill, which enabled Indian judges to try Europeans outside the three presidencies of Madras, Bombay and Calcutta (Indian judges were already presiding within the presidencies.) There was such an uproar – even a plan to kidnap Ripon – that it was watered down to state that half the jurors must be white in case of an Indian judge presiding.

Lord Curzon arrived in 1899 as Viceroy after a brilliant academic career at Eton and Balliol, extensive travel throughout Europe, the Middle East and Asia, and receiving the Gold Medal of the Royal Geographic Society for tracing the Oxus River to its source in Russian Turkistan. He had his knuckles rapped for his imperialistic scheme when he blundered into Tibet and slaughtered some 700 Tibetans. He was a no-nonsense administrator and earned the wrath of the Bengalis by blundering again when he vivisected Bengal, creating a Muslim East and a Hindu West. He was regarded as 'a regular jingo'. But he was not a racist. He loathed British indiscipline within the civil service and the army. He was outraged by the behaviour of white troops towards the Indians. An infantryman of the West Kent Regiment had raped an old woman in Rangoon, and the authorities closed ranks; Curzon banished the regiment to Aden at the entrance to the Red Sea – one of the direst outposts. Some drunks belonging to the 9th Lancers beat an Indian to death, and once again the regiment closed ranks. Curzon had every lancer recalled from leave, stopped their leave for the next six months and reprimanded the entire lot – a disgrace in military circles. He said, "The argument seems to be that a native's life does not count; and that any crime ought to be concealed and almost even condoned... I have set my face like flint against such iniquity."

When London asked him to 'recruit' 20,000 coolies to work on the railways in South Africa, he refused to be a part of the indentured labour system because, "In practice it means to India a full share of the battles and burdens of Empire, but uncommon little of the privilege and rights."

He extended irrigation, started more primary and secondary schools, and enthusiastically conserved India's monuments – it was he who restored the Taj Mahal, Fatehpur Sikri, the Pearl Mosque in Lahore, the Palace at Mandalay, and the temples of Khajuraho, etc. to their former glory. And he held the Great Durbar in

Delhi in 1902. The programme started on the 29th of December and went on for ten days. Some 173,000 visitors from all over the world. Military bands comprising 2,000 men; 67 squadrons of cavalry; 35 battalions of infantry, artillery and engineers; a total of 34,000 British and Indian soldiers. Marquees containing the biggest display of Indian arts and crafts. Britons and Indians decorated for their loyalty. State ball. Open-air service with prayers for all the peoples of India, climaxing with 'Fight the good fight with all thy might'.

Lord Minto undid the damage done by Curzon in Bengal by once again unifying it and appointing a Bengali to his own Executive Council. John Morley, Secretary of State for India, appointed two Indians to his India Council. They increased the Bengal Legislative Council from 21 to 53, with a majority elected rather than nominated, thus taking the first practical step towards the government of India by Indians.

King George V, at yet another durbar, held in Delhi in December 1911, announced that the capital would be shifted from Calcutta back to the historic old city of Delhi by the 1st of April 1912. India was overjoyed; but not the Bengalis or the British, for they had vested interests in Bengal.

* * * * * * * *

Edward Lutyens was entrusted with the task of creating New Delhi. Herbert Baker was his chief collaborator. Lutyens would create the Viceroy's House, Baker the government secretariat and Imperial Legislative Assembly. It was decided to give the entire project an oriental flavour. They used the same red and buff sandstone, white marble from Jodhpur, green from Baroda, black from Gaya, pink from Alwar, and yellow from Jaisalmer used by Akbar and Shah Jehan. Some 30,000 men were put into service. The Viceroy's House was bigger than Louis XIV's Versailles and had 340 rooms and cost £10 million. But the approach was somehow irrevocably flawed. As one ascends from the bottom of King's Way to the foot of Raisina Hill, the Viceroy's House disappears. The great architects had miscalculated the gradient. The capital city of India was completed in 1931. The building of Parliament House, more than anything else, is proof enough that the Brits did not even consider leaving India to the Indians. If they had, do you think they would have invested in the building of a capital city as late as 1931?

A word about the Indian civil service – ICS. In 1805, Haileybury College was founded to acclimatize the Brits to service in India. Just before the Indian Mutiny of 1857, entry to the civil service was thrown open to other universities: Oxford, Cambridge, Cheltenham, Marlborough, Clifton, Bedford Grammar School and Kingston. Between 1855 and 1860, some 60% of ICS men were Oxbridge graduates. Until the dawn of the 20th century, all were British middle-class. Once he came to India, the raw recruit would be in charge of some 4,000 square miles as a district officer who dispensed justice, collected revenue, dealt with brigands, famine and floods and sorted out communal problems. He was on the move some 100 days in the year, living in tents, socializing with the common villagers, making friends, swapping stories, learning languages and customs. These tours were the marvellous memories of India recalled many a time with true fondness around hearth fires in Britain in the days of retirement. The ICS was renowned for the integrity and efficiency of its British officers. They were answerable only to themselves, and occasionally to the officer above, who would visit them on his rounds. They were minor kings in their respective districts. They could do their job well and live in peace and happiness, or they could be despots and line their pockets.

William Herschel, an ICS man, pioneered the science of fingerprinting in Bengal long before Francis Galton. Brian Hodgson, Resident of Nepal, was the recipient of France's Légion d'honneur for his reputation in philology, ethnology and zoology. Allan Octavian Hume was a distinguished ornithologist and left his collection of 82,000 birds and their eggs to the Natural History Museum, London; he was the father of the Congress – born on the 28th of December 1885 with the blessing of the Viceroy, Lord Dufferin – which later evolved into the Indian National Congress. Hume remained its secretary until 1907. It was organized to channel popular protest into legal moderation, and later allowed the waters of nationalism to flow into it.

Before we leave the ICS, I must tell you that, in 1868, three Bengalis and one Bombayite passed the examination in England. The nation cheered – until someone said that three of them had lied about their ages. Surendranath Banerjea was one of the accused and he sued the Secretary of State in the court of the Queen's Bench and won. But later he was dismissed for sending in a false return. That proves that the Indian is corrupt unless otherwise proved. But all this 'foreign' education worked adversely for the British. The foreign-educated Indian returnee could speak English better than the English, he could use his cutlery with aplomb, and he could be as good an administrator or judge or warrior. He could even speak on such diverse subjects as world politics, socialism, equality, freedom and independence. This confused the Brit. The only way he could deal with this new kind of Indian was with irrational wrath, cold contempt, supreme arrogance, and devastating humiliation. If only the Brit had utilized such Indians in a more charming manner, he would not have been asked to leave.

* * * * * * * *

World War I. At the outbreak of war, Indian soldiers numbered around 280,000. The number recruited during the course of the war is 1,300,000, most of them volunteers. Indian soldiers fought in all the countries around the Mediterranean, France, Belgium, Persia, the Cameroons, Somaliliand, Trans-Caspia and north China. The number of British soldiers in India at the time was reduced to 15,000; 15,000 amongst 300 million people. If India had wished to rebel, it could not have had a more opportune moment. But even then Indians preferred British rule to any other.

By that time a good many Indians had been to Britain to study, observe and further their careers. They came to see that Great Britain was not as great as it was cracked up to be. They saw that the British in India lived an exceedingly grand lifestyle compared to the counterparts in their own country. The world was seeing a sociological change. Europe and America were calling for independence, self-government and democracy. The Indians started to wonder why their own country was missing out on these newfangled ideas. The Indians thought that they would be allowed to participate more in the governing of their country now that they had helped Britain win the war.

Edwin Montagu, Secretary of State for India, and Lord Chelmsford, Viceroy of India, put their heads together in 1917 and presented the British Parliament with a report in 1919 – which became the Government of India Act. The Viceroy's Executive Council was to have six members, three of whom were to be Indians. Each province was to have a diarchy with ministers answerable to a Legislative Council that would be elected. The Imperial Legislative Assembly was to have 146 members, 106 of whom were to be elected, and a Council of State of 61 members. Thus a Westminster-type parliament was ushered in with just one-sixth of the elected in both houses reserved for Europeans. All this took time, given the pedantic nature of legislation. Meanwhile Bengal was erupting with violence; Hindu against Muslim; both against the British. While Montagu and Chelmsford were trying to heal the wounds, an oaf called Sir Sidney Rowlatt issued a report on the 19th of July 1918 recommending his infamous bill that would authorize judges to try political cases without juries and allow provincial governments to intern people without trial – in effect, a continuation of wartime rigours. If only this bill had been presented after the 'Montford' reforms it would have been roundly defeated

272

by the majority Indian members. But this antedated the reforms. India was outraged.

Let us go step by step.

18th March 1919 – Rowlatt Act passed.

30th March – Gandhi's campaign of general mourning and prayer – in other words, a strike. Violence in some parts of India, contrary to Gandhi's wishes. A disillusioned Gandhi calls off strike on the 18th of April, stating that India was not prepared: "Himalayan blunder."

The agitation now centres around the Punjab rather than Bengal.

At about this time the Hindu extremist school of Tilak and co. were trying to incite the police and the army to rebel. The Pathans and the Punjabis were sharpening their knives and loading their guns. There was violence at Lahore and Amritsar: looting, burning, train-derailing, telegraph-line-cutting – the works.

9th April – Dr Kitchlew, the Muslim leader, and Dr Satyapal, the Hindu leader, the two chaps who could have restrained the people, are arrested on Ram Naumi, a Hindu festival day. Messrs Stewart, Scott and Thomson, bankers, are killed. Some other British were assaulted.

April 10th to 12th – Amritsar in the hands of the mob. Miss Marcia Sherwood, a doctor, was assaulted. Situation beyond police control.

Michael O'Dwyer was in charge of the Punjab. He belonged to the school of thought that maximum force in the beginning would avert a disaster. He wanted to impose martial law. He was not allowed to do so. He could only advise the military.

April 11th – Brigadier General Reginald Dyer arrives. Drum orders all over the city banning meetings and warning people that meetings will be fired upon. The general opinion is that this message was not broadcast in all parts of the city. But I don't subscribe to that. In India, anything and everything from one part is immediately known everywhere by physical or ethereal means. Such an important broadcast would definitely have been known by everyone.

April 13th – 4:30 p.m. Meeting held at Jallianwallah Bagh. Opinion is that it was some festival or fair day and that the people were just having a jolly party. That may be true as there were women and children present, but it is also true that it was also (turned into) a political meeting. It was held in defiance of the prohibition order and its leaders were agitators – this was confirmed later by courts of law. They were mainly Sikhs, a warlike people traditionally armed with swords, knives and quarterstaffs. Dyer ordered his force of 50 Baluchi soldiers armed with guns to open fire without any word of warning. He also had with him 40 Gurkhas armed with knives. About 1,650 rounds were fired. They killed or wounded 1,516 people – a very high strike rate, confirming that the soldiers fired into the thick of the people. The people could not escape as the ground was enclosed on all sides; and the soldiers fired with cool and calculated disdain.

Now, this is where the trouble starts.

1.   Dyer could have given the usual word of warning to the crowd, however unruly or unlawful they were, before firing.

2.　　　He need not have inflicted such a terrible retribution. After all, there were women and children at the meeting. He could have ordered a burst of fire over the heads or stopped after a token show of force. He did not. He admitted that he directed the fire to the most densely peopled areas of the ground. He also callously stated that, if it had been possible for him to take in the two armoured cars, he would have done so and opened fire with the machine guns with impunity.

3.　　　He did not make any arrangements for the care of the wounded or the dead.

4.　　　He later said that he deliberately inflicted such a monstrous outrage because he wished to teach the whole of the Punjab and entire India a lesson in obedience. He had no right to do so. "It was no longer a question of merely dispersing the crowd but one of producing a sufficient moral effect from a military point of view not only on those who were present but more especially throughout the Punjab. There could be no question of undue severity," Dyer stated to the Hunter Committee.

5.　　　He promulgated the wretched 'crawling order'. Indians – even those who lived in the street – were made to crawl on all fours down the street where Marcia Sherwood was assaulted. This was a dreadful insult indeed. O'Dwyer remonstrated with Dyer over this order.

6.　　　Dyer erected a whipping frame on the spot where Sherwood was assaulted and he ordered to be whipped Indians on animals or vehicles who failed to alight, Indians who failed to lower their umbrellas, and Indians who did not salute or salaam their British officers in Amritsar. Six youths were flogged simply on suspicion, without a trial. He behaved like someone out of the Middle Ages.

The Hunter Committee condemned Dyer but the House of Lords voted in his favour, 126 to 86, and the *Morning Post*, prompted by O'Dwyer and Sir Edward Carson, leader of the Ulster Protestants, launched a fund for 'the Man who saved India'. A sum of £26,317 4 shillings and10 pence was raised; Rudyard Kipling contributed ten of those pounds.

Rabindranath Tagore flung his knighthood back at the Raj. Gandhi flung his Zulu War medal and the Kaiser-I-Hind medal given to him for organizing and serving as stretcher-bearer to the British in South Africa during the Boer War and in Europe during World War I. Many other Indians gave up their privileges and positions in the British government.

The infamous Rowlatt Act was repealed – without having been implemented.

Postscript – O'Dwyer maintained that what he and Dyer did averted a disaster on a greater scale. He was proved right in 1921 at Moplah, when the Muslims and Hindus fought each other. The British pussyfooted around and, instead of the fewer than 1,000 killed in the Punjab in 1919, several thousand Muslims and Indians slaughtered each other at Moplah in 1921.

* * * * * * * *

After Jallianwallah Bagh, the Indian started to mistrust the British, and the writing was on the wall for the British to get back to their island.

Gandhi now seriously enters politics. He calls for 'non-cooperation', burning and boycott of all things British. Spinning becomes an obsession. He agrees to the Montagu-Chelmsford reforms that bestow a 'diarchy' system of government; more Indians will participate, but they will have no power! But the message is clear to the British. Get out! Amidst all this turbulence, the stupid Prince of Wales, the future King Edward VIII, decides to visit India. Of course, he is cold-shouldered by the masses. Riots. By 1922, tens of thousands of Indians were imprisoned.

February 1922 – Gandhi decides to personally supervise and rehearse a mass civil disobedience movement in the small district of Bardoli, near Bombay. It is a success. But in Chauri Chaura, 800 miles from Bardoli, the mob burned alive the police in their police station; those who gave themselves up were hacked to pieces. Gandhi calls the whole movement off. There is great discussion even now as to the wisdom of this decision. This could have been another 'Himalayan blunder' by Gandhi. India could have had its freedom then if the momentum had been maintained.

10th March 1922 – Gandhi is arrested.

18th March 1922 – the Great Trial. I am not going into this. All that I shall say is that what Gandhi said whilst freely admitting the charges of sedition constitutes one of the greatest speeches even made by a human being that I have ever read. (If only for this speech, you should read a book on Gandhi.) He was sentenced (reluctantly and with great respect) to six years' imprisonment by Mr Justice Broomfield.

In 1927, the Simon Commission was appointed to review the 'Montford' reforms. All the members were British. How stupid could they get? India was outraged.

12th March 1930 – 6:30 a.m. Gandhi and 78 members of his Ashram set off to the sea, 240 miles away. Gandhi had informed the government of his intentions. He was going to 'make salt'. The manufacture and sale of salt was an exclusive government monopoly, which also included a tax on the selling price. Salt is essential for the people of a tropical land. To the poor peasant the tax represented two weeks' annual income. As the cortège made its way through towns and villages, it swelled into thousands. Newspaper reporters and cameramen from all over the world followed Gandhi's every step and listened to his every word.

April 6th – 6:00 p.m. The strange entourage reached the town of Dandi on the Indian Ocean. At dawn the next morning, Gandhi stooped down and scooped up a piece of caked salt – which was later sold to a Dr Kanuga for a sum of 1,600 rupees. To the Indian those few grains of salt became a new symbol for the struggle for independence. Within a week people all over India were making salt. Lord Irwin clapped Gandhi into jail. "The honour of India has been symbolized by a fistful of salt in the hand of a man of non-violence. The fist which held the salt may be broken, but it will not yield up its salt."

1931 – Gandhi was now a world-renowned figure. Even the children in Britain were writing essays about him. He was invited to the round-table conference in London. He was a bigger hit with the British public than with its politicians, who were all, once again, a bunch of pedantic, conniving oafs who sought to set one Indian against the other. Given the mentality of the Indians, they succeeded easily.

1937 – provincial elections; the franchise included one-sixth of the population; women were given the right to vote. The Congress headed eight of the 11 polls. Typically, they refused to accommodate the minority groups, especially the Muslims. If only they had shown a bit of foresight at this vital stage of history, India would not have been bifurcated; Pakistan would not have come into being. Jinnah was justifiably miffed.

1939 – World War II. Without consulting a single Indian, Viceroy Lord Linlithgow declared war on Britain's enemies. Some 189,000 troops swelled to 2,500,000 by the end of the war: the biggest 'volunteer army' the world has ever seen, quite unprecedented in human history. The Indian political stalwarts, though justifiably offended at the lack of courtesy, volunteered to help if promised independence after the war. The British refused to barter. The eight Congress ministers resigned and, like petulant children, the Congressmen refused to cooperate with the war effort. The three Muslim regimes – Bengal, Sind and Punjab – snatched their God-given chance and backed the British. Jinnah thus strengthened his stature amongst the 90 million Muslims out of a population of 400 million and started to demand Pakistan.

* * * * * * * *

Hollywood had made 35 movies with the Indian theme by now, starting with the *Hindoo Fakir* in 1902 and carrying on to *Gunga Din* in 1939. Even before they entered the war, Roosevelt was campaigning for Indian independence. He had a few words on the subject with Churchill. But Churchill had a curiously incurable blind spot as far as Indian independence was concerned. In March 1942, Stafford Cripps, a socialist member of Churchill's War Cabinet, came to India and invited the Congress leaders to rejoin the Viceroy's Council – now acting as a cabinet of the Indian government – and promising India complete freedom within or without the British Empire after the war. The Congress should have accepted the offer, as the British could not have wriggled out of such a public announcement. But the fools did not, Gandhi referring to the offer with his famous quip about a 'post-dated cheque on a failing bank', probably because they thought that Britain would lose the war. Instead they launched the 'Quit India' movement. It was the wrong time to agitate, for the Japanese were knocking on India's frontiers in the north-east and had dropped a couple of bombs on Madras in the south. The British could not fight two enemies at once. So they quite rightly slung Gandhi and the whole Congress lot into jails across the country.

Unfortunately, there was a famine in Bengal in 1943. Some say that it was the diversion of food to the troops that caused it. Now the British had to fight three fronts. A lot has been said about who was to blame. The British were in power. They have to take the blame for lack of foresight, diversion of materials to the war effort and lack of an adequate and speedy response. Some 3,000,000 people died terrible deaths from starvation. Lord Wavell, the new Viceroy, visited the areas and diverted almost the entire war effort to getting food supplies to Bengal.

Soon after VE Day – even before the atom bomb was dropped on Hiroshima by the Americans, thus bringing about VJ Day – Churchill was kicked out of Downing Street and Clement Attlee, a former pupil of Haileybury, headed the new Labour government. He immediately sent a mission to India to prepare the nation for independence. The mission was to suggest various ways and means of reconciling the various political and religious groups. It was doomed right from the beginning. How can Indians ever agree about anything? Even at this stage of momentous history, they could not set aside their petty and shoddy personalities. If only the Congress had been generous towards the Muslims, there would not have been Pakistan. India would have been united; the British would have left. At the next election everything could have been sorted out democratically. Everyone would have been satisfied. But Jinnah was fed up with the Congress attitude. With some justification, he feared the Hindus. He ordered a 'Direct Action Day' on the 16th of August 1946. Hindus and Muslims fell on each other the way only human beings do; the streets stank with nearly 6,000 hacked and mutilated bodies, the likes of which turned the stomachs of even the 45,000 war-hardened troops who were drafted in to quell the riots.

The Brits were at a loss. They could find no solution. They decided that the best thing to do would be to announce a definite date for independence, hoping that that would get the various factions to get their act together. Wavell was recalled and Lord Louis

Mountbatten, Supreme Allied Commander in South-East Asia and a cousin of King George VI, was sent to India as the last Viceroy to sort things out.

Now, a lot has been said about our Louis. He did go out of his way to ingratiate himself with the Indian people, by taking morning horseback rides unescorted, by casually dropping into Nehru's house and chatting with guests, by insisting that at least half the number of his dinner guests must be Indian, by providing Indian vegetarian food in the Viceroy's House, etc. He liked Nehru and was fascinated by Gandhi, whom he respected. He disliked Jinnah.

When Louis was appointed to his glamorous post during the war, many of his colleagues laughed. Louis was just an egotistical windbag, albeit a handsome, glamorous one. He was a headstrong, impulsive, colourful, rash individual. He brought these qualities into play at this juncture of history. Acting on a whim – the second anniversary of the Japanese surrender to his forces – and without consulting Attlee or the Indians, he announced the 14th of August 1947 as the date of independence. The Indians should have been overjoyed. Instead they were aghast. They had not settled their infighting. Gandhi, now wearing the air of someone who has been completely defeated, suggested to his Congress colleagues handing over everything to the Muslims in order to save the unity of India. It is not as preposterous as it sounds. It was a sound moral argument. India would have had a Muslim as the first Prime Minister – Mohammed Ali Jinnah. It would have had Muslims in all the leading posts all over the country. So what? At the time of the next democratically held election, the people would have made their choices – both Hindus and Muslims would rule over different provinces under a single flag. But Nehru wanted to be the first Prime Minister. The other salivating Congresswallahs wanted to be in positions of power – and make good, doing naughty things.

No other option lay ahead except the division of the land into India and Pakistan.

The burden of carrying out this complex task fell to Sir Cyril Radcliffe, generally acknowledged to be the most brilliant barrister in England when he was summoned to the office of the Lord Chancellor of England one afternoon in the summer of 1947. He was told to divide Bengal and Punjab – to draw a line through the mud that would affect 88 million people. Cyril was stunned. Cyril did not even know where they were; indeed he didn't know much about India at all. When he landed in India, Mountbatten told him to finish the job by the 14th of August – now just a few weeks away. Cyril told him that he would not be able to inspect the land, that he would be liable to make mistakes – that it was impossible. Louis told him to get on with it. Cyril was a barrister and he was independent. He called on Nehru and Jinnah and asked them if it was imperative that he divide the land before independence. The two idiots told him that that was so.

The inevitable happened. After independence, millions of people found themselves on the wrong side of the border. During the course of this mammoth immigration, the largest in human history, thousands lost their lives due to religious intolerance.

* * * * * * * *

It is ironic that, when the prime motives of the British were trade and profit in the 17th, 18th and 19th centuries, India was blessed with Governors General and Viceroys with humanitarian principles; and when the entire world order was changing in the 20th century, to incorporate the principles of democratic self-government, the people in charge of government, both in India and Britain, turned out to be a bunch of short-sighted, bigoted, rash, pedantic, arrogant, incompetent idiots.

* * * * * * * *

The question of who is to blame for the partition of India always crops up. Let me put down my views...for what they are worth.

The Role of the British

     1.   World War I was fought on the principles of democracy and freedom. The world was awakening to the fact that self-government was an agreeable concept, that independence was worth dying for. Britain was the greatest power then. It was an enlightened power. It was aware of these concepts. Therefore, it should have given India its independence soon after the war ended in 1918.

     2.   The Indian movement for independence had gathered momentum soon after World War I. The slaughter of Jallianwalla Bagh happened in 1919 and India was outraged and up in arms. Britain should have gracefully walked out then.

     3.   Britain messed up things with Messrs Rowlatt and Simon. Gandhi stirred the nation and the

entire world with his Dandi march. Britain should have bowed out then.

But they had no intention of bowing out. How else can you account for the shifting of the capital to Delhi and the building of Parliament House, which was completed in 1932.

4.   Britain relented, released Gandhi from prison and arranged a round-table conference in London in 1931. It turned out to be a farce. They could have granted independence then – instead of charging the atmosphere and setting the delegates at each others' throats with religions, castes and princely states.

5.   World opinion was changing rapidly during the 1930s in the lead-up to the Second World War. Britain should have given India its independence at least then, when war was declared against Hitler in 1939. Then India would have gladly fought for the British. Instead, Indians were insulted grievously when they were plunged into war without any consultation.

6.   During World War II, when Roosevelt suggested that India be given independence, the British should have taken the hint.

7.   When they finally decided to go, they should have just gone and left India to its own inhabitants. It was no concern of theirs if different factions disagreed or slaughtered each other. It was no concern of theirs if the Indians did not know anything about self-government. It would have been their own mess, not a British mess.

The Role of the Indians

1.   In 1937, when the Congress won eight of the 11 provinces, they should have accommodated the Muslims more generously. Instead they behaved like selfish power-mongerers.

2.   The Congress government should not have quit their posts at the outbreak of World War II, leaving the field free to the Muslims.

3.   In 1942, when Cripps invited the Congress back into the fold, the Congress should have buried their differences with the Muslims and joined in. After all, India was promised independence soon after the war if they did so. The Congress should not have refused this offer and should not have launched the 'Quit India' movement.

4.   Soon after the war Attlee tried to reconcile the Hindus and the Muslims. They should have behaved like astute politicians and settled for a compromise.

5.   Jinnah should not have ordered 'Direct Action Day' in 1946, urging the Muslims to slaughter the Hindus. This really fuelled the feeling of hatred amongst both the Hindus and the Muslims.

6.   The Muslim League was only for Muslims. The Indian National Congress was for everyone; Muslims, Hindus, Sikhs, etc. were prominent office-bearers. It was the only all-India secular party representing the entire cross-section of the Indian population. Therefore, Jinnah's claim that the Congress was a solely Hindu party is so much poppycock. The ultimate falsity of this statement lies in the fact that, even after partition, India had a larger population of Muslims than any other country; many Muslims preferred to stay

on in 'Hindu' India. Jinnah acted the part of a shrewd and calculating rogue; he was a master poker-player – and he won his hand despite having no cards. The British and the Congress are guilty of not calling his colossal bluff. They should have stood by their guns and shunned the idea of partition. The scene would have been comical if it had not been so tragic, for the fact was that the great majority of these so-called Muslims were converts from Hindu under long years of Muslim rule. It is ironic that a nation was created for a bunch of converts – but then, you know how the saying goes: 'there is no greater fanatic than a convert'. Jinnah's ancestors were themselves converts.

7. In 1947, when independence was imminent, the Hindus should have taken up Gandhi's suggestion and handed over the government to Jinnah. The next election would have settled affairs; there would have been Muslim and Hindu majorities in different states – but one India. The usual excuse put forward is that, if Gandhi's plan had been implemented, the Hindu masses would have slaughtered the Muslims. This is the usual game of blaming the victim. The masses are unconcerned about who rules them. It is the politician who whips up feelings and goads them into activities of terrorism. Nehru, Patel, Azad and co. could have easily influenced them.

Going according to plan, thousands were murdered – including Gandhi. Who is to say that morbidity and mortality would have been greater or lesser if Gandhi's plan had been adopted? I am convinced that there would have been less bloodshed; there would not have been a twin migration of populations, especially across the Punjab, the province that accounted for the great majority of the killings. Of one thing, at least, we could have been sure: India would have been one; it would not have been partitioned; Pakistan would not have been on the maps of the world.

Then the Indian cricket side would have been invincible!

So, there you have it. A fatal combination of British opportunism and cunning, Muslim fanaticism and fear of the Hindu, and Hindu asininity and poltroonery – all of them shrouded by the web of expedience – caused the bifurcation of the then India and created the new nation of Pakistan.

Let me give my interpretation of the India-Pakistan conflict that has destroyed one of the most enchanting spots in the world.

The Indian princes were asked, cajoled and threatened to throw in their lot with India at the time of independence. They had no option, for geography dictated that that was the most logical thing to do. Finally, only Kashmir was left, its ruler dithering. Its ruler was Hindu, Hari Singh. The majority of his subjects were Muslim. Worried that the kingdom might eventually go to India as its ruler was a weak Hindu king, the Pakistanis, along with Muslim Afghan mercenaries, raided Kashmir. They had almost entered the capital city of Srinagar. They would have captured it if the Afghan mercenaries and Pakistani troops had not stopped at a nunnery to ravish the poor maidens. Meanwhile, Nehru was seething as he helplessly watched his beloved native place being stolen. Hot-blooded as he was, he wanted to rush in his troops. But Mountbatten advised him that it was contrary to international law. Nehru could not intervene until asked to by Hari Singh. Frightened for his life, Hari Singh eventually sent an SOS to Delhi asking for India's assistance. The Indian troops flew in, fought pitched and courageous battles and drove the marauders from Srinagar. It was only a matter of time before the invaders would be pushed back to their allocated border, as delineated by the departing British. The matter should have been settled then. But Nehru chose to appeal to the United Nations. Maybe he thought of projecting India as a righteous nation given to non-violence; maybe he wanted to cover himself in personal glory as an international statesman. Who knows what he was up to? The United Nations lived up to its reputation as specialists in colossal stupidity and monumental inertia. They asked the Pakistanis to return to the border and asked India to hold a plebiscite. Neither country has honoured the United Nations directive. The war still goes on between India and Pakistan.

India is legally right, for Pakistan is the encroacher. The argument put forward by non-Indians is that Kashmir has a predominantly Muslim population and should be allowed a free plebiscite to choose its status. So what if it has a majority Muslim population? Hari Singh, a Hindu, was their ruler; a quirk of destiny – but, nevertheless, a solid fact. The maharaja opted to throw in his lot with India when his kingdom was threatened. Kashmir is thus part of India. A plebiscite is out of the question.

If anyone is to be blamed it has to be the British, who had no business in vivisecting the land. They should have just quit and left India to 'God or anarchy'; whatever the outcome, the British would not have been blamed. Now we do blame them, and rightfully so. If they had wanted to create Pakistan, they could have done so with more care. Why the unholy hurry, all of a sudden, to leave India? Just because the egotistical Mountbatten plucked out a date from his hat. I am not going into that bit of hindsight about Jinnah being mortally ill. No one knew that at the time, so cleverly did the poker-player hide his mortality.

India and Pakistan have been involved in many talks. The UN resolutions have been put aside and a lot of water has flowed under the bridge. The net result is that India has lost territory the size of Wales to Pakistan, and a similar area to the Chinese.

The Indians will never ask for a plebiscite and will never give up their legitimate piece of real estate and the Pakistans will never give up their demand of the wilderness, their only reason being that the majority of people there are Muslims, not Hindus. This despite the incontrovertible fact that Pakistan treats the Muslims who have chosen to come over to Pakistan from other parts of India as second-class citizens. This unfortunate group of immigrants know and suffer this. The Muslims of India also know this – but adamantly and illogically choose to ignore it. The Muslims of India have a better deal within India than what would be meted out to them if they were to go over to their beloved Pakistan – a country given to regular doses of military dictatorship.

What about the future? It is impossible to foretell, but let us have a go, eh?

1.   Pakistan should give up its claim over Kashmir; it is ludicrous to claim a place on religious grounds. India should magnanimously give up Kashmir to Pakistan.

Either of the above moves would save both the countries a lot of heartache, and together they would be partners in their march into the future. But, unfortunately, neither move would save face.

2.   Or Pakistan and India could shake hands over a cup of tea and become *one*. Maybe Bangladesh, Nepal and even Sri Lanka would like to join in. After all, East and West Germany have united and all the European countries that have been slaughtering each other for centuries are trying their best to get their act together. It is all an inexorable cycle of events. Nations divide and unite – only to divide again and re-unite later.

3.   There is another option. Make Kashmir independent – like Switzerland. And, like Switzerland, develop it into an international resort for all kinds of people for all kinds of reasons...

What neither Pakistan nor India want is interference from other countries that seem to deem themselves as somehow morally superior. They may be militarily superior; but not morally so. Every country has its skeletons. The great USA still mistreats the autochthons of the continent, the Africans that it brought over, and various other minorities – Catholics, Jews. It interferes with business far away from home and gets scalded – Vietnam. Great Britain has a long history of cruelty and exploitation that it still practises on some of its minority citizens. It has its foolish Irish problem...that it says it is trying to solve. And it sent its soldiers millions of miles away to the Falklands – for what logical reason, I wonder? Pakistan and India are contiguous nations – not a million miles away. So, let not others even think of interfering. If Pakistan and India blow each other up...then let them.

But you are wasting so much money fighting each other, people say. Let me state a few facts a Lieutenant-Colonel cousin of mine told me. India spends 25 billion rupees a year to maintain its forces in Kashmir. A helluva lot of money, you say. Yes, it is – but what you do not know is that: a. we have to spend that money anyway on our forces, wherever they may be located; b. military expenditure is more or less the same whether they are fighting somewhere or just idling; c. the only extra cost is ammunition, which is only a fraction of the total cost, the main element being maintenance of the troops; d. 25 billion rupees represents only 0.1% of India's GDP! So, financially, our expenditure there is no big deal. In fact, if India chooses to increase that amount to just 2.0% of its GDP, Pakistan will become bankrupt – and the war will end.

* * * * * * *

CHAPTER 27
The Legacy

The Anglo-Indians

The Portuguese came to India not only to trade but to convert to Catholicism; cowled monks and tonsured priests accompanied the traders in their ships. They accomplished both by intermarrying with the natives – widows of natives they had slain in battle; now they had family who could help them barter in the local language. Many Indians were converted without the contract of marriage and adopted Portuguese names. These make up the majority of 'Portuguese' today – who make excellent cooks in restaurants in all the cities of India.

When the British landed on the north-west coast of India they had no intentions of proselytizing their religion. To help them with their trade they recruited the Armenians from the British settlements at Gombroon on the northern shore of the Strait of Hormuz; they knew Persian, the language of business in Mughal India at that time. When they had established themselves at Madras and Bengal, the Portuguese influence was waning; so they recruited some of the local Portuguese converts, conversant with local languages and well versed in the business of trade, to help them. These people of mixed descent were known as *Topasses* in Madras and *Firinghees* in Bengal. They made good mercenary soldiers to protect their rudimentary huts, which housed their goods awaiting shipment to Britain, from the marauding Marathas and Pindaris. Once business picked up, the British hovels were enlarged to incorporate warehouses, offices, living quarters and military barracks. British soldiers were brought in.

A round journey took some 18 months in those days and many of them resigned themselves to the fact that they might never see England again. The British in India had no women. So they took to mingling with the locals – either Portuguese of mixed descent or Portuguese converts. When the Portuguese population was drained they mingled with the regular autochthons. The British quarters were too small to accommodate the growing number of emigrants; they moved out and set up homes with their Indian wives. The East India Company paid the mother one pagoda (about eight shillings in those days) for every child born of a Briton; it was later raised to five rupees for every child. Thus the British were directly responsible for the mixed race of Anglo-Indians.

Let us see what happened.

1.   Many maintained seraglios, begetting illegitimate children who were either accepted and treated decently or abandoned as scrap to fend for themselves.

2.   Many married their Indian women. These women were converted to Christianity and taught the English language, customs and practices, and their children were Christians. These women were shunned by their own families for the rest of their lives. Thus, over the course of generations, they came to embrace alien English ways detached from the people of the soil, separated from them by speech, dress, religion, customs and habits. They lived a lonely life, their only female

companions being other Indian women in similar positions.

3. These children of mixed descent were brought up in an atmosphere of trade and soldiery; they knew the local vernaculars and Indian customs. So they were invaluable assets and made excellent partners to the British. Thus the British found help with trade, labour and defence. The Anglo-Indians, it can be said, laid the foundations for the evolution of company into Crown. Their loyalty was unquestionably with the British at all times.

4. All this changed in 1869 with the opening of the Suez Canal. Now the voyage to India was quicker, less expensive, less dangerous and less arduous. British girls now started to flow into India. Now the Briton in India could marry one of his own kind. If he still chose to marry an Indian woman, he was ostracized by his own company people. His and his family's lot was painful indeed. What happened to them?

a. They returned with their families to England – to be slowly absorbed into the British population.

b. They remained in India and became more Indian and were absorbed into the Indian milieu. Some of them are referred to as Indian-Christians.

c. Or they remained in between the above two classifications – a distinct race of Anglo-Indians. This is what most of them are today.

Whatever group they chose to belong to, they saw themselves as 'British' – even though they had never seen the white cliffs of Dover. They did not identify with Indians.

They acted as scouts, manned the guns, sprang to stirrup, dashed with bayonet wherever and whenever they were called. The 'sons of the soil' were given preference in government jobs for their loyalty. Some of them had been sent to England and returned as commissioned officers to serve beside their parents.

Slowly the Anglo-Indian population surpassed the British.

Two events altered the course of Anglo-Indian history.

1.   During the latter part of the 18th century there was much dissent even within the ranks of the British soldiers. The troops mutinied in Madras, Bengal and Patna. At this time, ill-treated and oppressed half-castes in Hayti and San Domingo had turned on the French and Spaniards. A mindless fear set into the hearts of the British. What if the Anglo-Indians started to side with the Indians and drove them out?

2.   The Britishers were making tons of money, returning home and purchasing estates and Parliamentary seats. This made the company officials in Leadenhall Street envious. Why should they give posts to the 'sons of the soil', the Anglo-Indians? Why couldn't they send or sponsor their own relatives and friends?

Agitation was set in motion. The paranoid company passed three resolutions.

1.   The first to be sacrificed were the defenceless and friendless wards of the Upper Orphanage School at Calcutta, established by the East India Company for the orphans of British military officers. They were prohibited from coming to England

for further education and qualifying for the covenanted services.

2.   The second were the sons of a native Indian – the Anglo-Indians. They were prohibited from employment in the civil, military and marine services of the company.

3.   The third were local Indians. They were disbarred from civil, military and marine services too.

Thus, within the space of ten years (1786 to 1795), the Anglo-Indians were summarily stripped of the chance of honourable careers. They were deprived of education and civil and military livelihood. They were reduced to the status of a proscribed and downtrodden race. If a person was not descended from European parents on both sides, he could work only as a fifer, drummer, bandsman or farrier.

Just look at the absurdity of it all.

1.   The hopes and desires of (deceased) parents were dashed. The duty and affection of parents, the elementary dictates of humanity, were ignored.

2.   A full Indian child could be sent to Britain to be educated, but a child who had only one British parent could not.

3.   Illegitimacy in Britain meant forfeit of inheritance, not civic rights and political equality. But illegitimacy in India deprived them of *all* rights.

4.   Britain's Indian sons could be sent to England for education and employment but they could not return to India and work for the company that received its charter from the Crown.

5.   The half-Indian sons were summarily discharged from military service. Since they were

uneducated and had had no opportunity to learn a trade, they could not find any employment.

6.   The only employment open to them was as mercenaries. The Anglo-Indians entered the services of the Indian rulers – Mysore, Hyderabad, Oudh, Sindhia, Holkar, etc. Some raised their own irregular infantry and cavalry and offered their services to anyone who would pay.

Were the banished Anglo-Indians bitter against the British? No. When the Marathas under Baji Rao regrouped and warred on the British, a proclamation was issued summoning all British and Anglo-Indian men to return to the company's forces. Every one of the Anglo-Indians returned to the fold – even those who were serving the Marathas as mercenaries.

The Anglo-Indians realized that they could no longer depend on the military for employment. They looked to mechanical, industrial and agricultural pursuits as apprentices, for all education was rudimentary, private and Church-run. The Apprenticing Society was formed in Calcutta. Other institutions were started around the country. A few petitions were sent to the British Parliament enunciating the plight of the Anglo-Indians, but nothing came of them. Britain was more interested in what was happening in Ireland and France.

In the 1830s, English supplanted Persian as the language of the courts and Britain needed all its people to prepare for possible wars with France. Both these events helped the Anglo-Indians into positions of employment not open to them previously. But then the overland route to India was opened and educated and adventurous Britons came over to India. They once again displaced the Anglo-Indians. Their position was worsened yet again when the Suez Canal was opened, bringing in more Britons – men and women. Whereas, hitherto, Britons were consorting with the Anglo-Indians, now they shunned the half-castes for the full castes from Britain. In the 1850s the company started educational institutions for the Indians – but not for the Anglo-Indians.

The grievances were somewhat redressed in the latter half of the 19th century with the coming of the railways, the opening up of inland rivers for transport and the post and telegraph system. The Anglo-Indians set about building and manning posts in these enterprises, for they knew the language and could work under Indian conditions better than their half-brothers from Britain.

During the Indian Mutiny of 1857, they once again fought for the British. During World War I they fought in all spheres.

What about the Anglo-Indian women? It seemed that they had distilled in them the very best physical features of both races. They were beauties. They wore European clothes, bobbed their hair, applied lipstick and preferred the Tommy soldier to the native Indian.

The half-British half-Indian people were given the name 'Anglo-Indian' only at the time of the census in 1911. Before that they were known as half-castes, country-born, Indo-Britons, East Indians or Eurasians.

The Anglo-Indians could and should have thrown in their lot with the Congress in 1885, but they dithered. For centuries they couldn't decide who they were. They were born and bred in India; yet they insisted on regarding themselves as British. They were initially ostracized by the orthodox Indians but, during the latter part of the 20th century, they became as accepted as anyone else. They were ostracized by the British at various times and were never accepted by them despite their efforts in assiduously aping their manners.

Due to their behaviour they are a sort of lost race; not Indian, not British. They are Anglo-Indian.

They are Indian in one way – their cuisine; they love curry.

As independence drew near, they were a very worried and confused lot. Many emigrated to Britain, Canada, America and Australia. Some asked for a separate state in India only for Anglo-Indians. Of course, it was refused. There was a lot of bitter infighting amongst them: Anglo-Indians from the north looked down on those from the south; people of Portuguese and Dutch descent were insulted by those of British descent; etc. After independence the Indian constitution safeguarded their position by recognizing them as one of the six official minority groups – but then this produced a stigma of inferiority.

The Anglo-Indian community produced a number of great people. Sir Eyre Coote, commander-in-chief of Clive's army; James Skinner, founder of the most famous Indian cavalry regiment; Sir John Hearsey, commander at the time of the mutiny; Lord Roberts, Supreme Commander in the Boer War; Lord Liverpool, Tory Prime Minister; Elihu Yale, benefactor of the American college; etc.

* * * * * * *

When I was in Doveton Corrie Protestant High School, Madras, we had a few Anglo-Indian boys in our class. Somehow they seemed a class apart. They seemed to smell – we thought they didn't bathe every day, as we did; their breath seemed to smell of decaying food – we put it down to their beef and pork diet. They were never good at studies, managing just to scrape through; they didn't take much interest in sports, either; they were naughty and insubordinate to the teachers; rarely would they act the bully with us. They had girlfriends – we did not. They didn't mix with us – they preferred their own company. The Anglo-Indian girls were, of course, very beautiful and fetching. The ones I got near to smelt the same as the boys. They didn't do well with their books, either. Some were good athletes.

I think that they are best employed in the following situations:

a. Hotel receptionists, managers, captains and waiters.
b. Airline stewards and hostesses.
c. Modelling.
d. They would make good actresses if they chose to learn Indian languages.
e. Their physique, which is better than Indians', should make them excellent athletes and sportspersons if only they had the aptitude. Some have made the Indian hockey and cricket teams.

Anglo-Indians are very rare in the professions. Maybe we have to look for parental attitude here. Indian parents encourage, cajole, threaten and beat their children into performing well academically; a matter of family and social pride. The Brits take a more lackadaisical attitude, which the Anglo-Indians seem to have adopted.

* * * * * * * *

The Indian-Christians
Anglo-Indians have a bit of British blood, however diluted, sloshing within. The Indian-Christians have as much of it as a flaming polar bear, for they are straight converts. They originally belonged to the lower classes of Hindu society – the Sudras or labouring class, the untouchables or scavengers, and the hill tribals – and were treated like dirt by their fellow co-religionists. Therefore they were ripe for the plucking by the Christian missionaries. Can't blame them, really. Whereas the Anglo-Indian is fair-skinned, the Indian-Christians are very dark-skinned, almost like the Australian aborigines. They usually have an Indian *and* a Christian name; they use either. Their food and sartorial habits are Indian. They often participate in Hindu ceremonies and rituals and are as susceptible as the Hindus to superstition. The Anglo-Indian is not really religious and is not an eager churchgoer; the Indian-Christian is virulently evangelical. The latter look upon India as their home; they are not pretenders.

The Indian-Christian is very much more academic, and many of them are professionals. They are more artistic and athletic than the Hindus – probably due to the Christian influence.

* * * * * * * *

What has India contributed to Britain?

Well, about 1,000 words in the *Oxford English Dictionary* are straight transliterations of various Indian words: e.g. *pariah*, from Tamil, denoting a low caste; or corruptions of such words: e.g. *Blighty*, from the Hindi *bilayati* (meaning foreign), or *juggernaut*, from Jagannath; or words that the British created out of their Indian experience: e.g. civil servant. A sample of the ever-expanding Indian vocabulary in English: bangle, bungalow, cheroot, chintz, chutney, cot, dinghy, dungaree, gymkhana, jodhpurs, khaki, loot, musk, punch (the drink), pundit, pyjamas, sandal, shawl, swastika, thug, veranda, yoga.

Millions of Indians have settled in Britain as proprietors of corner shops, newsagents, restauranteurs, hoteliers, public transport staff, advertisement agents, stock market brokers, politicians and all the professions; the NHS would collapse overnight if it were not for the Asian doctors. Most of the professionals were trained in India with Indian money and resources; the British are getting expert labour at cheap prices. Now we have generations of Indians who have not seen the sands and shores of India and are thoroughly absorbed into British society, irrespective of their colour. Indian antiques and artefacts, legal or loot, adorn various houses and museums.

Brighton Pavilion, Sezincote House in Gloucestershire, Kidderpore Avenue in London, Ranjit Singh's Koh-i-Noor diamond, the final resting places of Rammohan Roy in Bristol, two members of the Tata family in Surrey, the Gurkha regiment – these are some of the connections between India and Britain. Indian food, fashions, customs, philosophy and medicine are being adopted by people all over the world. The most popular foreign food in Britain is Indian. In recent times Bollywood films have become popular in the West

Two things I hold against the British. One is the mindless bureaucracy and red tape that bedevils the smallest of transactions between people and government that India is still unable to shed. The other is the Victorian prudery with regard to sexual relations, which has been widely accepted by Indians; Indians refuse to believe that the so-called Victorian lifestyle only existed in books, not in real life, where all sorts of shenanigans were more the norm than the exception. India was a country of free sex, polygamy, polyandry and various other delightful and exciting ways to indulge oneself in before the confounded Muslims and British came in and spoilt everything by taking the zing out of life.

* * * * * * * *

CHAPTER 28
India now

Geographically, India occupies a pretty strategic position in Asia. To the east, across the Arabian Sea, are Arabia and Africa. To the west, across the Bay of Bengal, lie Burma, Malaysia, Singapore and Indonesia. To the north lie the great Himalayan mountain ranges that separate India from Russia and the rest of Asia, including China, Tibet, Nepal and Bhutan – and Pakistan and Afghanistan. To the south lies the Indian Ocean, with nothing below it; Sri Lanka is a small dewdrop to the south-east. So you can see why the foreign powers love to have a footing in India in their frightful vision of security, xenophobia and domination.

India lies in the northern hemisphere, between 8° 4' and 37° 6' latitude and 68° 7' and 97° 3' longitude. It measures 3,214km from north to south and 2,933km from east to west. Total land area – 3,287,263 sq. kms or, let us say, 3.3 million sq. kms. India has lots of mountains, rivers, deserts and fertile lands and the climate varies from place to place in this vast subcontinent. The south-west monsoon hits the country between June and September; the north-east scours the country between October and December. Summertime is between April and July; winter is between October and February. The best time for foreigners to visit the country is between November and March, when the heat is somewhat bearable; at other times the poor foreigner will be roasted – 'well done', in culinary terms. But if the visitor is touring somewhere near the icy Himalayas, then it is best to avoid those months as he/she will be frozen meat. The Nilgiris reach up to the skies more than 7,000 feet. We get both the monsoons and it is chilly in December. So the best time to come here is between January and June, though August and September and October can also be fairly pleasant.

India has 28 States, six Union Territories, and one National Capital Territory (Delhi), together teeming with nearly 1,000 million people comprising Nordic Aryans, Dravidians, Mongoloids, Proto-Australoids and Negroids, with an average life expectancy of 63 years, a sex ratio of 935 females to 1,000 males, an over-60 population of 6%, and an average literacy rate of just over 50%. The average population density is around 275 persons per sq. km – ranging from nearly 7,000 in the big cities to ten in Arunachal Pradesh. The urban/rural population ratio is 25%/75%.

Let's split the crowd. The figures are rounded.

Group	Population	Percentage of total	Rate of increase
Hindu	730 million	82%	23%
Muslim	120 million	12%	33%
Christians	20 million	2%	17%
Sikhs	17 million	2%	26%
Buddhists	7 million	1%	36%
Jains	4 million	0.5%	5%
Others	4 million	0.5%	5%

By 'Others' is meant nearly 75,000 Zoroastrians, 6,000 Jews and several thousand Adivasis, tribals, etc.

So, even though Buddhism originated in India, there are very few of them here. And, though Pakistan was created for the Muslims, there are quite a number of them still in India. Now you can see that Jinnah was speaking rot and the spineless Congress did not have the guts to call his bluff. By the way, the population of Pakistan is 150 million.

And the Muslims are procreating at a faster rate than the Hindus. We are not too worried about the Buddhists…for the moment.

Bombay – 13 million. Calcutta – 11 million. Delhi – 9 million. Madras – 6 million.

There are 18 officially recognized Indian languages and some 1,700 'mother tongues'. Roughly, about half the population knows Hindi. The other half speaks a variety of tongues. Now you can see the absurdity of adopting Hindi as the national language. It is rot because half the population does not know it and does not wish to know it. History has dictated that English is the language most widely spoken or understood in the world – including India. So English should be the national language of India. If the fuddy-duddies at the time of independence wanted to have an 'Indian' language, they should have adopted Sanskrit. No one would have objected to that.

India's principal imports are petroleum, oil and lubricants, chemical elements and compounds, pearls and precious stones and non-electrical machinery mainly, coming from OPEC, the EU (including the UK), and the USA. The chief exports are textiles, cotton yarn, fabrics, ready-made garments, handicrafts, gems and jewellery, machinery, transport and metals, going mainly to other LDCs, the USA, and the EU (including the UK).

Foreigners are bemused as to why a 'poor' country such as India has opted to join the 'nuclear club'. I'll tell you why. No one likes to be treated like an irresponsible child. No one likes to be told what to do – what one can and cannot do. How can an entire nation of peoples be made to conform according to the dictates of another? If the collective pride of a nation is thus belittled, it bristles. The so-called 'Big Five' – the USA, UK, France, Russia and China – chose themselves to be neat cosy members of the exclusive club. Industrial powers such as Germany and Japan refrained from joining on the assurance of nuclear security from some of the members of the Big Five. South Africa did not bother about membership. Countries such as North Korea, Israel, Pakistan and India were suspected at one time or another of having nuclear capability. India burst the bubble by detonating a 'peaceful' nuclear device in 1974 – much to the astonishment and consternation of the world. India waited until 1998, however, to demonstrate that it was also capable of manufacturing nuclear weapons. Furthermore, it showed that its technological ability to simulate tests with supercomputers was also on a par with the Big Five. The Comprehensive Test Ban Treaty (CTBT) is a load of eyewash. It enables the Big Five to do whatever they like and prevents the others from doing likewise. In other words, the Big Five think that they are the only chaps responsible enough to play with their toys. The others are irresponsible kids, barbaric dimwits. Well, India isn't. Throughout the history of India, it has never extended its borders or annexed foreign land. We could have kicked the Pakistanis out on several occasions. We chose not to. When we kicked them out of the erstwhile East Pakistan we could have taken over, but we graciously handed it to the disgruntled peoples of the territory, who went on to create Bangladesh.

We know that Pakistan is going in for nuclear weapons. Why should we wait for them and then embark on our programme? Whether we use a nuclear weapon or not is an entirely different matter. The point is that we do not like to be treated like dimwits and we do not want to be told what *not* to do. By the way, India has always categorically stated that it will never be the first to use nuclear weapons.

I know that India is a veritable cauldron of corruption in every sphere of public and private life. I know the Indian mentality of dishonesty, discourtesy, uncleanliness, rodomontade, unpunctuality, slovenry, sloth, procrastination, superstition, waste, arrogance, toadyism, priggism, lack of compassion – do you want me to go on? If only we were not cursed with those qualities we could have ruled the world.

But, in spite of it all, we have managed to achieve what we have within 50 years of independence. If you ask me, that is the greatest miracle of humankind. Let me enumerate a few of those miracles.

1.   India's population of nearly 1,000 million are self-sufficient in food production. Which western country can boast of that? They cannot perceive the logistics involved as their populations are relatively low. The problem here is akin to the problem everywhere else – maldistribution and corruption. The agricultural sector accounts for 65% of the workforce and yet contributes just 27% of GDP.

2.   The smallest village can be reached by some form of transport. India has more than three million kilometres of road – though the national highways network comprises only 2% of it. It has a total rail track of nearly 63,000 route kilometres, carrying more than 11 million passengers in 7,550 trains every day, and employing some 1.6 million people. (It is beside the point that a good many of them are sinecures.) It is dead cheap to travel by rail. I travel by train from Coonoor to Madras, a distance of 600km, at a cost of only 220 rupees. By bus it is only 150 rupees. India has 11 major ports and 139 minor ones, 45 shipyards and 17 dry docks, along its 5,560 kilometres of coastline. Besides, it has nearly 15,000 kilometres of navigable waterways – rivers, canals, backwaters, creeks, etc. Air India has a fleet of about 30 aircraft operating to nearly 50 foreign destinations, and Indian Airlines operates its 60 aircraft to 75 domestic and 17 international airports. Now several private airlines operate alongside. In the near future all the major and minor cities will be connected by air. (Hopefully the air fares will be intelligently priced.) This gigantic network enables one to post a letter to the remotest corner of India for the paltry sum of 3.00 rupees. India has 150,350 post offices – one for every two kilometres.

3.   We do have freedom of the media. Here are some mind-boggling statistics: 39,149 newspapers and periodicals in 100 languages and dialects – though most of it is rubbish, like publications elsewhere in the world.

4.   I do not hold our education system in great esteem. It is a load of rubbish. It is a potent form

of exploitation. But if you want to educate yourself, there are 590,421 primary schools, 171, 216 upper primary schools, 98,134 higher secondary schools and junior colleges, 6,569 colleges for general education, 1,354 professional colleges and 226 universities dotted across the country.

5. Foreigners are stunned that India has forests, mountains and greenery. Well, it has 416,516 sq. km of reserved forests, 223, 309 sq. km of protected forests and 125, 385 sq. km of unclassed forests, with over 45,000 plant species and 81,251 animal species – the greatest a country can boast of. Besides, India has 83 national parks and 447 wildlife sanctuaries, covering 4.5% of the country, where it is illegal to kill anything. It has 166 species of crop plants.

6. We do not want to go into arts and literature. India is well known for its diversity all over the world. The cultural fame of India is literally lost in the mists of time.

* * * * * * * *

I have visited many countries. Let me say this. India would be paradise on earth if it were made clean and if its inhabitants learnt cleanliness, courtesy and compassion. This, of course, will never happen. India will languish despite having the potential to be a truly great nation.

The trouble with India is that it is full of Indians...

* * * * * * * *

CHAPTER 29
Indian Princes

Let us take a glimpse into the surreal world of Indian rulers. Let us probe into their vices and eccentricities, their indulgences and prodigalities, their folklore and myths – the stuff that dreams are made of, and the basis of titillating literature and Hollywood movies.

The Nizam of Hyderabad, a devout Muslim, presided over 20 million Hindus and three million Muslims in the largest landlocked state in central southern India. He was five foot three and weighed under 100lb. He lived on an unvarying diet of sweets, fruits, cream, betel nuts and opium, all but the last of which were tasted by a servant, for he lived in constant fear of being poisoned – a common paranoia amongst rulers. He wore cotton pyjamas and grey slippers bought for a few rupees in the market. He ate off a tin plate, squatting on a mat. He smoked the cigarette butts left behind by his guests. The English Resident who visited him every Sunday was given a cup of tea, one biscuit and one cigarette. His bedroom was not unlike that in a slum dwelling, with battered furniture. The palace was full of cobwebs and substantial layers of dirt coated everything. To save electricity bills, he turned down the current; no electrical apparatus would work – not even the ECG machine brought by a Bombay doctor to give him a medical check-up! It was customary for the nobles to make a symbolic offering of a gold piece to the Nizam, who would bless it and return it; but not so this Nizam. He simply pocketed the gold pieces.

Yet, he was the richest man in the world at that time. Wrapped in an old newspaper in one of his drawers was the fabulous lime-sized Jacob diamond of 200 carats that he used as a paperweight. Trucks sank up to their axles and, rotting in his untended gardens, carried solid gold ingots. Sapphires, diamonds, emeralds and rubies sprawled like coal in a cellar in the palace rooms. Just the pearls he secreted away would have covered all the pavements of Piccadilly. Basements and attics contained millions of pounds rolled in newspapers carelessly lying around as food for the palace rats. With the coming of the automobile, the Nizam had a new fetish. He simply confiscated any vehicle that took his fancy. He had hundreds of cars he never used. He also had his own private army and air force.

He also collected something else – pornographic photographs. He had cameras placed in the walls and ceilings of his guest rooms, including the bathrooms, and recorded the sexual exploits of his visitors. When a British Resident told the Nizam that he might not have an heir as his son was probably a homosexual, the Nizam ordered a fetching female to be brought into the room and ordered his son to perform to refute the insinuation.

He donated $100 million to the British during World War I, for which he was accorded the title 'Exalted Highness' – the only ruler in India to be so honoured. He was one of only five Indian rulers to be given a 21-gun salute. He dreamt of an independent, sovereign nation. But in the end he had to go, unloved by his people, and Hyderabad was integrated into the Indian nation at the time of independence.

Maharaja Hari Singh, a Hindu, was another who was accorded a 21-gun salute. He ruled over the Vale of Kashmir in north India amongst the great Himalayas, probably the most beautiful spot in the whole of India. The majority of his four million subjects were Muslim. He was a weak and self-indulgent ruler, loathed by his subjects, whom he regularly imprisoned. He was a bisexual. He was caught in the act by a gang of blackmailers when he was performing with a woman not of his harem; the slush money he had to pay drained his treasury. When he returned to his kingdom, he decided to switch to the company of young men.

He too had an army. At the time of independence he too dreamt of presiding over a sovereign nation. What happened at the time of partition is told earlier.

The Maharaja of Baroda was another 21-gunner. One of the maharajas was miffed that the British had ordered a 21-gun salute to his British Resident, a colonel. So he ordered a pair of cannon in solid gold for his own salute. Now the Resident was miffed, and he forwarded a stinky report to London accusing the maharaja of indulging in slavery. The maharaja had had enough of this common colonel, consulted his priests and astrologers, ground up a suitably big diamond and slipped the dust into the colonel's soup – whereupon he developed a bellyache and was rushed to hospital, where the truth was revealed. The maharaja was deposed and sent into exile. But the Maharaja of Patiala (whom we shall meet later) was a friend of Baroda. When the Viceroy who had signed the decree of exile visited Patiala, he had his cannons stuffed with miniscule amounts of gunpowder so that they would sound no louder than vehement coughs.

Baroda was obsessed with gold and precious stones. His royal attire was made of spun gold by just one family in his kingdom, whose nails were long and notched like a comb to caress the gold threads. Amongst his collection of diamonds was the historic Star of the South, the seventh biggest diamond in the world and the diamond given by Napoleon III to Empress Eugénie. His tapestries were made of pearls, rubies and emeralds. The accoutrements of his ceremonial elephant were of gold – harness, howdah, saddle-cloth, and the ten chains from each of the pachyderm's ears; each chain was worth £60,000! He entertained his guests by organizing elephant fights. Two mammoths would be driven to fury by lance thrusts and goad each other until one was dead.

The Raja of Dhenkanal had a different programme with his elephants. He organized the public copulation of select elephants from his stables!

Talking of elephants, the honours must go to the Maharaja of Mysore, the fourth 21-gunner. During the Hindu festival of Dassera, 1,000 elephants would be draped with elaborately woven blankets of flowers, their foreheads studded with gold and jewel plates. On the back of the strongest bull elephant, on a pedestal of gold draped in gold-brocaded velvet, sat the maharaja on his massive throne. Once a year at the autumnal equinox the maharaja was in seclusion for nine days, at the end of which he would be brought out, mounted on an elephant, to the Mysore racetrack, bathed, shaved, fed and anointed by Brahmin priests. Then he would mount his black horse and gallop round the track, lit with thousands of torches, to the applause of his subjects. His 600-room palace dwarfed the Viceroy's House. Exquisite three-dimensional paintings adorned the walls. Twenty rooms housed his collection of stuffed tigers, panthers, elephants, bison, etc.

The fifth recipient of the 21-gun salute was the Maharaja of Gwalior. He ordered a chandelier from Venice to surpass the largest one in Buckingham Palace. Someone doubted the strength of his ceiling to support such a weight. He solved the problem by hoisting his largest elephant onto the roof; the roof did not collapse and the chandelier was installed! His passion was electric trains. His trains ran over 250 feet of solid silver rails on a gigantic table at the centre of the banquet hall, with special tunnels for tracks into the royal kitchen. He sat at the control panel and shuttled the comestibles around to his guests on the train set. He also massacred 1,400 tigers and published a book, *A Guide to Tiger Shooting*.

The Maharaja of Jaipur visited his treasure, which was buried in a hillside in Rajasthan, once in a lifetime at the start of his reign to embellish himself. One of his necklaces was composed of three tiers of rubies, each the size of a pigeon's egg, and three emeralds, the largest of which weighed 90 carats. The maharaja adorned his turban with the largest topaz in the world, nestling amongst 3,000 diamonds and pearls. The Maharaja of Bharatpur's obsession was ivory and hunting. He had his tiger skins stitched together and carpeted his reception rooms wall-to-wall with them. He held the record for duck slaughtering: 4,482 in three hours in honour of Viceroy Lord Hardinge. He owned the most exotic Rolls-Royce in India – a silver-plated convertible. He also had an RR done up as a shooting brake for his hunts, in which the Prince of Wales and Louis Mountbatten went for a *shikari* (hunting expedition) in 1921.

Surely the most extraordinary vehicle must have been that belonging to the Maharaja of Alwar – gold-plated exterior and interior, ivory steering wheel, gold-brocaded cushions, the body a perfect replica of the coronation couch of the King of England! One of the Alwars believed himself to be a reincarnation of the god Rama and ordered his theologians to calculate the size of Rama's turban so that he could wear it. He always wore silken black gloves to prevent contamination from mere mortals. Lady Willingdon had accumulated a sizeable collection of precious stones by casting her eyes on the fingers of her princely guests, who naturally gave their baubles to her. She eyed the Alwar's heavy diamond. Alwar gave it to her. She slipped it onto her finger and – for reasons unknown – returned it to the Alwar. The Alwar called a waiter and meticulously washed the ring, in front of the gathering, before restoring it to his divine finger. He played a bit of polo. Once he had a disobedient pony drenched in kerosene, and personally set fire to it in public. He was also a hunter with a novel method of baiting his animals. He would enter any of his subjects' houses, requisition a child and tie the child to a stake as bait – all the while reassuring the frightened parents that he was a good shot and that their child was quite safe. He was also a voracious homosexual. Any soldier who wished to be an officer had to sleep with the Alwar and, once an officer, he was expected to participate in depraved sexual orgies, some of which ended in sadistic murders. He was eventually sacked and exiled.

The Maharaja of Benares had to be awakened each morning to the moos of a sacred cow, on which he had to cast his morning eye. Once when he visited the Nawab of Rampur he was assigned to the quarters on the second floor. The nawab hoisted a cow up to the maharaja's bedroom window!

The Maharaja of Kapurthala visited the palace of Versailles. He proclaimed that he had been Louis XIV in an earlier incarnation, imported French architects and decorators, built himself a miniature Versailles at the foot of the Himalayas, filled it with Sèvres vases, Gobelin tapestries and other French antiques, dressed his Sikh retainers in powdered wigs, silk waistcoats, knickers and silver-buckled slippers, and proclaimed French the language of his court.

The Nawab of Rampur preferred to hold audience in a hall the size of a cathedral, sitting on a throne surrounded by white-marble nudes; the gold brocade cushion on which he sat had a hole leading to a chamber pot to enable him to carry on his affairs of state without interruption.

The ruler of Orissa bought a bed from an antique-dealer in London because it was a replica of Queen Victoria's wedding bed, and had it studded with jewels.

The Nawab of Junagadh, a minor potentate, had apartments equipped with servants, telephones and electricity. He celebrated the weddings of the inhabitants of these luxurious abodes – which few of his subjects could afford – with invitations to all the princes and dignitaries of India including the Viceroy. Some 150,000 of his poor subjects lined the route of the nuptial cortège, led by his own bodyguard and royal elephants in full regalia. The celebrations were rounded off with a lavish banquet, after which the bride and bridegroom were escorted to their well-appointed bridal suite to consummate their union. The entire charade cost £60,000, a sum that could have sustained 12,000 of his 620,000 subjects for an entire year. Who resided in these apartments? you may ask. The nawab's pet dogs!

In May 1947, the Viceroy's political secretary was a missionary's son. His name was Sir Conrad Corfield. He loathed Gandhi and the Congress. He was firmly on the side of the Indian princes and had personally gone to England to plead on behalf of them with the Earl of Listowel, Secretary of State for India, in the famous octagonal London Office. The princes had surrendered their powers to the British Crown; when India became independent, his argument was that the princes should revert to their original independent status; they could then be free to work out their future with either India or Pakistan. Corfield was technically right, but in practice it was totally unfeasible.

He lost his plea and returned to India. In June, he ordered a bonfire to be lit, witnessed by a circle of British bureaucrats. The bonfire was of paper: four tons of secret documents listing the idiosyncracies of the Indian princes. Corfield was protecting his friends from blackmail after the British left.

Not all of the princes were bad. Some of them were enlightened due to Western education and extended to their subjects privileges unknown in British India.

Baroda banned polygamy, campaigned for the untouchables and made education free and universal before the 20th century. Bikaner created lakes and gardens in his desert kingdom for the enjoyment of his people. Bhopal offered sexual equality. Mysore had scientific establishments, dams and industries. Jaipur had a world-class observatory. In the 1940s, with the world order changing, Patiala closed his father's notorious harem; Gwalior married a commoner and moved out of the palace.

Why did the British indulge the Indian princes?

1. Whilst two-thirds of India was directly under the Viceroy, one-third was not. In theory, the British could depose an Indian ruler on some pretext – disloyalty, mismanagement, cruelty to people, sedition, connivance with the Congress, etc. In reality, the rulers could get away with anything – as long as they were loyal to the British Crown and paid up their dues. The Congress was stirring up the people to achieve independence. The Brits had their hands full dealing with them. They simply could not have coped if the Indian kingdoms joined hands with the independence movement. They were happy and much relieved that the princes were on their side. Why were the Indian princes for the continuance of British rule? Because, if India achieved independence, they would lose most of their privileges, for India was to be a secular state. More importantly, they would be accountable for their actions. This they did not like. The Congress abhorred them as much as the princes feared the consequences of Congress rule. They were virulently anti-Congress and thus anti-independence. For the moment most of them were

rotters getting away with literally murder. They enjoyed their despotic rule; the British allowed them to get away with it. It was a simple policy of ranging the princes against the Congress movement; in other words – to use a cliché – *divide and rule.*

2. The princes' loyalty took more tangible forms. We have already mentioned the Nizam of Hyderabad's substantial contribution to the British war effort – $100 million. The Maharaja of Jodhpur's lancers led the charge against the Turks at Haifa in 1917. Bikaner's camel corps fought alongside the British in China, Palestine, Egypt, France and Burma. Gwalior contributed three battalions and a hospital ship in 1917. The First Jaipur Infantry was led by the Maharaja at Monte Cassino, Italy, in 1943. The Maharao Raja of Bundi was accorded the Military Cross fighting in Burma.

3. African and Native American chiefs were palmed off with pinchbeck jewellery and tacky trinkets. The Indian princes, for the services rendered, were showered with decorations. Oxford and Cambridge conferred honorary degrees on the princes and their progeny. Their crowns were embellished with the Order of the Star of India or the Order of the Indian Empire. They were given nine- to 21-gun salutes. (425 minor princes had no gun salute at all). Some princes were given the honour of riding as ADCs at Edward VII's coronation. Fidelity was thus rewarded.

4. The opulence of some of the Indian princes far surpassed that of the British monarch. A British official in India, of whatever class of society, would not have even dreamt of such princely hospitality

and remuneration. The British Resident was treated like royalty; in other words, he was bribed to look the other way. It is easy to look the other way when you know that you have 'earned' a fortune to buy a fancy house in Britain, when you are supplied with endless hunting expeditions, when you are given free coupons for female companionship.

Why have I given an exordium about the Indian princes? Because one of them, the Maharaja of Patiala, a Sikh, had something to do with cricket.

Until 1900, it was customary for the maharaja once a year to appear before his subjects naked except for a diamond breastplate, his penis in full and royal erection. The subjects cheered this demonstration, as it was supposed to drive away evil spirits from the kingdom. How he managed to sustain the feat of priapism in public is quite beyond me. Amongst the Sikh's collection were a pearl necklace insured by Lloyd's of London for $1 million, a French De Dion Bouton (the first automobile to be imported into India in 1892), 27 Rolls-Royces, 500 of the world's best polo ponies, a roomful of silver trophies, hundreds of animal skins and a seraglio of several hundred inmates to cater to his changing tastes.

During the last decades of the 19th century, Rajendra Singh was the maharaja. He realized the importance of cricket as a means of promoting his ties with the British and bettering his perks. He put together a team that included Ranji, Mistry, Brockwell, Hearne and leading Parsee, Hindu and Muslim cricketers of the day. Thus, Patiala was the first princely patron of cricket in India. His aim was to bring the best English and

Australian cricketers to India. Rajendra died at the age of 28, however, in 1900. Just a week before his untimely death he had scored 21 runs in 8.5 minutes. The princes were always sloggers. They would have made good one-day cricketers. But it was beneath their status to field!

Rajendra's son was Bhupendra Singh. He inherited his father's propensity for cricket. He was a slogger too, once smashing 86 runs comprising fours and sixes only. He shaped Indian cricket between the two wars. Let us get to know him.

The two pastimes of the princes, Hindu, Muslim or Sikh, were sex and sport and the acknowledged master of both activities was the Sikh, Sir Bhupendra Singh, the Magnificent, the seventh Maharaja of Patiala. He stood at six foot four and 300lb. His sensual lips, piercing eyes, enormous waxed moustache and supremely arrogant stance encompassed all the folklore of his ilk. He could eat 20lb of food; a couple of chickens were a teatime snack. When he was not slaughtering animals in his kingdom he was galloping across the polo fields of the world at the head of the 'Tigers of Patiala', annihilating the opposition.

As he matured, he supervised the recruitment of his harem, accumulating a total of 350 winsome ladies. The walls and ceilings of his private rooms were decorated with erotic art; a manoeuvrable silk hammock enabled him to perform the more complex sexual callisthenics. During the summers the harem moved outdoors, where they would be stationed – bare-breasted like nymphs – around the swimming pool, whose waters were kept cool by floating chunks of ice.

The seraglio was visited by jewellers, perfumers, hairdressers, dressmakers and teams of French, British and Indian plastic surgeons to alter the physiognomies of certain members of his entourage according to the latest London fashion magazines. He also had a laboratory to produce aphrodisiac scents, lotions and philtres based on silver, gold, iron, pearls, herbs, spices, vegetables and certain anatomical parts of animals and fowls. He even treated himself with radium to increase his sexual prowess. Alas, the malady that plagued him was not lack of virility – but boredom.

It was said that he had to have two women before breakfast! And he would go to any lengths to procure them – abduction, rape, or even buying them. He would imprison or murder complaining husbands and fathers, punish his official pimps if they failed to supply him with regular fodder; he even made indecent advancements to his young stepmother, who fled to British India. One 12-year-old died as a result of rape; he burnt women who fled his harem; punished some by shoving red peppers up their vaginas; even raped the daughter of a European minister. When a 200-page charge sheet was presented to the Viceroy, Lord Irwin, he dismissed it, saying, "His Highness does not deny youthful indiscretions and is willing to make monetary amends."

You see, he was an important ruler in the crucial Punjab area; his friendship was vital to the British, both for political and pleasurable reasons.

So, now you have had a glimpse of what life was all about with the Indian princes.

Let us see their part in Indian cricket.

PART THREE –
A HISTORY OF INDIAN CRICKET

*Who would think that a little bit of leather and two
pieces of wood
had such a delightful and delighting power!*

Mary Russell Mitford

* * * * * * * *

CHAPTER 30
Interlude – School Time

Well, I am not David Copperfield.

Some can fill volumes about their childhood – or so it seems, if one is to go by the size of their autobiographies. Till the age of 17, when I enrolled at Stanley Medical College, Madras, I don't seem to have much to say at all. Not that I was some sort of dope or put in suspended animation; it is simply that nothing 'braggable' happened.

I was born in the rice town of Nellore in the State of Andhra Pradesh at the start of the second half of the 20th century – a fact I have always resented. This is a terrible era; not that earlier eras were any better. Human beings have always behaved abominably towards each other and towards nature. It is just that, perhaps, there was more scope for romanticism then – or so I feel.

My father was a doctor in the State's government service. If you are at all familiar with the devious machinations of Indian government service, you will probably know that one who has chosen to be affiliated to such a body is doomed to the life of the proverbial nomad – an itinerant peddler of whatever he or she is dubiously peddling. One is shifted from place to place like peas on a plate. I suppose it is to prevent the human tendency of soon becoming a despot if left too long in one place; it may be to prevent one from stagnating in the one habitat, like a pig in quicksand; it may be to teach the poor public servant the logistics of moving house and adapting to new environments; or it may be just one of those sadistic notions that give the mindless, bureaucratic sinecures their jollies.

Who knows?

Anyway, my parents thought it best that we (you see, they had three children: me, the eldest bum, a younger brother and a sister) be plonked in a metropolis that had socially approved educational facilities – Madras. We were left to get on with it under the guidance of our maternal grandmother, a completely illiterate person but God's last word in human patience, forbearance, sacrifice and diplomacy – all of which qualities she needed often to bring into play during all those long years.

Our grandmother was widowed quite early in life, even before her only daughter was married. And her status as a human being had been relegated to the background – like backdrop scenery. She was maintained by my parents till she died in her sleep some ten years ago. Her lot was much better than the lot of other widows in India. She was given the responsibility and independence of raising us three without the interference of my parents. Therefore she filled a vital post. Her duties were acknowledged by one and all.

Compare her to the young widow of one of my father's brothers, who got himself killed in a whirlpool in the river when he went for a swim. She had two little daughters that she had to bring up whilst living with her parents-in-law and several brothers- and sisters-in-law in the same house...on all of whom she was totally dependent. Her status was just one level above that of servant. She now spends her twilight years passed on from one daughter to the other and to members of her original family with as much frequency as a volleyball in one of those matches you see on television between 20-foot-tall black giants.

We went to Doveton Corrie Protestant High School in Vepery, Madras. We lived in Ritherdon Road (where the school was) for a few years and then shifted to a parallel road called Clemens Road in a sort of railway compartment flat – front door leading into the living room that led into a bedroom that led into a dining room that led into a kitchen. A bathroom and toilet were on the side. Looking back now, they must have been small rooms; a cot in the living room for me; two cots in the bedroom for grandmother, brother and sister. (In India we call them 'cots'; in Britain they are 'beds'. In India we call the mattress a 'bed'; in Britain they call a mattress a mattress.) We had big built-in shelves. I remember that my brother – who was a bit of a runt – used to sleep on one of them.

We used to visit our parents for the holidays. In those days we started school in January. Once the climate got to the point of frying eggs on the bonnet of a car – oh yes, my parents did have a car: a black Ford Prefect – or of melting the tar on the road – oh yes, India does have tarmacked roads – we used to go to wherever they were stationed.

The months of May and June were – and are – the hottest months of the year. Then back to school. Then we broke for the winter – December. In between we used to have a week or so off for Easter and Michaelmas. If our parents were stationed close to Madras, we used to go home. Our half-yearly exams were before our summer holidays and our final exams preceded our winter holidays. Now, of course, everything is topsy-turvy. Children seem to have holidays before exams and they seem to be studying some rot or other all the time.

Holidays! Excitement. Packing. Bus to Central Railway Station, Madras – that beautiful red-brick bastion of British architecture. The queuing for the tickets. A little hole in the wired grill through which someone mysteriously pushed our tickets to my grandmother. Then the hustle and bustle. Red-turbaned coolies rushing about. Hawkers selling things we didn't even know existed. The uniformed ticket-collector at the entrance who checked our tickets. Platform 6. Howrah Express. Ah! The divine smell of coal and steam. The exquisite sound of screeching metal wheels and spouting steam. If it weren't for the fact that I would have been scalded, I would have loved to enter into those enthralling clouds of white steam. Scramble for the seats. Window seats, naturally. Never mind the tons of soot. Window seats. Don't fight. Each of us takes turns. Once we are ensconced, we jump down and run to the engine. Huge, black steam thing. Giant wheels. Powerful axles – or whatever they are called. And then the main attraction. Black-faced engine-drivers shovelling coal into a monstrous boiler. Why is it that children are always fascinated with a steam engine? Don't know. Today we have streamlined diesel engines. Pfft! Nothing to them. Nothing to see. Just one big metal box totally lacking in character. You can't even see the driver. It is as if there was no driver. All run by robots or computer or some such nonsense. See what I mean when I say that it was more romantic in a previous era? The children of today don't know what they are missing – they have to go to museums where these things are preserved. But it is not the same thing, is it – gazing at a majestic steam engine and actually travelling in one!

Of course, we travelled third class. Wooden plank seats and backrests. Nowadays they have done away with third class. An exercise in self-deception. In society there are three classes. But in trains there are only two. You see, we didn't have this duplicity in those days. Third class was bloody well third class. Whistle. Scramble on board. Stick our necks out as far as they would go. Must see the signal lights changing from red to green. Then shift our eyes to the stationmaster or guard, or whatever, and see him change his red flag to green, put his whistle to his lips and blow. The hypnotizing sounds of the massive engine coming to life, steam all over the place. And then the monster comes to life and moves to a delightful clanging of all the parts of the machine. We are on our way!

The station slowly slips by. We emerge from the massive curved roof into the sunlight. Railway workmen are either working or strolling by, doing and checking whatever they are supposed to be doing and checking – all of them straight out of the minstrel show.

We see the massive chimneys at Basin Bridge Junction, which always heralded to me the real start of our journey. In a few minutes we leave habitation behind. Miles and miles of reddish-brown sand, fields of whatever they are growing, the odd hamlets, the ubiquitous red-striped tiny temples, half-starved cows, buffaloes, goats and dogs, human beings of similar constitution working, ambling or in a state of weakened somnolence. The excitement of a passing train that screams by with a terrific rattling, hurtling dangerously close.

Ah! Now is treat time! It is hardly 30 minutes since we set off and only an hour since we have had our fill at home before departing to the station. But we are ravenously hungry. Open stainless steel tiffin-carrier. The smell of the idlies – steamed rice cakes – on which are smeared oil and spicy chilli powder. Once we demolish those, we open the next tier and devour the dosas – thin pancakes made of rice and dhal flour – with fried masala potatoes. Then we open the next tier and finish off the bananas. Then we screw open the silver-plated water-carrier and wash all the comestibles down with tepid water. Happy now.

The train covers about 25 to 30 miles an hour, stopping at innumerable stations, at every one of which there is a troupe of hawkers going from compartment to compartment, carrying their delicacies or fountain pens or watches or kitchen utensils or whatnot. Tea, tea. Coffee, coffee. Masala vadai. Poori potato. Curd rice. Lime rice. Cool drinks.

We arrive at Gudur Junction, where the train most conveniently waits for 30 minutes. Gives us time to rush up to the cool drinks counter and get glasses of that delicious, mouth-watering, ice-cold pink liquid: rose milk. Then we go to the Higginbotham book counter and fill our eyes with the comics on display. If we have enough put by, we buy ourselves a *Phantom* or *Tarzan* comic. If we haven't then we harass grandmother till she has no other alternative but to either kill us or give us the money. She invariably chooses the non-criminal option.

We finally reach our destination. We alight with loads of baggage. Indians never travel light. A coolie runs forward and grabs our belongings. He takes us to a bullock cart. The contrivance is called a jutka. It is amazing how much it can accommodate. I have seen jutkas with a dozen people crammed in – just as you see a Maruti 800 today with eight people. On the way home, I keep a keen eye out for the cinema posters plastered on every available inch of wall space. My favourite actors are Nageswara Rao and N T Rama Rao. I make a note of their films and the cinema houses – theatres – they are playing at. The streets are crowded, dusty and dirty. Smell of spices, fruits, flowers, and human excretions mingle in tantalizing cocktails – unknown to the likes of Christian Dior.

We reach home. Daddy is not home. He is invariably at the hospital. Mummy is there. She hugs and kisses us. I really don't remember me actually running up to her to be hugged or kissed.

We always had a dog at home. He is jumping all over us, licking us to death. His name is Bullet. We have had a series of dogs – Tony, Caesar, etc. We have also had a menagerie of chickens, ducks, guinea fowls and turkeys on and off. My sister was good with them. The crazy girl had names for the fowls and they would respond to her; they would follow her about like amiable dogs. It was quite a sight. All the non-vegetarian waste – chicken and mutton bones – would go for the dog, and the vegetarian waste for the feathered pets. Someone told us that ducks like urine. So we used to hold onto our urine as if our lives depended on it and early in the morning we would rush out and pee in a big aluminium dish. The ducks did relish their early morning drink.

The chickens were a source of joy. We had dozens of them, and a few of the hens would always be in the family way during our holidays. Mummy would know when the hen was going to brood. The hen would come puffing up its feathers and cluck-clucking in a characteristic tone searching for an ideal place – below the bench, in a cupboard, in a cardboard box, under the deal-wood box 'sofas'. It would settle down. It would lay an egg and not get up. We would lift up its tail every day and count the eggs, number and date them. When a dozen or so were in place the hen would sit for 21 days, warming them up. It would occasionally venture out to forage. Twenty-one days pass. All of us would crowd around it, expectant and excited. We would bend down and listen. Finally we would hear the little chirps under the mother hen.

We cannot wait. We lift up the tail of the resentful hen and see what is happening. A tiny crack in the eggshell; a little beak appearing; the shell cracking wide open; the beautiful chicken with closed eyes, wet with goo. A miracle. A miracle indeed. How many times have we watched the obstetrical goings-on of the hen and how many times have we been equally fascinated? And then, when all have hatched, we shed tears for the casualties; there are always a few who fall by the wayside; the eggs are spoilt, the foetus has under- or mal-developed, the foetus has died at birth. The mother hen proudly walks out. With what care it tends to its brood! Human beings are definitely among the also-rans. How it watches out for the eagles and falcons!

How it clucks its warning and spreads its feathers and gathers its rushing, frightened children in tender protection. City folk today are sadly unaware of such goings-on; they glibly say that they have seen it all on the Discovery channel. But is seeing on a screen the same as living it? Many are prepared to swear that there is little difference.

We wait for daddy. We hear his car arriving. We run and hug him. He lifts us off the ground. I am in front; my brother is hanging onto his back, and my sister is on one arm. I do remember running to daddy. The dog is yelping its head off and jumping up, demanding its rightful share of daddy's attention. He pats it and scratches it and talks to it. The dog is now happy and quiet. Then he turns his attention to us. I don't remember our parents welcoming us with any presents.

When we have all settled down, I ask about the cinema. India is the greatest producer of films. It has to be, what with its many languages and population running into unfathomable millions. In those days, cinema was the only and most excellent form of entertainment for all ages; the only pan-Indian addiction that even precedes cricket. So we spend the holidays devouring films; returning again and again to the ones we like.

Our paternal grandparents are even more avid cinema-goers than we. Invariably we visit them during either our summer or winter holidays. Our grandfather too is a doctor. When he gets fed up with his hectic practice, he tells his assistant that he has to do a 'house visit' and secretly we set off to the theatre in his privately-owned jutka. It is a military operation. First he asks us which film we would like to see. Invariably he has seen it. He tells us that it is good and wouldn't mind seeing it again. He tells us to come down the side of the house and meet him away from the house; his clinic is in one part of the house. We are hiding in the jutka. After what seems an eternity he shuffles out and quickly jumps into the jutka. Quick! quick! we urge the driver. He lays his whip lightly and tickles the bull's private parts. It charges down the road. When we reach the theatre, the owner, who is a patient of my grandfather, greets him and orders special cushioned chairs for us – there are only benches in the theatre – and also orders a round of lime sodas for us.

The lights dim. The newsreel is shown. Some nonsense going on somewhere. Who wants to see that! Adverts. Cinthol soap. Colgate toothpaste. OK. OK. Get on with it. Ah! The Indian Cinema Certificate comes on, stating the name of the picture and the number of reels. Good. It has 21 reels: a good three-hour film. We are not being short-changed. Our hero and heroine appear. We are in another world. We laugh along with them. We cry along with them. We rescue heroines from dastardly villains by fighting alongside the painted lover. We race with the tortured hero in a jalopy to the hospital to save a worthy soul. We suffer every minute with them. The more we suffer and cry the more we like the film. An Indian trait. Tragedies are more popular than comedies. We return the next day and suffer and cry again. It is a common sight to see and hear people, both men and women, sobbing loudly in Indian cinema houses. All the members in our very extended family – both my father and mother are one of 14 siblings – are very emotional beings, shedding tears as if they were on tap.

Thank God, I am not so. Brave front. Oh yes. It is a front. Certain things bring a lump to my throat and a tear to my eye.

A bond of genuine friendship. Charlton Heston epic, *Once upon a Murder*; a white senator and a black police chief embrace each other, recognizing in each other the long-lost childhood friend.

Telugu mythological film, *Sri Krishna-Arjuna Yuddham*. Lord Krishna brings gifts to the five Pandava brothers. He gives material gifts to the four; he seemingly ignores his favourite, Arjuna – to Yudhisthira's consternation; Lord Krishna later on bestows a divine embrace on Arjuna – and Yudhisthira lets drop a tear of relief, understanding, appreciation and ecstasy.

A good deed – performed under a veneer of cynicism. *Casablanca*; our friend Bogart listens to the woes of a damsel in distress who has no money to escape to America. He arranges that her boyfriend wins the necessary money at his roulette table to enable them to purchase exit visas from Claude Rains, the police chief. The bartender, on learning of the good deed, rushes to Bogart and kisses him; Bogart pushes him away muttering, "You crazy Russian!" and tubby Sakall applauds Bogie's gesture of goodwill.

We never had any 'holidays' in the Western sense of the word. Our holidays were visiting family members, attending marriages and going on pilgrimages. The only 'outing' I remember in my entire childhood with regards my parents is going for a picnic. I was about eight years old. One evening we – along with a platoon of parents' friends – set off in a number of cars to the riverside and had our pre-packed dinner on the banks. I remember crossing a little stream whose waters were so clear that I scooped up the water in my palm and drank it.

Another thing I remember. My father took me to see a drama of one of the innumerable episodes in the Hindu epic, *Mahabharata*. The actor who played Krishna was daubed in blue and I remember that he had a lovely voice; he was also an expert at whistling the various Sanskrit stanzas. The entire audience – including me – was in ecstasy. Daddy, of course, was openly crying with sheer joy.

We never went to a place by ourselves to sightsee or relax.

The only other outing I remember is when my grandmother's sister, whom we called 'grandma', and her husband took us to the zoo in Madras. It was twilight. The gates were due to shut. The wild cats were roaring. Grandpa was missing. The zookeeper was urging us to leave. What to do? We were frightened out of our wits. It was eerie. At last grandpa turned up.

There used to be a 'supermarket' in Madras next to Central Railway Station, called Moore Market. Lovely red-brick, single-storied structure where there were shops galore selling everything under the sun. The outer perimeter was full of new and second-hand books, magazines, comics, etc. The inner perimeter sold everything else – haberdashery, toys, clothes, shoes, tin trunks, trinkets, furniture, cutlery, etc. And behind the complex were the meat and fish freezers, pet shops and repair shops to mend anything under the sun. The bloody fools set fire to it to get the space to construct a multi-storied monstrosity. It was our grandmother's favourite outing for shopping. We would stare wide-eyed at the items on display. We couldn't afford most of them. We could afford to look at them.

School. I only remember studying and playing and private tuition. Thrice a week a Brahmin teacher clad in khadar (coarse cotton, home-spun Gandhian style) would come to coach us – in all the subjects, especially the dastardly language of Hindi. Though I 'studied' Hindi until I was 15, I never understood the damned language. My method of passing an exam was to mug and regurgitate without comprehension. This strategy always worked; I used to scrape through with the minimum marks.

The teacher was famous for three things:

One; he would be presented with a plate of two slices of thick-sliced bread on which was spread an inch layer of ghee (clarified butter) on top of which was sprinkled a generous layer of sugar; our mouths would water.

Two; he would screw our ears up or the skin of our thighs and bring tears to our eyes when we committed a mistake.

Three; he would extract the snot from his nose, roll it into balls, and eat them. To this day, I cannot tell whether he did it intentionally or in a dream-state. We used to watch hypnotized by the twins – fascination and nausea – at this novel, seemingly esculent hors d'oeuvre.

Up to the ninth standard, when I was 13 years old, I had Anglo-Indian female teachers. Two of them were very fetching, with enormous breasts, and like any boy I was fascinated with the twin mounds. I was always up there – not on the breasts but academically – but never achieved the first rank.

I remember three fights in school – all of which I won. I was big for an Indian. Five foot ten. In school I must have been about nine stone. Now I am 11.

I was good at cricket and hockey and represented the school in both the games; first-change bowler of medium pace and three-down batsman; left back in hockey. The only events of note are:

Cricket. We played Don-Bosco High School, renowned for its snobbery. They batted first and made 98. I took four enemy wickets for 30. We went in and were soon three for ten, staring defeat. I had a word with my partner and told him to let me have the majority of the batting. I was not going to let the blighters win. I stroked the balls all over the place and scored 62 and steered our side to a win.

Hockey. We had a Past versus Present match. I excelled myself. It was just one of those days. The Past players were huge; but not one of them could get past me, and when I hit the ball it flew to the other end as if on wings. We won. After the match, some of the opponents congratulated me.

What about my brother and sister? Well, they hovered about, stuck at an uncertain evolutionary stage, my own opinion being a cocktail mix of Martian, human being and slug. When they dared to try and approach the hallowed pedestal of my existence, I firmly put them in their place with a thump or two. It was only after I left home and went to stay in a hostel at the age of 16 for my pre-university course at Loyola College, Madras, that I came to see them metamorphose into something resembling our species. Once their status was confirmed I took them presents whenever I returned for holidays, took them to the cinema and even brought them back to Madras for holidays – for then they were living with my parents. In such magnanimous ways indeed did I show my approval!

It was at Loyola College that I learnt to play tennis. The college had 13 tennis courts. I started at court no. 13, the one for beginners, and within the year I was playing at court no. 3, displaying a difficult-to-get-at fast serve and a searing down-the-line return of serve that left the opponent stranded in despair at his service line.

It was at Loyola that I learned to be self-sufficient in all ways; budgeting, cleaning, washing, cinema, studies, sport. Every child should be kicked out of the house as soon as is possible, to experience the priceless twins of independence and responsibility.

* * * * * * * *

CHAPTER 31
Mr Rangachari

So, I had to meet this chap called Rangachari.

A sports editor of a magazine recommended him to me. Ranga was supposed to be an encyclopaedia on Indian cricket.

I set off from my hotel in an auto-rickshaw. Triplicane, a suburb of Madras smack near the city centre. It has a predominantly Muslim population. Rangachari – one could tell by his name – was a Hindu Brahmin. I alighted at no. 21 Ettines Road. It was a narrow road; busy, busy, busy. Shops and residences all mixed up. Pavements taken over by street vendors selling flowers, footwear, plastic items, pinchbeck jewellery, strange herbs, shiny stainless steel ware, fruits, etc. A garish green mosque was blaring prayers from the loudspeakers in its minarets. A Ganesha shrine seemingly sprouted out from the pavement and a few devotees were clutching their ears, squatting and arising, squatting and arising, to complete the stipulated mystical number of ritual callisthenics. A couple of women whose profession could not be doubted were flaunting themselves in no subtle manner. By God, they were ugly. A leper was sprawled in a corner with his bowl in front of him. Buses were plying with the drivers' fingers stapled to the horns. Auto rickshaws were darting here and there with an alacrity that would put rabbits to shame. Two motorcyclists were carrying on a leisurely conversation in the middle of the road, blissfully aware of their contribution to the mayhem all around.

No. 21 was slap bang in the midst of this cacophonous frazzle.

The front door was open – to let the air and the dust in. I didn't have to knock. A male monster of about eight lazily appeared, looked at me as if I were something the cat had brought in, and disappeared. A female monster appeared, giggled and also disappeared. A woman then appeared and asked me to sit down.

"I am Dr Mohan," I said; "I have an appointment with Mr Rangachari."

"Yes. Please sit down," she said. "He has just gone out. He will be back in a few minutes. Would you like a cup of coffee?"

"No, thank you."

'A few minutes' in India could mean anything from five minutes to three hours. Should I wait or skedaddle? I decided to wait.

The woman disappeared. Suddenly there was a crash. I heard the woman's voice screeching at the monsters. The monsters were shouting back, trying to shift the blame – possibly to God or destiny. The screaming ended just as abruptly as it had begun. A dishevelled man appeared, smiled a sickly sort of smile, sat down and started to scratch his belly.

"You are Dr Mohan?" he asked.

"Yes."

"You want to know about cricket?"

"Yes."

"My father is an expert."

"So I have heard."

"You ask him the score of India-Pakistan match in 1962 and he will tell you."

"Amazing."

"You are from England?"

"I was in England for some time."

"What were you doing there?"

"I was a doctor."

"But you want to write about cricket?"

"Yes."

"Very unusual. Do you want some coffee or tea?"

"No, thank you."

We heard a sound. I turned around and saw a man in his late sixties cross the threshold.

"'Allo, 'allo, 'allo, Dr Mohan," he said with evident joy.

"Hello, Mr Rangachari."

"I had to go out for some paan." (This is betel leaf stuffed with betel-nut, lime and spices to aid digestion – the habit of chewing the concoction is widespread in India). "Sorry to keep you waiting. Do you want some coffee?"

"No thank you."

"This is my son, Chandru," he said, pointing to the slob; "where are the others? Viji! Viji! Ramani! Ramani! Come. Come. This is Dr Mohan I was telling you all about. He has come to get some details about cricket. This is my first daughter-in-law, Viji, and this is my second daughter-in-law, Ramani. My first son, Pratap, is at the office, Larson and Toubro. This is my second son; we are looking out for a job for him. Where are the children? Come. Come. This is Raghu. Say 'good morning'. Good. This is Devi. They are my first son's children. And these are Ramu and Radha, my second son's children. So I have four grandchildren. They all live here."

So, there were four monsters in the household.

I was later to find out that Mr Rangachari had lost his wife a few years ago.

Now the paramount question was: how were we to conduct our proceedings in such an atmosphere?

"You are from Madras?" Mr Rangachari continued. "Vepery! Doveton Corrie...then Stanley Medical...then you went to England? How many years you were there...17 years? Long time... You have a family? *No?*...No... Why not? You don't know about children...very good, very good they are... Who will look after you later? See me...I am happy because of them... You have any brothers and sisters? Oh, both in Madras? That is good... What about your parents? Where they are? Oh, sorry...are you sure you do not want coffee? What about tea...or a cool drink? No? So, what do you want to know? History of Indian cricket? Big topic...big story... Where are you staying...in 'otel? You said that you have brother and sister here... Oh, I see. How long are you going to stay?... I think about one week...at most... You take notes? Oh, tape recorder...that is good... Then what do you do? You listen and write...and then? Oh, you put it into computer... Yes, yes...nowadays everything is computer... My grandchildren want computer...in my days we had only valve radio... Progress, you see...progress..."

I managed to convince him with great diplomacy that it would be best if he came to my hotel room and we discuss the subject of cricket. I would arrange for an auto-rickshaw to pick him up at ten o'clock every morning – if that was convenient for him. I was staying in a vegetarian hotel; so nourishment, if needed , would be acceptable to him.

"Woodpark 'otel!" he said. "Good masala dosais and good coffee."

So that was that.

* * * * * * *

CHAPTER 32
The Evolution of Indian Cricket –
The Parsees; The Hindus; The Muslims

The Useful Cricketer
I am rather a 'pootlesome' bat –
I seldom, indeed, make a run;
But I'm rather the gainer by that,
For it's bad to work hard in the sun.

As a 'field' I am not worth a jot,
And no one expects me to be;
My run is an adipose trot,
My 'chances' I never can see.

I am never invited to bowl,
And though, p'raps, this seems like a slight
In the depths of my innermost soul
I've a notion the captain is right.

In short, I may freely admit
I am not what you call a great catch;
But yet my initials are writ
In the book against every match!

For although – ay, and there is the rub –
I am forty and running to fat,
I have made it alright with the club,
By presenting an average bat!

June 1892

Ranga presented me with a fascinating story. The intrigues of Indian cricket could match and even surpass the skullduggery of national or international politics.

I have edited his narration. The terms 'English' and 'British' are used as synonyms – with apologies!

* * * * * * * *

The English traversed the globe with their football and cricketing paraphernalia. What were they supposed to do when they were not double-dealing and fighting? All work and no play...

Remember that they came to India in 1600. They must have stuck their stumps into the first patch of ground they beheld and got on with it. But a game has to be recorded or mentioned on paper to anoint it with the necessary authenticity. That was the game played off the Gulf of Cambay in 1721; it became the first milestone in the history of Indian cricket. Needless to say that it was an English game played by the English; the native Indians were merely spectators and must have been either awed or suffered hernias due to unbridled laughter.

It was the native Bengalis who first took to the game of cricket – just as they were the first to take to many things English: literature, education, art, business, politics, etc. But, of course, there are no recorded details. The recorded fact is that, in 1792, the Calcutta Cricket Club was formed, making it the second oldest club in the world after the MCC. And in this famous club a match was held on the 18th and 19th of January 1804 between the Old Etonians and the Rest of Calcutta, meaning the members of the East India Company, all of whom were English. One Robert Vansittart distinguished himself by taking seven wickets and slamming a century, thus inflicting the shame of an innings defeat on the poor old Rest of the Calcuttans. So that was the first hundred on Indian soil. It also heralded the sport of gambling, the Etonians defying the odds of 2-1 against. The Madras Cricket Club joined in the act the same year.

No doubt some Indians did try to learn the game. And just as surely were they ridiculed for their efforts to imitate the English, and probably punished for having the audacity to do so. The cheek of the dark-skinned people, indeed!

The Parsees

Now, enter the Parsees. After Muhammad had done his bit and vanished from the scene, he spawned a few overzealous proselytizers who ran amok in the 6th century. Some of the Persians fled before the incoming hordes and headed towards India for sanctuary. The local king generously gave them sanctuary, provided they did not in turn impose their funny religious ideas on the local populace. A deal was struck. Thus the Persians, who were Zoroastrians, were allowed to stay and practise whatever it was they practised alongside the Hindus – who practised whatever it was they practised. They came to be known as the 'Parsees'. Over the centuries they have evolved into great business entrepreneurs – the likes of the Tatas and the Wadias, etc.

When the English set foot in India, the Parsees were their eager business collaborators – for, in spite of the fact that they had been Indians for generations, they still continued to consider themselves as 'foreigners'. Such was their total insulation from Indian society. They threw in their lot with the conquerors. The English, of course, quite happy for the local support, cultivated the community and showered them with gifts, lands and titles. By 1908, three Parsees were anointed as hereditary baronets; by 1943, 63 Parsees had been knighted. Now, how much of all this stemmed from the fact that the Parsees were fair-skinned is left to conjecture!

Let us get on with cricket, however. The Parsee boys of Bombay hovered around the boundary as gleeful ball-pickers to the Englishmen, who occasionally cracked a few boundaries. As a reward for such unstinted service to the game, the noble Englishmen let them occasionally handle the bat and ball as a sort of favour of the gods – which they did with evident ecstasy. The Parsees took to the game. They skilfully constructed bats from deal-wood boxes and logs and balls from waste cloth and string, and started in earnest to take on the might of the British Empire. And this they managed to do in 1877 at the Bombay Gymkhana.

"You see," said Ranga, "you have to understand that Bombay was an island then and the English were afraid of the French. So they built a fort and cleared the area around it to the sea to have good visibility and a clear range of fire. This was the 'maidan'. Being Indian, you know the game *gilli-danda*. You can say that it is Indian cricket, for it uses a three-foot stick to hit a six-inch piece of wood instead of a ball. So, when they saw the English play cricket, the locals soon took to it."

"Did the Parsees form a team?"

"Yes, they started the Oriental Cricket Club in 1848. Then someone must have objected to the title and it was changed to the Zoroastrian Club in 1850. Soon many other clubs were formed, and they played tournaments."

"Who were the rich Parsees in those days to fund these clubs?"

"The same as today. The Tatas. There were many others too."

"When did the Hindus take to cricket?"

"1866. Bombay Union Cricket Club. But only those of the Prabhu caste could join."

"Somehow I am not surprised," I said.

"Then, in 1877, the Marathis formed the Hindu Club. But the English had formed the Bombay Gymkhana in 1875. Do you know what 'gymkhana' means?"

I shook my head as a negative answer.

"It is from *gend-khana*, meaning ball-house. They took over nearly 5,000 square yards of the maidan – nearly a quarter of its 185,000 square yards – to play their games of cricket, tennis, etc. The Parsees and Hindus used one part of the field. But when there were polo matches, the English used the area of the locals."

"But that would have spoilt the area for cricket!"

"Exactly. Until 1879 polo was played in another part of the maidan. But from then they joined the Gymkhana and used that part of it used by the locals for cricket. The Parsees and the Hindus complained.

"The Parsees, having a better knowledge of English, had the temerity to petition the governor. Where are we to play cricket – with your damned donkeys all over the place? Thus started a protracted epistolary battle between the Parsees and the English, which began in 1879 and carried on until Lord Harris, who was governor of Bombay at the time, doled out patches of land along the waterfront to the Parsees, the Hindus and the Muslims."

"Strange, isn't it? The game of polo was invented by the Indians and cricket by the English. The English wanted to play the Indian game whereas the Indians wanted to play the English game. When did the English play against the Indians?"

"1877, the Parsees versus the Gymkhana. Though the Parsees led in the first innings, they lost the match. But they had acquitted themselves well. Because of the trouble with the polo-players, no games were played between the teams until 1884."

Though round-arm had been legalized in 1828 and overarm in 1864 in England, the Parsees were still bowling underarm – for some reason I cannot fathom.

"You think the trouble with home umpires is recent?" went on Ranga. "In 1885 the Parsees asked for a Parsee umpire."

"The request was disallowed," I said.

"Naturally. You cannot have a native giving an Englishman out. It was not until 1911 that a Parsee umpire was allowed. In 1886 the Parsees were invited to tour England. Since they were a rich community, they invited Robert Henderson from Surrey to coach them."

The Parsees lost 19 of the 28 matches and won one during their historic tour of the land that gave birth to the game. At Lord's the Parsees lost by an innings and 224 runs. Some consolation lay in the fact that the great W G Grace played against them on that occasion, scoring 65 and taking seven for 18 and four for 26. Another match was at Windsor Great Park, against a team captained by Prince Victor, grandson of Queen Victoria. The Princes' XI were skittled for 90 with the two princes, Victor and Albert, making 24 and 11 respectively. But alas! The Parsees fared badly and lost.

They were entertained at Cumberland Lodge by invitation of the Queen. She had a soft corner for India and even had a faithful Indian servant/confidant.

The Parsees were stunned at the difference in behaviour between the English in India and the English in England towards the 'lesser races'. Here it was all genuine warmth, friendship, curiosity to learn, praise, appreciation, conviviality and civility. Back home in India it was scorn, apartheid and humiliation.

"After their tour of England, the Parsees were granted a piece of land – 425 square yards on the newly reclaimed Kennedy Sea Face, a couple of miles from the Gymkhana grounds," went on Ranga. "Since the Parsees were rich enough to buy out the English, they levelled the ground and built a Parsee Gymkhana. The Parsees returned to England two years later, in 1888."

This time they won eight, lost 11 and drew 12; very creditable indeed. At the Scarborough game the opposition needed four runs with four wickets in hand with half an hour's play left. The gallant Parsees scalped three wickets for three runs and managed a draw! At Eastbourne our Parsees followed on but managed to compile a huge second innings total and went on to win the game handsomely by 66 runs!

The hero of the tour was one Dr Mehellasha Pavri, a medium-pacer who took 170 wickets at an average of 11.66. If one can discount the Indian propensity for exaggeration, Pavri bowled with such truculence that he once sent the bails flying a full 50 yards and on another occasion achieved the feat of somersaulting a stump so that it pitched itself! He was from a little town called Navsari in Gujarat, the same town that brought forth the Tata family – and the Mehta family, one of whom is Zubin. On his English tour he carefully watched Lockwood and Sharpe of Surrey.

Ranga continued, "In 1889-90, G F Vernon from Middlesex brought over a group of Englishmen, of whom only three had played first-class cricket; Lord Hawke was one of the tourists. Their matches were against Englishmen in India. But the Parsees managed to wangle a match against them in Bombay. This was the first great cricket match in India between the locals and the foreigners. About 12,000 Orientals, including women and chanting priests, congregated on the perimeter. Framji Patel was captain."

First Innings: Vernon's Eleven – 97; Parsees – 80.

Second Innings: Vernon's Eleven – 95; Pavri an incredible seven for 34.

The Parsees had to make 78 to win. They won with four wickets in hand. A comprehensive victory. Pandemonium. Pitch invasions; garlanding of players; later, tumultuous parties of celebration of an unprecedented event in Indian and cricketing history.

It was the only defeat of the tour for the Vernons. The English ire was up. The damned natives had beaten them! How could that possibly be? We have to show them. Still, a sense of fair play prevailed, and the English sent a congratulatory note to the victorious Parsees, who danced and sang through the night.

Lord Hawke returned in 1892-93, this time with all 11 first-class players, including Stanley Jackson (who first ignored Ranji and then selected him for Cambridge and who later became governor of Bengal). They played two matches against the Parsees.

1st match: Pavri took 10 wickets and the Parsees won by a thumping 109 runs.

2nd match: The proverbial nail-biting finish, with the Parsees losing by seven runs.

This time, the Parsees reacted a bit differently. Angry noises and gestures; the women openly weeping. You see, even then, the Indian crowd could not take defeat sportingly. The English community had saved face, and heaved a sigh of relief.

Indian crowds have always been boisterous. In fact, in 1890 a match had to be cancelled due to the *tamasha* of the crowds.

In the same season Lord Harris had managed to persuade the local English to pit their full strength against the Parsees in what came to be called the Presidency matches – held either at Bombay or at at Poona Gymkhana Clubs. Between 1892 and 1906, 26 matches were played; the Parsees won 11, the English won ten, and five were drawn.

"Lord Harris is generally regarded as the father of Indian cricket," I said. "Can you tell me something about him?"

"His real name was George Robert Canning," said Ranga. "He was born in 1851 in Trinidad, where his father was governor. His family had connections with India. His great-grandfather fought against Tipu Sultan and took his share of the booty. He later became Baron Harris of Belmont and Seringapatam. *His* son fought against Napoleon at Waterloo. *His* son in turn became governor of Madras after a stint in Trinidad. Our Lord Harris, the 4th Baron, grew up here in Madras and was sent to Eton. He played for Eton and Cambridge and then went on to captain England and become the president of the MCC. In 1890 he was appointed governor of Bombay. He did very little governing; he was busy organizing and playing cricket. When the Parsees sent him a letter about the polo business, he calmly turned their request down. You must understand that nearly 1,000 Indians were playing cricket in the maidan then and that Harris sided with a handful of polo-players."

"Because they were British."

"Exactly; and this whilst he was busy organizing cricket matches between his team of military officers and civilians and the team of Lord Wenlock, the governor of Madras – ignoring a famine that raged through the province.

"Remember that the Indians were petitioning the English for suitable ground to play the game on. Lord Harris finally, in 1892, apportioned land to the Islamic and Hindu Gymkhanas. Let me tell you something else about Harris. The same year, an Indian was elected to the British Parliament…"

"Dadabhai Naoroji."

"Yes. But Harris was disgusted and scandalized at the reality of a native sitting in the hallowed House of Commons. Soon after this momentous news of Naoroji, the Parsees invited Harris to play a match against them. He refused."

"Maybe he thought it would be bad for the Empire if his side lost!"

"Harris was an irresponsible governor. In 1893 Hindus and Muslims were butchering each other whilst he was playing cricket in Ganeshkind. He refused to come to Bombay to calm the situation. He finally came to Bombay – only to play a cricket match!"

Lord Harris certainly did a lot for cricket, but not for the Indian. What little he did he had to do, for he had no other option. When he finally left his post, most Indians were happy to see his back. Harris was a dipsomaniac and a lousy bigot, who often aired his opinion that the Indians, of whatever community, hovered somewhere about the hogs in the evolutionary nature of things.

Why the senior inter-schools tournament in Bombay, the coveted Harris Shield, should be named after such a one is anybody's guess.

The Hindus

Today people pay a lot of money to come to the cricket stadium to watch their favourite teams at play. In those days it was free. How could you charge people simply walking in from the streets into grounds that were open on all sides? It was impossible to take a 'gate'. As the game grew to attract thousands, temporary bivouacs and *shamianas* were erected and spectators charged. This has mushroomed into the present massive, enclosed, concrete sports stadiums all over the country.

"Seeing the Parsees playing, the Hindus started up the Bombay Union Cricket Club," continued Ranga. "A certain Ramachandra Vishnu Navlekar of the Prabhu caste was the initiator and he restricted membership to those of his own caste. And then, in 1877, the Marathis started the Hindu Cricket Club."

"Did the English play the Hindus?"

"Oh yes. In 1882, the Hindu Cricket Club played against and defeated the Carlton Cricket Club. Seeing their proficiency, the Bombay Gymkhana played against the Hindus in 1883 and won. But in 1887 the Hindus won."

"What about the other cities?"

"The Princes of Natore and Cooch Behar, together with Sarada Ranjan Ray, the principal of Vidyasagar College, started the Calcutta Cricket Club. The Madras Cricket Club was formed in 1846 at Chepauk thanks to the unstinting efforts of the Nayudus and other influential people. The other important centres of cricket were Poona and Karachi. By the beginning of the 20th century, Bangalore, Lahore, Aligarh, Allahabad and Nagpur all had their respective cricket clubs."

"Did the English give a part of the maidan to the Hindus as they did to the Parsees?"

"In 1892 they allotted a plot of land to the Hindus on the Kennedy Sea Face. Jivandas, a Gujarati merchant, donated 10,000 rupees to construct a gymkhana . . . Do you know any cricketers of that era?"

"The great C K Nayudu, Nissar…"

"Have you heard of Palwankar Baloo?"

"Vaguely. He was a spin bowler, wasn't he?"

"Yes. Let me tell you about him. But before that, let me tell you about myself. I am an orthodox Brahmin. In fact, you cannot get more orthodox than our caste. My forefathers were temple priests. My father was the intermediary between human beings and their gods at the Kapaleeswarar Temple. But that was not for me. I was the eldest son and, according to tradition, I was supposed to become a priest – a *pujari*. But I refused. I became a chartered accountant and immersed myself in cricket. I played for my school and college and wanted to play for Madras State. But I contracted tuberculosis and was in a sanatorium for five years. Since I could not play cricket any longer, I made it my hobby to learn and follow the game."

"How did your parents take your decision to opt out of the traditional profession?"

"In the usual manner. They ranted and raved and threatened. I stayed mum and refused to become a priest. In the end they had to come round. Why am I telling you that I am a Brahmin? Because, as you know, we are not supposed to mix with other castes. But do you know who looked after me when I was coughing up blood in the sanatorium? An untouchable ward boy. It was he who wiped the blood off my chin; it was he who massaged me with oils. It was he who washed me and my clothes and the latrine. And it was he who fed me when I was too weak to eat. Since then I have thrown this caste nonsense overboard. It is a sin; it is a crime. We Hindus will never prosper until we get rid of this abominable caste system. Do you know who Palwankar Baloo was? An untouchable."

This is the story of India's first great spin bowler.

The village of Palwan is on the west coast of India, north of Goa. It was home to an untouchable family of the Chamaar caste, who specialized in goods that were deemed to be tainted by the Hindu caste system – leathers. The Chamaars were tanners and dyers and made shoes and saddles. Since the caste Hindus would not do certain jobs, the Chamaars filled in. They went to where they could find work, usually the English factories and cantonments. Baloo's father moved from the stifling conditions of his village to the anonymity of a town called Dharwad in the interior of south India. Baloo was born there in 1875. Poona was rapidly developing into an important English base. So Baloo's father moved there. After a short stint at school, Baloo's first employment was on the cricket field. The Parsee Cricket Club paid him three rupees a month to sweep and roll the pitch. In 1892 Baloo shifted his operations to the Englishmen at Poona Club, where he was paid four rupees. He must have been gifted, for in his spare time he practised with the ball, bowling slow left-arm spinners. Soon the Englishmen were asking him to bowl to them in the nets. A certain Greig, a fairly good batsman, was the one who encouraged him by asking him to bowl to him. Baloo was eventually paid 12 rupees a month for his extra duties.

A match was fixed between the Poona Hindu Club and the European Gymkhana Club. Of course, the Hindus had heard about Baloo, but how could he be picked? The cricket ball would be tainted. It would have to be washed, with proper incantations, before a caste Hindu could use it. What if Baloo's shadow fell on them during the course of play? Could he have tea with them? Whilst the Hindus were discussing such profound problems, Greig put it about that it would be foolish of the Hindus not to include a bowler of Baloo's calibre. That shifted the Hindus. If the English themselves held Baloo in such regard... (Another version is that it was the Parsees who were eager to enlist him.)

Baloo was chosen to play – and won the match for the Hindus! He won many matches for the hidebound Hindus.

"Do you know that Tilak himself praised Baloo?" asked Ranga. (Bal Gangadhar Tilak was a ferocious nationalist freedom fighter.) He continued, "We now come to 1896. The Poona plague. Baloo left Poona and came to Bombay and joined the Hindu Gymkhana. You must understand that at that time, at the turn of the 19th century, there were many Hindu clubs based on caste. The only reason Baloo was accepted was because of his prodigious talent."

"What about the rich Hindus? Did they not sponsor cricketers then?" I asked.

"They did. Various companies sponsored teams. The manager of the Bombay Berar and Central Indian Railways was an Englishman called Lucas. He gave Baloo a job – only to play cricket. Baloo played for the Railways and the Hindu Gymkhana. The princes also sponsored teams. Patiala, Holkar, Baroda, Bhopal, Udaipur, Jodhpur. Remember the Prince of Cooch-Behar and Natore of Calcutta? He invited Baloo to play against the all-white Calcutta Cricket Club. The Indians won the match, to the chagrin of the English, thanks to Baloo's bowling.

"1906.   Bombay Gymkhana versus BBCI
Railways. Greig verus Baloo. Greig made a century.
Then came the big match. The Hindus versus Bombay
Gymkhana. The Hindus put up a decent 242. They had
drafted in Erasha, a fastie. He skittled the Europeans out
for 191, taking six for 77. Baloo, three for 41. Second
innings: Hindus 160. The Europeans were shot out for
102. Baloo and Erasha divided the ten wickets equally
between them.

"Can you hear the roar of the crowd?" asked
Ranga. "Can you hear the drums? Can you see the
dancing in the streets? Can you see the garlands around
the cricketers' necks? The lowly Indian had finally
defeated a full-strength English side. Was the match the
harbinger of greater things to come? You must note that
the Hindus allowed Baloo – and his brother Shivram,
who also played in the match – into the dining area and
sat alongside them. Was this going to herald the end of
caste distinctions?

"1907.   BCCI Railways against Bombay
Gymkhana. The crowds came to see their Baloo taking
five wickets and winning the match. This was followed
by a return match; Hindus versus Europeans. The same
result but more emphatically so. The Hindus won by
238 runs and Baloo took 13 wickets and wielded the bat
for 50-odd runs.

"In 1907 the Triangular Tournament was
introduced between the Europeans, the Parsees and the
Hindus. The Hindus never won the tournament in the
early years but Baloo was consistently the leading
wicket-taker. 1910. Three Palwankar brothers played
for the Hindus – Baloo, Shivram and Vithal. Shivram

and Vithal were working for the Greater Indian Peninsula Railway.

"1911. The Europeans thought that it was time to allow an All India Team to tour England. Six Parsees, five Hindus and three Muslims were selected. The great Ranjitsinghji of Nawanagar was asked to lead, but he refused. He never played for India; perhaps he thought it was beneath his dignity after having played so much in England. Perhaps he deemed himself an Englishman. So Maharaja Bhupendra Singh of Patiala was captain. He was a good batsman. Baloo was in the team. Shivram was in the reserves and eventually played. Vithal was not picked for he was too young.

"The All India Team fared badly because the Maharaja was busy elsewhere, socializing with the VIPs. One cannot imagine the excitement the tour must have caused in India. And can you imagine an untouchable playing in the hallowed cricket grounds of England? Against Oxford, Baloo took five wickets for 87; against Cambridge, eight for 103; and against the MCC at Lord's, four for 96.

"On that momentous tour, Baloo took an incredible 114 wickets at an even more incredible average of 14.84. Baloo was a phenomenon. He was mobbed and celebrated. He was a true hero of all India. At long last, the untouchables had something to brag about. When they returned from England, do you know who gave a welcome speech to Baloo in Bombay?"

"No."

"Ambedkar."

1912. The Muslims join the fray and the Triangular becomes the Quadrangular.

1913. Baloo was now 38 years old. Another of his brothers, Ganpat, joined the team and they thrashed the Europeans. The four brothers played together during the following years of international and national turmoil. In 1919, the youngest brother, Ganpat, died of tuberculosis.

"Now I shall explain the captaincy," said Ranga. "Baloo was the Hindu hero. But could an untouchable be made captain? That was a bit too much for the Hindus. So, though the media backed Baloo, the Hindus did not. Pai was made captain. In 1920, Baloo was not picked, Pai was indisposed and Deodhar was made captain. Like Pai, Deodhar was a Brahmin. But Deodhar was junior to Shivram and Vithal, both excellent batsmen. Shivram and Vithal stood down in righteous protest. The Hindus beat the Muslims. The next match was against the Parsees. The media was crying for the Palwankar brothers. They were reinstated. Pai was still captain – but Baloo was made vice-captain. To avoid any trouble, and possibly because Pai himself thought it fit, he left the field and handed over the captaincy to Baloo – who, by all accounts, did a magnificent job, though the Parsees managed to draw the match in a nail-biting finish."

"Did any of the Palwankars captain the team?" I asked.

"Bombay cricket management passed from the Brahmins to the merchants. They were more amenable to change. At last, in 1923, when both Baloo and Shivram had retired, they offered the captaincy to Vithal. It took the Hindus ten years to accept an untouchable as a captain. In his four years as captain, he led the Hindus to three victories against the Europeans and lost once to the Muslims. Vithal retired in 1929 at the age of 40. Thus ended 30 years of the Palwankar brothers' involvement in Indian cricket. Baloo was a world-class bowler. He could bowl slow and medium-fast and spin the ball. He knew every trick. He could bowl six different balls in an over, and that was what mesmerized the batsmen. Baloo could also wield the willow – to a small extent. Shivram was a proficient batsman and an excellent fielder. Vithal was the consummate batsman and thinker of the game. He was an untouchable who should have been a Kshatriya.

"But even Vithal was tainted with communalism. Let me give you an example of Indian petty intrigue. A Madrasi called Ramaswami had scored a quick hundred against the MCC a few weeks before the Bombay MCC-Hindu match in 1926-27. Ten minutes before the Bombay match, Vithal, the captain, asked Ramaswami to stand down; Vithal wanted a fellow Bombayite in the team. Ramaswami answered that he would if the selection committee asked him to do so. Vithal backed off. Ramaswami made one run in the match. Such pettiness still dogs Indian cricket. Do you know C Rajagopalachari?"

"What?" I was thrown.

"Rajaji."

"Of course. First Governor General of India, Chief Minister of Madras and originator of the Swatantra Party."

"C R was a Madras Brahmin. He was close to Gandhi. He didn't like Nehru. He was a politician and a philosopher and he was very erudite. He wrote many books on religious philosophy and his versions of the Hindu epics are still selling very well. I was employed as a chartered accountant by one of his grand-nephews. One day we were talking about cricket, and I told him that I had written an article about the Palwankar brothers and given it to *The Hindu* and the *Indian Express* newspapers. They did not publish it. When I asked them they said that they had never heard of the Palwankars and besides, who wanted to know about them? No public interest. As soon as I told him this, he got up and went to a big roll-top desk and pulled out a notebook.

"'I too am a cricket lover,' he said, 'and I have been reading Rajaji's notes. People know him as a great philosopher-statesman but he was also interested in cricket. This is what I call fortuitous. I was reading this chapter only a week ago, and as soon as you mentioned Palwankar Baloo the hairs on my neck stood on end. Rajaji knew him and, seeing that he was a cricketing hero, well respected and cultured, he drew him into politics. This explains Baloo's involvement in politics, especially in matters concerning caste. At the time of the Round Table Conference in London in 1931, Rajaji asked Baloo to oppose separate electorates. Baloo agreed. He even wrote a letter to the British Prime Minister airing his views. This must have been at the instigation of Rajaji. If it was, then it can only mean that Baloo was an influential figure in caste politics at that time. It also says here that a certain M C Raja and a P Baloo met Gandhi and Ambedkar to resolve the deadlock between the two when Gandhi fasted for the untouchable cause at Yeravda jail in 1932, only a month after he returned from the disastrous Round Table Conference in England. Raja was a famous freedom fighter and also sided with Gandhi for his views on Harijans (children of God, as Gandhi preferred to call them). But I did not know Baloo. Baloo wholeheartedly agreed with Gandhi and disagreed with his fellow untouchable Ambedkar on the issue of their caste. He was the ideal person to negotiate between the two. So Rajaji pressed him and Baloo and Raja acted as go-betweens. They met Gandhi at Yeravda and finally persuaded Ambedkar to sign the pact, especially since Gandhi had given more seats to the Harijans than Ambedkar had asked for. It was an unexpected windfall. On the 24th of September, four days after the beginning of the fast, the Poona Pact was signed.'"

"In 1935, Ambedkar reneged on the pact," continued Ranga. "He began to clamour for separate electorates and even threatened to embrace another religion. Baloo was furious. So he stood against Ambedkar in the 1937 elections. The Congress threw its weight behind Baloo – Nehru, Patel, Munshi, Rajaji canvassed for Baloo. Ambedkar won marginally, only because the vote was split by a third candidate."

I never did like Ambedkar. The trouble with him was that he always wanted to be the focus of attention. He was an opportunist. He could have used his brains in a better way. After so many decades, there seems to be a sudden resurgence of interest in Ambedkar. People are putting up statues of him all over the place, and they have even made a film about him.

"It was in the same year 1937," continued Ranga, "that Rajaji spoke out vociferously against communal cricket. He said that the Quadrangular Tournament was against all that he, Gandhi and the Congress stood for, that it divided people, that it was morally wrong and an abomination. We come to 1940. World War Two. Hindu-Muslim strife. Voices were being raised against playing communal cricket matches. The Hindus did not know what to do. They sent a delegation to the highest 'court of appeal' – Gandhi. Rajaji was present at the time in Wardha and immediately wired Baloo to come. Gandhi clearly stated that he was against communal matches. The Hindus pulled out; the other three teams participated but the tournament was a wash-out. Out of respect for Gandhi, the princes withdrew their support from the communal games. But loyalty is short-lived. In 1941 the Hindus joined the fray and won the final against the Parsees. Baloo continued to speak at meetings against separatism, for the abolition of the caste system and for the upliftment of the underprivileged.

"Palwankar Baloo, Chamaar untouchable, Harijan, cricketer, national hero, politician, Congressman, gentleman, died in 1955. Vithal died in 1971."

"What is your opinion about the communal matches?" I asked.

"I don't like them," Ranga replied.

"Do you think that they foster camaraderie or dissension?"

"Despite what anyone, including the players themselves, may say, I am of the opinion that we see ourselves only as belonging to a particular family, sect, community, religion or country. We will never think of ourselves as one people with common goals. Therefore there will always be tension on and off the field amongst players and spectators. Do you mean to say that Indian and Pakistani players are true friends?"

"That is what they insist on saying in public."

"Ah…"

"Can I ask you about the ward boy who looked after you in the sanatorium? What was his name?"

"Raghu."

"What happened to him?   Did you keep in touch?"

"Five years after I was discharged he contracted tuberculosis. I visited him regularly. Within two years he was reduced to a skeleton and died; I was one of the pall-bearers at his funeral."

The Muslims

"The Tyabjis and the Lukmanis, rich Gujarati merchants, started a Muslim Cricket Club, which in 1890 evolved into the Muslim Gymkhana," said Ranga. "In 1891 they were allotted 425 square yards of land next to the Parsee Gymkhana along the Kennedy Sea Face. Amidst the Hindu-Muslim riots of 1893, the Gymkhana was inaugurated.   (Within a few months the Hindus inaugurated theirs.) In 1912 the Muslims reached the proficiency required to join the Europeans, the Parsees and the Hindus and the Quadrangular Tournament was born.   The Muslims drafted in players from all over India, whereas the other three teams were local Bombayites. But from 1916 they too were allowed to have 'foreigners'. In those days, the cricket season commenced in June and reached a climax in September, when the Quadrangular was played. It was the most popular sporting event of the year – the Bombay Cricket Carnival.

"It took the Muslims 12 years – 1924 – to win the championship. Syed Wazir Ali blasted 197 runs and Botawala bamboozled the Hindus by scalping eight of them. Do you know who proposed the toast at the celebrations afterwards?"

"Mmm. Let me guess. Someone big…Muhammad Ali Jinnah?"

"Correct. But at this time he was all for Hindu-Muslim unity and made his sentiments clear in his speech. Their next triumph was in 1934, when they once again beat the Hindus. The following year they thrashed the Hindus again, by a margin of 221 runs, the brothers Wazir Ali and Nazir Ali each slamming scorching centuries. 1936. Hindu-Muslim riots in Bombay. The Muslims wanted very badly to complete a hat-trick of triumphs over their Hindu rivals. But they were defeated by them in the semi-finals, and the Hindus went on to win the final handsomely against the Europeans.

"In 1937 it became known as the Pentangular when 'The Rest' was added, made up of a gallimaufry of Indian Christians, Anglo-Indians, Buddhists and Jews. The Pentangular was played at the new Brabourne Stadium, named after the governor of Bombay and built by the Maharaja of Patiala."

"Was this when Rajaji spoke out against the communal sport ethic?" I asked Ranga.

"Yes, because he saw that this was just another aspect of the divisions in Indian society and that it would augur no goodwill. Coming back to the Pentangular, the Hindus pulled out because their community was not granted more seats than the Muslims. The Muslims won the final. They won it again by defeating a disorganized and disunited Hindu team in 1938. 1939, the world was at war, but the Pentangular carried on. The Muslims were once again eager to complete a hat-trick but, again, they were thwarted by the Hindus. There was great jubilation amongst the Hindus, as at this time there was much Hindu-Muslim tension, with Jinnah whipping up Hindu-Muslim animosity in his quest for a separate Muslim homeland."

"In 1940, Gandhi stated that he did not approve of communal cricket, the Hindus abstained and the Muslims won," I filled in.

"Yes. Who was president of the Indian National Congress?"

"Maulana Abul Kalam Azad."

"Correct. Despite the Congress leaders and many of the princes voicing their dissent against communal cricket, the tournament went ahead in 1941. The greatest crowds were for the Hindu-Muslim semi-final. The Hindus won and went on to thrash the Parsees by ten wickets in the final. What happened in 1942?"

"The Quit India movement."

"Correct. So, no cricket amidst the carnage. 1943: cricket resumed. Quite contrary to expectations, The Rest defeated the Muslims in one of the semi-finals, thanks to a magnificent 248 by Hazare. The Hindus defeated the Europeans in the other. The stage was set for a first-time final between the Hindus and The Rest. And it turned out to be superb. The Hindus defeated The Rest, Vijay Merchant scoring an unbeaten 250 and Vijay

Hazare a phenomenal 309 out of a second innings total of 387, made after following on.

"1944. Gandhi-Jinnah talks break down. Total impasse. Hindu-Muslim final. Hindus, 203; Muslims, 221. Second innings: Hindus, 315. The Muslims won the nail-biting encounter. Whilst wickets tumbled around him, the opener Ibrahim stood his ground and, with help from Abdul Hafeez, Gul Mohammed and Mushtaq Ali, managed to engineer a win 20 minutes before close of play. The Pentangular of 1945 was not played until early 1946 due to war celebrations and visiting foreign teams. The Parsees, surprisingly, defeated the Muslims but lost miserably to the Hindus in the final. With the inevitability of Pakistan's creation, the Pentangular had finally reached its end. The Cricket Carnival, staunchly supported by many and equally scathingly referred to as an abomination by many others, was finally cremated. The Brabourne Stadium witnessed a Zonal Quadrangular, the teams made up of all denominations – or abominations."

"The history of Indian cricket seems to centre around Bombay. Did the other towns and cities have such Quadrangular matches?"

"They did. Sind and Karachi were famous venues. Other places had Triangulars, for they did not have many Parsees about."

Communal cricket was the most popular form of Indian sport in the early 20th century. There is no doubt about that, as the gate receipts prove. Even after the Ranji Trophy national championships were started in 1934-35, the Quadrangular was the better attended. Was communal cricket bad for India? Yes, because it was divisive. The competition was unhealthy. And the various factions never saw themselves as belonging to one nation, India. The Europeans looked down upon the Parsees, who looked down upon the Hindus, who, in turn, looked down upon the Muslims. How could such an attitude be right in any context? The inhabitants of India were never a nation. It was the British conquest that welded them (artificially) into one. The welding points were, are and will forever be brittle.

* * * * * * * *

CHAPTER 33
Patiala; C K Nayudu; Vizzy; Willingdon; Amar Singh; Nissar; Mushtaq Ali

Indian princes saw the advantages – and panache – that cricket could bring them. This is where Patiala comes into the picture. It was a middling state of 1.5 million Hindus, ruled by a Sikh. Its rulers had always been pro-British; it had sided with the British during the Mutiny and would side with the British against the Congress movement for independence. Rajendra Singh saw the importance of sports to butter up the British. He had the best polo ponies and teams in the country. He also played cricket. His son, Bhupendra Singh, carried on his father's passion for cricket – no doubt influenced by the fortunes of Ranji. He built the Bardari Palace Oval, larger than Lord's, with a charming clubhouse. It is said that elephants were used to roll the wicket. He put together a team called the Maharaja of Patiala's XI that provided winter employment for English, West Indian and Australian cricketers as players and coaches – the likes of Rhodes, Larwood, Tarrant, Constantine, etc. Exactly how much cricketing they did is open to conjecture; I suspect that it was one helluva holiday – sightseeing, shopping, hunting and sex.

In 1911, Bhupendra took a team to England – just before King George V and Queen Mary came to India and announced the shifting of the capital to Delhi. Patiala's XI won only two of the 13 matches, Meherhomji making 1,227 runs and Baloo taking 114 wickets. The two greats, Sydney Barnes and Gilbert Jessop, played against the Indians.

Patiala was busy meeting the right people to safeguard himself and his state and to further his status amongst the princes. It seemed to pay off. He was never punished for his atrocious behaviour and he was Chancellor of the Chamber of Princes from 1926 to 1930 and then again in 1934 and 1935.

Let us fast forward to the 1916 Quadrangular match between the Hindus and the Europeans. Remember Greig? The man who practised against Baloo? He was given out, stumped for a duck off the bowling of a debutant by the Hindu umpire, Pai. The Englishman refused to accept the decision, claiming that a Hindu umpire was 1) incompetent and 2) communally and racially biased. The European umpire at square leg ruled 'not out'. Pai stoutly disagreed. Greig strode back to the pavilion and complained to Chunilal Mehta, who called in the Hindu captain and the umpire, who both stuck to their guns. Play was resumed. The Europeans won the match, with Greig making 55 in the second innings. After the match Greig wrote a nasty letter, which was approved by the Bombay Gymkhana and sent on to Pai. This episode led to 'neutral' umpires from the communities not playing.

"Do you know who the debutant bowler was?" asked Ranga.

"No."

"Let us move on. Patiala helped to pay the costs of the 1926-27 MCC tour of India, captained by A E R Gilligan; Tate was one of the tourists. Lord Harris, president of the MCC, presiding over the Imperial Cricket Conference, gave his imperial sanction to the tour, which two Calcutta Britons had lobbied for to boost cricket in their city; they didn't like Bombay getting all the glory. Twenty-six of the 34 matches were first-class.

"Let me tell you about the two-day match against the Hindus in Bombay at the Gymkhana. Some 25,000 people witnessed the proceedings. They were stunned by Guy Earle, who blasted 130 runs in 90 minutes with eight sixes and 11 fours; one of his shots crashed through a glass pane in the pavilion. The MCC made 363 runs on the first day. The next day the Hindus were 84 for three, their key batsman, Vithal, back in the pavilion. Silence greeted the tall, tough, dark and dour individual strolling to the crease. His first scoring shot was a two; the next landed on the roof of the pavilion. What followed was a literal mauling; a lion shaking a cloth doll in its jaws. Balls were ricocheting off his bat into the pavilion, onto the pavilion, smashing clocks, glasses, scoreboards, trees, spectators... In 116 minutes he made 153 runs. Let me give you some statistics.

"First 50:   16 scoring strokes, 4 sixes and 5 fours.

"Second 50:   17 scoring strokes, 3 sixes and 5 fours.

"Third 50:   16 scoring strokes, 4 sixes and 4 fours.

"Forty-nine strokes providing 122 runs.   He established a world record with his 11 sixes in a match; a record that was beaten only in 1962-63 by John Reid. who hit 15 sixes for Wellington in New Zealand.   It wasn't mindless slogging.   A lad of 15 watching the match regarded it as the best innings he had ever seen: Vijay Merchant. The match was drawn.

"The mesmerized crowd departed in a state of shocked euphoria, having listened to the euphony of willow against leather.

"That day the Indians lost their awe of the Englishman; he was not a god; he could be slogged. The thrall of the European was dented. The Brits, who until then had almost looked down on the Indians as a bunch of jokers, acknowledged and applauded the Indian who had taken the battle to them. Who was he?"

"I know now. C K Nayudu."

"Cottari Kanakaiya Nayudu, a Telugu, born and brought up in Nagpur in north India; his father was a contemporary of Ranji. After captaining Modi Cricket Club he made his debut for the Hindus in the Quadrangular Tournament of 1916 at the age of 21, when he was embroiled in the incident with Greig; it was off his bowling that he was stumped. He took four for 27. His first runs in first-class cricket were a six. Between 1916 and 1939, in 52 innings, he slammed 2,156 runs at an average of 45.87. He lived and breathed cricket. He was a brilliant fielder and could turn his arm with medium-pacers. The crowds adopted him as 'C K', the first great Indian cricketer, acknowledged as such by all Indian denominations. In 1923, the ruler of Holkar made him a captain in his army – which explains C K's stern military bearing and attitude, his ability to outswear a trooper and his fortitude against pain. Once a vicious ball shattered his teeth. He refused medical aid, calmly brushed aside his teeth from the wicket, and was visibly miffed when the bowler eased up on the next delivery."

"So C K was the second Indian hero after Baloo."

"Not really. You know that bowlers can never be real heroes. Only batsmen have the copyright to such fame. So, according to all historians, C K was the first glamour boy of Indian cricket.

"Let me give you an instance of Indo-English relationships. A week after the historic match, the MCC played against a combined Hindu-Muslim eleven. C K was at the wicket. The English thought he had been bowled, but the ball had rebounded off the wicketkeeper onto the stumps. C K was walking off when his partner, Vithal, the captain, appealed to the umpire, a Parsee named Warden, who ruled 'not out'. The English were furious and were petulant in the dressing rooms and restaurant; the English had no faith in the competence and fairness of Indian umpires. Then, in another match against the Bombay Presidency XI, when Deodhar made a gallant 148, two boys, one Hindu the other Muslim, ran onto the field in ecstasy and laid their caps at Deodhar's feet in homage. The European umpire, Higgins, kicked the caps away. The captain, Gilligan, apologized to the crowd for Higgins' reprehensible behaviour."

At the end of the tour Gilligan was convinced of the status of Indian cricket and suggested a board of control. In February 1927, Gilligan, Grant-Govan, a businessman, and the Maharaja of Patiala held a meeting at the Roshanara Club in Delhi, and a Board of Control for Cricket in India (BCCI) was formed in December 1928, with Grant-Govan as president and Anthony De Mello as secretary, and India was admitted to the Imperial Cricket Conference in 1929.

"Let us come to 1930. India was in a state of turmoil. Gandhi's Dandi march. Widespread arrests. What do you know about Willingdon?"

"Willingdon was governor of Bombay," I replied at this sudden question, "between 1913 and 1918, governor of Madras between 1919 and 1924, and became Viceroy in 1931. He played for Cambridge, Sussex and the MCC, of which he was once president. When he was governor he organized cricket matches of mixed sides – English and Indian – and threw open the Willingdon Sports Club in Bombay and the Willingdon Club in Madras to all. He was against racial discrimination. Unfortunately, he metamorphosed into a 'jail 'em, flog 'em, fine 'em, shoot 'em' policy man when he became Viceroy. He wanted Ranji to captain India; we know that Ranji didn't want to have anything to do with cricket in India. Duleep was offered the job; Ranji censured him. Though Duleep played in a few tournaments in India – in one of which he neatly executed the first reverse sweep in cricketing history – he never captained a side. He went on to play a dozen times for England between 1929 and 1931. Patiala applied for the job, but he was up for various misdemeanours and Willingdon never liked him."

"That will do, thank you," said Ranga. "Now a new figure appeared over the horizon. A banished member of royalty, who was not even fit to qualify for a place in a first-class cricket side."

Vizianagaram was a substantial state in south India. A quarrel between uncle and nephew forced the uncle to leave the kingdom and live on estates near Benares in north India; his status was akin to a member

378

of the landed gentry, a zamindar. He was not a ruling prince. But he adopted the title of Maharajkumar of Vizianagaram. He may have lacked princely clout but he had panache. He was another who recognized the influence of cricket with the British; he had his own cricket pitch. He put together a team called the Maharajkumar of Vizianagaram's XI and toured India and Ceylon in 1931. Two members of his team were the legendary Jack Hobbs and Herbert Sutcliffe, who only showed their brilliance occasionally on the tour. His team won 17 of the 18 matches, what with C K and Deodhar also playing for them.

Two players of eminence emerged from this tour – Amar Singh and Mushtaq Ali. The tour was slightly marred by an incident not rare in Indian cricket. In the final of the Moin-ud-Dowlah Tournament, Amar Singh dismissed four batsmen with lbw decisions. Vizzy (as he was known to the English) was furious and complained to the tournament committee. The committee, quite rightly, told him to get lost.

After the tour, the overseas players were richly rewarded. The Indian players – amateurs – were given blazers, statuettes, trophies. Hobbs gave a pair of silver hairbrushes to Mushtaq Ali when he took 11 wickets in one match. Everyone was happy. Did I tell you that Vizzy played for his team? He was never a first-class cricketer; a poor batsman, but he insisted on coming in at number three. When he dropped himself down the order, he scored 71 – the only significant score he made. He was in the team only because of himself. Hobbs, as a purely thanksgiving gesture, muttered that Vizzy would make a good captain. The seed was sown. Vizzy became obsessed with the idea. He buttered up Willingdon with a donation of 50,000 rupees. But Willingdon was firmly of the idea: as in politics, so in cricket. The English were the only ones who could rule India; therefore only an Englishman could knit an Indian team together.

MCC versus India – 1932

India was to tour England in 1932.

Enter Bhupendra Singh. He offered to pay all expenses for a whole month for the trials at Patiala for the 50 cricketers. The selection committee became pawns in Patiala's hands. Patiala was captain, Prince Gyanashyamsinghji of Limbdi was vice-captain and Vizzy was made deputy vice-captain – a novel post indeed. A fortnight after the announcement, Vizzy petulantly resigned his post and, for reasons not quite known, Patiala also resigned. Porbander, brother-in-law of Limbdi, and no cricketer, was made captain.

In mid-April 1932 the absurd Indian team arrived in England to play the first Test series between England and India. The maharaja scored six runs in four matches and resigned. The Prince of Limbdi, now captain, made 154 runs in 17 innings with an average of 9.62. C K was the mainstay; he scored 1,618 runs in first-class matches at an average of 40.45 and took 65 wickets at an average of 25.53.

But let us follow the nuances singular to Indian cricket. Limbdi had sustained a back injury making a hundred against the Eastern Counties and could not play the first Test at Lord's. He nominated C K as captain. But Wazir Ali was not pleased. He didn't mind a prince captaining but, if it was to be a plebeian, why not he? I wonder if it had something to do with C K being a Hindu and Wazir a Muslim! Porbander was awakened at 4:00 a.m. on the morning of the Test by Wazir and his coterie. They would not play under C K. The telegraph wires burned between England and India. Finally Patiala ruled that C K would lead.

Saturday, the 25th of June 1932. Three-day Test Match. England versus India. Some 24,000 spectators, a good number of whom were Indian immigrants. England, captained by Jardine, batted first. It had a strong batting line-up – Sutcliffe, Holmes, Woolley, Hammond, Jardine, Paynter, Ames; two fasties in Bowes and Voce and a couple of leg-spinners in Robins and Brown. Eight runs on the board. Start of a Nissar over. Holmes' off stump went walkabout. After 20 minutes of play the scoreboard showed an unbelievable statistic: England were 19 for three against a side that had just entered the Test arena. Then it was 101 for four. They were all out for 249. The damage had been done by two fast bowlers – yes, India had genuine fast bowlers then.

Nissar was a strapping six-foot Punjabi and could swing the ball both ways. Amar Singh, a Sikh, could also swing the ball and, according to Hammond, "Came off the pitch like the crack of doom" – exceptional praise indeed. India were 153 for four at lunch on the second day and seemed quite comfortable despite C K being out for 40. But then followed the (inevitable) collapse; six wickets for 36 runs. England made 275 and declared at noon on the third and final day. You would have bet your money on a draw, wouldn't you? Well, you would have lost your money. India sank without a trace.

C K acknowledged the overall superiority of England and made a few comments about the Indian physical (un)fitness, inabilty to hold catches and lethargic fielding – the banes of Indian cricket even today. C K, even at the age of 37, was a fitness fanatic and gave of his utmost in all departments and the English came out in fulsome praise of not only his cricketing abilities but also his leadership. C K's 32 sixes on the tour rank second to Constantine's 37 in 1928. He was honoured by *Wisden*, which nominated him as one of the 'Five Cricketers of the Year'.

But Wazir, aged 29, was envious and whipped up an anti-C-K feeling, criticizing his leadership. One of his cronies was Amar Singh, who disliked C K for his cold, aloof, no-nonsense disciplinarianism. The two factions never closed ranks against the enemy, England. The Indians divided themselves and allowed the British to rule.

The rancour travelled with them to India.

Between old Mughal Delhi and new British Delhi, created by Lutyens, a new cricket ground came into being – the Feroz Shah Kotla. Vizzy built an impressive pavilion and named it after Willingdon. The inaugural match was between The Rest of India under Vizzy and the 1932 Indian team that went to England. As C K walked out to bat, he was booed by some of his own players sitting in the pavilion.

* * * * * * * *

CHAPTER 34
Merchant; Amarnath

India versus MCC – 1933-34

Ranji died. Patiala was elected Chancellor of the Chamber of Princes. He had ideas of controlling cricket again. But the Willingdon-Vizzy axis must have worked behind the scenes for Patiala found himself cold-shouldered. At an emergency BCCI meeting in Delhi on the 1st of May 1933, three zones were created: the East Zone, represented by Alec Hosie; the North Zone, by E L West; and the West Zone, by H D Kanga, the Parsee. So, two of the three selectors for the Indian team were English. It prepared for the 1933-34 England tour to India. A Test Match was allowed only if the board was guaranteed a certain amount of money. Only Bombay guaranteed the sum. When Secunderabad tried to get into the act, Madras and Calcutta pulled up their socks, and thus the three biggest cities in India hosted the first ever Test series in India.

Except for Jardine, the team had no famous names. It is said that a clerk took this quite personally and sent off a telegram telling them that such a team was an insult to India and signed it as from 'the Indian Board of Control'. Remember that the infamous 'bodyline' tour had just been completed and that Australia was threatening to cancel their tour to England. Lord Hawke was also worried about the team. But in the end, as usual, the Indians backed down; after all England's regular captain was coming.

It was not until 1971 that England honoured India with its best team.

But let us not rush. Patiala was down but not out. His second son, who had been proclaimed heir apparent, was showing signs of becoming a genuine batsman. He had been coached by Leyland, Waddington, Brown, Kilner and Tarrant. In one of the preliminary matches he scored 49 with C K helping him; C K himself made a century and showed the rest of the team that the English were not unbeatable. At Amritsar, the son scored 66; his partner was an unknown called Lala Amarnath who made a splendid 109. Patiala wooed the British in his inimitable style: hunting, banquets, dancing girls – the whole lot. Naturally the British didn't have the heart to wound their generous host – they honourably dropped the catches offered by his son. Patiala even managed to win over the implacable Jardine, who included Patiala in the MCC team for a match in Delhi (!) – much to the chagrin of Willingdon. But all this wining/dining/womanizing/hunting did not get Patiala what he wanted. His son was not picked until the third Test at Madras, where he scored 60. C K was appointed captain.

The 15th to the 18th of December 1933. The first Test at Bombay saw the introduction of two youngsters, Merchant and Amarnath – and two oldsters: Jamshedji, at 41 years the oldest Indian to make a Test debut, and Ramji, ten years older than his brother Amar Singh. The Indians, besides all this communal badgering, fumed that two of their selectors were Englishmen and were incensed that Jardine insisted that both umpires be Englishmen – the old charge of Indian untrustworthiness.

India – 219. Nothing spectacular from anyone. England – 438; Bryan Valentine making 136 on his Test debut in India. Indian second innings: both openers cooling their heels in the pavilion with the score on 21. Enter the young debutant Amarnath to join his captain. C K went up to him with a word of encouragement. That seemed to suffice. Amarnath played one of those brilliant innings that is remembered by friend and foe alike – a hundred in 117 minutes. C K went down the pitch to congratulate his partner, not noticing that the ball wasn't dead. Elliott, the wicketkeeper, could have run C K out. He looked at his captain; Jardine shook his head. Thus was a major incident avoided. The crowd invaded the pitch; garlands were heaped on the hero of the moment; hysterical women removed their jewellery and thrust them into his hands, princes of the land felicitated him with wads of money and the band played 'God save the King'.

What followed was the now familiar collapse. India folded for 258. England won by nine wickets.

But the Indian press and the Indian people were unconcerned. It had its hero. It is the same today. Amidst shattering team defeats, there are spectacular individual achievements.

The Calcutta Test was drawn. The Bengalis were furious that no Bengali was in the team and stayed off in droves.

Madras Test. England – 335. Amar Singh, seven for 86. India – 145; Verity seven for 49. England challenged India with a lead of 451. India could manage only 249.

The now familiar witch-hunt was on. Four Tests (one in England, three in India) – three defeats, one draw. Who was to blame? The captain, of course. He didn't know how to get the best out of his players; he didn't know anything about bowling changes and field placings; he was arrogant and aloof. Jardine had the same problem with his players, some of whom he treated with disdain because of class differences. The essential difference between the English and the Indian was this: where the English players gave of their best despite what they thought of their captain, the Indians visibly pouted and deliberately underachieved – a trait that is sadly existent even today.

The total profit for the board from this tour was a measly 3,000 rupees. Patiala, overjoyed at his son's 60 in the Madras Test, threw in a bit more slush money and announced the donation of a trophy: a Grecian urn, two feet tall with a lid representing Father Time, the design of which was submitted by De Mello and valued at £500, for the Indian National Championship – akin to the County Championship in Britain. He proposed that it be called the Ranji Trophy. But Vizzy objected. Who the hell was Ranji? He had done nothing for Indian cricket. He proposed to call it the Willingdon Trophy and had got a trophy, designed by Lady Willingdon, made of gold. By the time these machinations were completed, the matches of the Ranji Trophy were under way.

Nawanagar was a piddly little state, famous for nothing but droughts, famines and plagues. The ruler of the state adopted Ranji as his successor. But the plan backfired and another became ruler. He was younger than Ranji; so poor Ranji had no chance. But luck was on his side. The young ruler died of typhoid. By this time, Ranji was a world-famous cricketer. He moved in exalted circles; he had the proper contacts – besides the proper breeding. So the British officials made Ranji the ruler on the 10th of March 1907. When the Chamber of Princes was set up to bring the princes together in 1912, Ranji was made Chancellor.

The Ranji Trophy is the most prestigious bauble that Indian cricketers fight for each year. Yet the prince – arguably the greatest cricketer India has ever produced – to whom it is dedicated never played first-class cricket in India and chose not to do anything to further the game in India. I have mentioned his exploits on the field when he played for Cambridge, Sussex and England in an earlier chapter.

The 4th of November 1934: Madras, captained by C P Johnstone, versus Mysore under Major M S Teversham, which Madras won. The final was won by Bombay, and Patiala's trophy was presented by Willingdon. Vizzy got his own back by organizing a Silver Jubilee cricket tournament in commemoration of King George V, winning it and accepting Lady Willingdon's Trophy presented by his pal, Lord Willingdon. Amidst all these shenanigans Patiala managed to dust some of the Australians off their shelves and bring them to India for a winter tour in 1935-36; the Australian pensioners won two and India won two – a drawn series.

Meanwhile the Cricket Club of India had been formed, with Patiala as president and Bombay as its headquarters. (The board's headquarters were in Delhi.) Bombay was expanding. Land was being reclaimed from the Arabian Sea by the government. De Mello strolled into the governor's office and asked, "Your Excellency, which would you prefer to accept from sportsmen; money for your government or immortality for yourself?" Brabourne had little difficulty in choosing. He sold the land to the CCI for just £1 per square yard. Thus was his name immortalized – the great Brabourne Stadium.

MCC versus India – 1936
The Indian tour of England was looming. The Nawab of Pataudi, who had scored a century against the Australians playing for England, refused to captain India due to the fact that several factions were fighting each other. The players were still divided into pro- and anti-C-K camps. Patiala's son was not captain material and was booed in Bombay because he captained the Hindus instead of C K. That left only Vizzy. He had already sewn things up by buying votes all over the country during the course of his politicking.

Vizzy was captain; his wildest dream had come true. There was no vice-captain. He arrived in England like a king with his entourage; two servants and 36 items of luggage. Luncheons with Stanley Baldwin, the Prime Minister, at the House of Commons, and the Royal Empire Society at Hotel Victoria, where Lord Hailsham, the Lord Chancellor, nicknamed him 'Vizzy'; generous bribes to English captains and players to bowl a few long hops at him – and a knighthood. He was now Sir Gajapatiraj Vijaya Ananda, the Maharajkumar of Vizianagaram.

While Vizzy was greasing everyone and being greased, C K captained India against Lancashire. Lancs. was set 199 runs to win. Vizzy was so anti-C-K that he ordered Nissar to aid the Lancs. team by bowling full tosses. After Nissar conceded ten runs in two overs, C K took him off and bowled India to victory. The atmosphere was such that anyone insulting C K was immediately Vizzy's pal. Baqa Jilani, knowing the situation, insulted C K at breakfast one day and was rewarded with a cap. Vizzy took his cronies to Paris and showered them with gifts – leaving C K and his gang behind.

Amarnath had scored a century in each innings against Essex but then had lost form. Against the Minor Counties, Merchant and Mushtaq Ali put on a stand of 215 runs in 140 minutes and Amarnath was waiting to go in. But Vizzy told him to stand down and sent him in with only a few minutes' play left. Always a volatile character, Amarnath exploded with choice expletives. The Vizzy-Willingdon axis sent him packing home despite pleas from some of the players, including C K, and apologies from Amarnath.

Just before the first Test, some of the senior players, fed up with Vizzy's tactics, or the lack of them, demanded that either C K or Wazir be made vice-captain, that selection should be a team effort, that players should be respected and that there should be no preferential treatment of players. One of the players had objected when he was not given a seat when the team was photographed!

Sycophancy. Humiliation. Partiality. Obsecration. Obsequiousness. High-handedness. Brutality. Corruption. Bribery. Self-aggrandizement. Edacity. Rodomontade. Lack of integrity. Lack of team effort. Lack of incentive. No sense of personal or national pride. All of which qualities plague the Indian team even today.

First Test, Lord's. India, 147. G O Allen, five for 35. England, 134. Amar Singh, six for 35.

The next time India secured a first innings lead was in July 1971 at Lord's.

India, 93. England won by nine wickets.

Second Test, Old Trafford. India, 203. England, 571 for eight declared; Hammond a superb 167. India, 390 for five. Bad light.

This was the Test that established the Merchant-Mushtaq duo as opening batsmen – though neither of them were specialist opening bats till then. This happened because the regular opener, Hindlekar, was injured. Merchant was the equivalent of Gavaskar – methodical, sound, the embodiment of concentration; Mushtaq was more like Srikkanth – an explosive swashbuckler. Merchant and Vizzy didn't get on. The story goes that Vizzy asked Mushtaq to run Merchant out. As they went out to bat, Mushtaq told him of the conspiracy; they had a good laugh. The two put on 226 in 150 minutes: Merchant 114, Mushtaq 112. But it was Mushtaq's day. The first 25 runs came in 20 minutes; the 50 in 45. He was walking out to the likes of Larwood and thumping him on the up; he was converting overpitched balls into full tosses and slamming them all over the ground. Old Trafford had not seen anything like it. Even the England players were applauding him. Mushtaq wasn't keeping an eye on the scoreboard. He was slogging away as if he was playing maidan cricket back in India. When he was in his 90s Hammond came up to him and said, "My boy, be steady, get your hundred." Neville Cardus was over the moon: "The feline silkiness conceals the strength of some jungle beauty of gleaming eyes and sharp fangs." That day saw 588 runs being made – a record in Test cricket.

Third Test, Oval. Merchant and Mushtaq made 81 and 64 in the two innings. But the honours went once again to Hammond, who made a scintillating 217, and to C K, whose 81 came near to overshadowing Hammond. He was hit fiercely in the ribs by Allen, but refused to retire; he walked out to the fast bowlers and hooked them to the boundary. C K's knock averted an innings defeat. He was 41 years old and that was to be his last Test.

Two Tests lost; one drawn. In the years to come India would have worse tours, losing all five Tests. Would India have fared better without the dissensions? Neither in politics nor in cricket could the Indians unite.

* * * * * * * *

Merchant was named one of the 'Five Cricketers of the Year' by *Wisden*, only the second Indian after C K Nayudu, for scoring 1,745 runs on the tour, 1,300 as an opening bat. Cardus dubbed him 'India's good European'.

Bradman scored 28,067 runs from 338 innings at an average of 95.14.

Merchant scored 13,248 runs from 229 innings at an average of 71.22.

Today there is a lot of cricket about. In those times it was just weekend club cricket during the winter with half a dozen first-class matches thrown in. Between 1929 and 1935, Merchant played about five first-class matches annually. When the Quadrangular carousel was suspended due to political tension, he didn't play for nearly four years. He had only played 24 first-class matches in six seasons before he went to England in 1936, where within a space of five months he played 23 matches. Indians were just not used to playing so much cricket. During the England tour, only two maintained their fitness: the redoubtable 41-year old C K Nayudu, and 25-year-old Vijay Merchant.

Merchant's figures before England were 24 matches, 1,778 runs, average 52.59. After England, his figures were 47 matches, 3,523 runs, average 51.80. He never fell below 50 in his entire career, which spanned a good 15 years.

How did he prepare for England? He knew that the weather conditions in England would swing the ball, sometimes during the whole day. How do you duplicate those conditions in India? The early morning mist flowing in from the Arabian Sea onto a dew-soaked pitch in Bombay. He had the fastest bowlers having a go at him in the nets. He even built a concrete pitch in his garden and had Amar Singh tearing down at him. When he was in England he asked Jack Hobbs to coach him. He was so meticulous in his approach to the game even in his forties. Such was his ardour for perfection.

Whilst the other players were exhausted after the England tour, Merchant hammered four centuries in four matches, 614 runs in all, at an average of 130.

* * * * * * * *

CHAPTER 35
Duleepsinghji; Mankad; Hazare

Ranji's successor was Digvijayasinghji, the new Jamsahib of Nawanagar. His brother was Duleepsinghji. Whilst Ranji didn't care a hoot about Indian cricket, these two brothers did. They brought Bert Wensley from Sussex and put together a good team. They won the Ranji Trophy in 1936.

Vizzy had disappeared under a cloud of disgrace and Patiala was back at the controls. He helped Digvijay become president of the board in June 1937 after Nawanagar lifted the Ranji Trophy. The Brabourne Stadium in Bombay was now completed and Patiala, who had just then been forced to shell out 10,000 rupees to an Anglo-Indian for seducing his wife, opened it with an inaugural match between the Cricket Club of India and Lord Tennyson's team, made up of a bunch of retired crocks. Nevertheless they still managed to beat India, captained by Merchant. Tennyson won the first two matches, India the next two; the decider by Tennyson.

But let us savour the inevitable skulduggery that flavours Indian cricket. C K was unavailable for the first match, being away on a world tour. He was available for the second and was willing to play under the young Merchant and was included in the team. But Patiala wanted a Patiala player, Mohammed Saeed, in the team; C K learnt about his exclusion in the newspapers. C K was adored by the Bombayites; they went berserk. They were pacified with the news that there would be an extra fifth match in Bombay with C K as captain. But by this time C K had had enough. He bowed out of the game. Meanwhile Digvijay was incensed; he was president of the board and no one had bothered to intimate him of this extra Test. He resigned.

As far as Merchant was concerned, it must have all been too much for him. He managed to scrounge only 98 runs in nine innings. But there was a hero for India. Another instance of the team performing badly with an individual shining in its midst.

Duleep had spotted a short, stocky 19-year-old lad who was a medium pacer. He batted at no. 11. Duleep and Wensley watched him and saw prime material. They soon got rid of his batting weaknesses and made him open the innings; they also saw that his real talent in bowling would be slow spin, rather than medium pace. They taught him about flight, variation of spin and pace, and made him give up his off-breaks and switch to leg-breaks. He also developed a disguised fast one that went with the arm – the freak ball that whipped through. And thus was born India's first great all-rounder. It had fair spinners in Mushtaq, Baloo and Warden. But this lad was India's first world-class slow left-arm spinner of the ball. It can be said that he started the trend of spin bowling for India.

India, in those days – 1926-1937 – had world-class fast bowlers in Nissar, Amar Singh, Ramji, Jehangir; it was a decade of Indian fasties – hard to believe for those who have been brought up with the idea that India's claim to fame was through spin. Even today we bemoan our inability to produce genuine pace bowlers.

Nissar and Amar played only six and seven Tests, and took 25 and 28 wickets respectively – all in England against the best sides in the world. Nissar took five wickets in an innings three times, Amar twice. They could have returned better figures if Indian fielding were more diligent and internal politics less prolific. Just to emphasize their roles, let me state that, between them, they used to bowl over 100 overs in a Test Match. The Tennyson tour was the last for Nissar and Amar. Amar died of pneumonia two years later at the age of only 30. Nissar lived to see the magic of spin established in Indian cricket.

It is also hard to believe that Indian batsmen of those times were more comfortable against fast bowling than spin; yet it was so. They were flabbergasted by opposition spinners. Now, of course, Indian batsmen lick their lips when they see spinners coming on.

Let us return to the stocky lad. In his first match he scored 86 and took three for 23. In the final of the Ranji Trophy that Nawanagar won, he made 185, 100 of them in fours. During the Tennyson tour, he headed the batting and bowling averages of both sides: 62.66 and 14.53 respectively.

Who was he? Mulvantrai Himatlal Mankad, known as 'Vinoo' by his chums, the son of a Gujarati doctor who cast aside academic qualifications for his love of cricket.

Lord Tennyson was given Patiala's special hospitality of sightseeing, shooting, gifts and pleasures. A few weeks later hundreds of wives, harlots and paramours, fairly active participants in polygamy and concubinage, cast aside their jewels, shred their clothes, banged their heads against the walls, wailed like proverbial banshees and shed copious tears. Bhupendra Singh, Maharaja of Patiala, had joined his ancestors.

* * * * * * * *

The results of the first five years of the Ranji Trophy: Bombay twice, Nawanagar, Hyderabad and Bengal once each. But the Indian people preferred to attend the Quadrangular and Pentagular Series based on religions, where both the spectators and the players were fired up.

World War II saw the end of international participation for Indian cricket. It was now that the Ranji Trophy came into its own.

Lord Linlithgow, the Viceroy, representing the Emperor, without even a show of decent protocol, without any parley with the Indians then elected to the Legislature as a prelude to self-government, with the abrupt arrogance of the British of those times, made a mockery of democracy and thrust a population of nearly 400 million people into a war several thousand miles from home – a war that was fought for the principles of democracy, independence and self-government. That announcement on the 3rd of September 1939 proves that Britain was not even considering relinquishing its hold on India; New Delhi was barely seven years old. Thus was the world's greatest volunteer army in human history recruited – two and half million Indians fought in the various spheres of war for the British simply because India was a colony, simply obeying an Imperial order.

Australia, New Zealand, the West Indies and India saw little of the madness that consumed Europe.

There was no international cricket for the duration of the war; but, whereas the other countries suspended their domestic engagements, India did not. Indian cricket was to experience a renaissance in the art of batting.

But let us once again enter into the politics of cricket. D B Deodhar was a contemporary of C K. Though he was a renowned cricketer, somehow he never got to play for India. He was a Hindu from Poona and played in the Quadrangular tournaments. But Bombay's Hindu Gymkhana treated him shabbily; you see, he was an outsider. The presidency of Bombay included Bombay city (which had by now surpassed the earlier importance of Poona), Poona and other cricketing centres in Gujarat and Maharashtra. The Bombay city coterie, with their now usual attitude of arrogance, showed scant respect to the 'outsiders'. So Maharashtra and Gujarat broke away from Bombay and formed their own teams. Deodhar, a Maharashtrian, had had enough of this nonsense and started to look around. He found a 24-year-old Protestant Maharashtrian. He was under the aegis of the Maharaja of Dewas, a 15-gun-salute ruler of some 83,000 subjects. The maharaja took a fancy to the wife of his son, Vikram Singh. She scorned his advances with regal disdain. He tried to poison his own son but failed. He banished his daughter-in-law and proclaimed that his son was illegitimate and therefore not the legal heir. He seemed to belong to the same ilk as Patiala, the difference being that he was not as wealthy. He soon frittered away his treasury and fled to Pondicherry, a French State, where the British could not get at him. Our Vikram Singh was installed as ruler of Dewas. His brother-in-law was the Raja of Jath. Both were cricket fans. They brought Clarrie Grimmett over as coach and asked him to see to the young Protestant. They wanted him to be a leg-spinner. But Grimmett saw that he would never be one. He was a medium pacer, in which capacity he had taken six for 54 against Tennyson's team in the final match. He came in to bat at number nine; the only significant occurrence when he was at the crease was an earthquake that frightened the trousers off the Englishmen. He had a funny stance, hands wide apart, bat firmly tucked in between his pads. Grimmett's method of coaching was to throw tennis balls at him from ten yards and shout instructions as to how to play them. He was even sent to England on a private tour to watch Bradman, Hammond and Hutton.

In the first match at Poona Club, Maharashtra versus Western India, the former made 543 for eight declared – a record – and our protégé took seven for 94. The Maharashtra rabbits had won their first Ranji Trophy match in five years. The next match was against Baroda. Baroda made 303. C.S Nayudu, C K's brother, was playing for Baroda and thought he could run through the opposition with his leg-spinners. He was in for a surprise. At the end of the second day, the unknown Maharashtrian entity was still at the crease with 165 to his name. He was still there at lunch on the third day; in fact he was there till Maharashtra declared at 650 for nine, our man surpassing Wazir Ali's 222 and Amarnath's 241 and amassing a personal score of 316 not out in seven hours – the first Indian to score a triple century in India. (Duleep had done so in England.) He also established a record 245 for the ninth wicket with Nagarwalla. In the semi-finals against Southern Punjab, he made 155. In the final against the United Provinces, he made a paltry 53. But Maharashtra lifted the Ranji Trophy.

In one season he had scored 619 runs at an average of 154.75.

Who was he? Vijay Samuel Hazare.

Vijay Merchant had scored 456 runs at an average of 114.

The stage was set for a battle between the two 'Vijays'. Vijay means 'victory'.

1940-41 season. Merchant played only two matches: 109 against Maharashtra; 137 against Ceylon. Hazare – 117 against Gujarat; 164 against Western India; 137 against Madras; 182 against the Europeans.

1941-42 season. Merchant – 243 not out against the Muslims; against the Parsees he slammed 221; 170 not out against Nawanagar; 153 against Sind. In that season, he made four consecutive scores of over 150 – a record. A total of 932 runs in seven innings with an unbelievable average of 233. Hazare had now left Maharashtra, who then sank like the Titanic, and was now under the wing of the Maharaja of Baroda. He made only one century.

1942. The 'Quit India' movement. The Congresswallahs were slapped in jail. The Hindus withdrew from the Pentagular. So Merchant was cooling his heels attending to his family business...as a merchant. Hazare accumulated 398 runs that season without once scoring a century. C S Nayudu rewrote the record books, taking 40 wickets in four matches at a truly incredible average of 12.85.

1942. Famine in Bijapur. Cyclone in Bengal. Brabourne Stadium staged a match to raise funds. The total of 1,376 for the first two innings is a record. Merchant was bowled for one by Mankad and for six by Hazare. Hazare scored 250.

1943-44. Merchant – 62 versus the Europeans. Hazare – 248, broke Merchant's record of 243. The next week, it was shattered by Merchant scoring 250 against the Rest in the final. Let us stay with this match awhile. Merchant had declared when he reached 250, with the Hindu score on 518 for eight. Hazare had bowled nearly 50 overs of medium pace and Merchant guessed that he would be tired. Any human being would be. He was proved right. Hazare made a measly 59 and the Rest were skittled out for 133 and made to follow on. Tired and humiliated, they slumped in no time to 60 for five. Hazare was still there hanging on for dear life. He was joined by his brother Vivek. You would have gone home; the result was a foregone conclusion; you wouldn't have bet a penny on the Rest. You would have lost your bet, but you would have missed one of the most glorious days of cricket ever played anywhere in the world. Vivek stayed with this brother for five and a half hours presenting the deadest of bats for a grim 21, while Hazare batted and batted and batted for six hours and forty minutes to score 309 runs out of a total of 387 – one of the more remarkable statistics of the game. The Rest still lost by an innings, but who would grudge Hazare his day? It was textbook cricket; it was an exhibition of concentration and dedication. Only once did he, uncharacteristically, lift the ball for a six in that massive total.

In spite of the match not being broadcast, Indian jungle drums started to beat and people started to pour into the great Brabourne Stadium. When Hazare finally walked back to the pavilion, the ecstatic Indians indulged in their peculiar whim of *darshan*, which meant even just a glimpse of their hero. Merchant went into the dressing room and ushered Hazare onto the balcony, and he uttered the words that Merchant had coached him to say. The crowd, satisfied, departed on a wave of euphoria. They would tell strangers on the street about what they had witnessed; they would tell their grandchildren that they were present on that historic day.

The next week, Bombay played Baroda. Both the Vijays scored centuries. But the question everyone was asking was, "When will Merchant reply to Hazare?"

The answer came at the end of the year, when Bombay played Maharashtra in the Ranji Trophy. Merchant put on a stand, still unsurpassed – for the sixth wicket – of 371, with 19-year-old Rusi Modi making his debut with a brilliant 163. When he came in to sup his cup of tea on the second day, the scoreboard had 240 against his name. "Could he beat Hazare's 316?" was on everyone's lips. Merchant was tired. He thought of playing safe and seeing out time. His colleagues gathered round him and said that, if he was tired, so were the bowlers. That decided him. Twenty minutes before closing time, he reached 300; 10 minutes later he had crossed 316. That night he slept with a smile. He walked out the following morning and carried his bat to the end. The record was his; 359 not out. Bombay were 735.

Rest of India versus Western India. Merchant injured his finger and did not bat, but Hazare compensated the crowd with 233 and 87.

That season Merchant made 865 runs in five innings; average 288.33. Hazare, in six innings, scored 248, 59, 309, 101, 223 and 87, thus becoming the first Indian to score more than 1,000 runs in a season.

When did the two Vijays play together? Early in the 1944-45 season, in a match between the CCI and an English Services XI that included Jardine and Compton. It was a fun match and both the Vijays enjoyed themselves by scoring double centuries. Compton was impressed.

Another fellow was making his mark on Indian cricket: Rusi Modi. He scored 160 against Sind and along with Merchant's 84 set up a 205-run stand. In the next match both of them established an as yet unbeaten record stand of 373 for the third wicket, Modi scoring 210 and Merchant 217. Modi followed this up with a 245 not out against Baroda. In the semi-final, he made 113. The final was between Bombay and Holkar. Holkar was led by the still-around C K Nayudu. He had in his team his brother, C S, Mushtaq Ali and...Dennis Compton, who happened to be at Mhow, 14 miles from Indore. Rusi Modi made 98 in a Bombay total of 462. Holkar replied with 360, Mushtaq making 109. Now Merchant had a reputation; he either failed or scored a double century. He had failed in the first innings, making only four. True to form, in the second innings, he made good with 278 – an epic innings lasting for just over eight hours, comprising a third wicket stand of 226 with Modi making 151 and a fourth wicket stand of 246 with Cooper contributing 104. He thus made 1,000 runs in the season and became the only player to score four double hundreds in a season in India – he had made 221 against the Parsees earlier. Bombay were all out for 764, made in 670 minutes. Only New South Wales making 770 against South Australia in 1920-21 has scored more runs in a second innings.

Holkar was left to make the trifling sum of 867 to win. An Indore merchant offered the incentive – 50 rupees for every run a player makes beyond a century. Mushtaq scored a century. Compton walked over, congratulated him and told him that they could still win the match. But Mushtaq was never a cautious fellow; he just had to play his shots. He was out for 139. Compton soon ran out of partners. Only the no. 11, a chap called Rawal, held out. While he stolidly kept his end, Compton got the runs. They put on 109 for the last wicket. Compton's final score was 249 and Holkar was beaten by 377 runs.

Did Mushtaq and Compton get the prize money from the Indore businessman? No. The blighter had simply vanished.

That match was played over six days without any rest day. A total of 2,078 runs had been scored, and 694.5 overs had been bowled. The entire 33 hours of play was broadcast by All-India Radio. Throughout that marathon match, there was only one commentator – a Parsee, A F S Talyarkan, the first cricket commentator in India. Subsequently, when AIR suggested a team of commentators, A F S packed his bags and left in a steamy cloud of indignation and vanity.

On April Fool's Day 1945, Merchant led an Indian team to Ceylon. Merchant was run out for 36 and Hazare top-scored with 70. But Mankad saved the day by taking eight for 35, giving India the vital first innings lead in a drawn match.

The questions to be asked were:

a. Could the Indians perform as well on pitches outside India?

b. Could the Indians perform against class opposition?

We shall have to wait and see.

* * * * * * * *

CHAPTER 36
1945 – 1947; Independence

World War II was over. Hitler had taken the easy way out. Japan was wreathed in radioactive fall-out. Britain got to know all about spartan living. Russia dug in with its Communist theory. America was now kingpin. India was a hotbed of turmoil. There was much political ill feeling, with strikes and riots being the order of the day.

As a sort of diversion an Australian Services side toured England for five 'Victory Tests', a series which was drawn 2-2 despite the anonymity of the Australian team and the almost full-strength England side; remember, Compton was still in India. On the way back they stopped over in India to play three matches. The first two were drawn and India won the last match at Madras.

But questions were being asked.

a. The Indian batting was shown to be brittle against foreign opposition despite the exploits of the Vijays and others during the war years.

b. It was all about individual achievement. Let me give you an example. Merchant, in 11 seasons, had averaged below 100 only thrice; yet Bombay had won the Ranji Trophy only twice.

c. Matches were being decided on first innings scores. Bombay once scored 645 runs in two days and Baroda replied with 465 for six in two days. The match had to be decided on the spin of a coin – Baroda won. The Indians did not seem to know Test Match cricket

tactics, where a first innings lead is immaterial.
d. Why had Merchant insulted Mankad by underbowling him?
e. Merchant seemed to think that a draw was a win. He played safe even in ludicrous circumstances. Once the Aussies were left to make 113 runs in 20 minutes. Despite the ironclad situation, Merchant ordered his bowlers to bowl wides.
f. Both the Vijays were playing safe textbook cricket, rarely lifting the ball. The more flamboyant Mushtaq and Modi, however, did not seem to be consistent. Young players were emulating the Vijays.

Thus it came to be that the Indian people came to expect large scores from safe batsmen and also to feel that a draw was akin to a win – a philosophy that still hovers over the playing fields of India.

1945 – Ceylon versus India
The weather spoilt the game. Ceylon made 107, with Mankad taking eight for 35, and India replied with 179. Ceylon rebounded to a certain extent, with Sathasivam making 111.
Draw.
It was time for some real cricket.

1946 – MCC versus India
The plots thickened behind closed doors.
India was due to visit England.

The board held a meeting at the Connemara Hotel in Madras. Duleep was voted out of the selection committee; Pankaj Gupta, a hockey man, was elected tour manager; Pataudi was elected captain.

How did Pataudi come to be captain? After all, he had opted out in 1932 and 1936 and had not played any serious first-class cricket for ten years – and he was 36. Britain at last got round to the fact that it had to give India its independence. But the princes held out, screaming for dominion status. It was absurdly illogical. But the Chancellor of the Chamber of Princes was the Nawab of Bhopal, father-in-law of the Nawab of Pataudi. It seemed a good time for a prince to captain India. Maybe that would, by some convoluted means, give a signal to the British to grant dominion status.

India played 29 matches, won 11, lost four and drew 14 – its best record until 1986.

Three Test Matches. Two drawn, one lost.

Merchant, aged 36, was a vegetarian and found appropriate nourishment hard to come by. He lost a stone and was ill. But still he topped the Test averages: 245 runs at 49. He also topped the tour averages – 2,385 runs at 74.53 – and became the first Indian to score more than 2,000 runs on a tour. The following figures will illustrate his grit in the face of adversity – adversity against food, against the capricious English weather, against internal politics...and against English bowling. At Leicester he scored 111n.o. out of a total of 198 and 57 n.o. out of a total of 107. Against Lancashire he made 93 not out and 242 not out and a masterly 128 in the last Test.

Hazare, aged 31, was second in the averages: 1,344 runs at 49.77. But, unlike Merchant, he was an all-rounder. He opened the innings with his medium pacers along with Amarnath. He bowled 604 overs and took 56 wickets. His one big score was against Yorkshire, where he made 232.

Remember Amarnath – the fellow who last played a Test in 1934 and was sent packing in 1936 for throwing a few choice expletives at Vizzy? Well, he was now 35 and opened the Indian bowling with his awkward run-up and delivery action. He didn't do much really. In the first Test he had figures of five for 118; in the second he took five for 96.

Mankad, aged 29. He was overshadowed during the war years by the two Vijays. He was the first Indian to achieve the double of 1,000 runs and 100 wickets in England; the last tourist to do it was Constantine in 1928. He bowled 1,160 overs and nabbed 129 wickets at an average of 20.76, displaying his considerable abilities at flight, spin and guile. His tally of runs was 1,120 at 28.00 despite being shuffled from opening bat to number nine by his captain. Arthur Gilligan rated him the best spin bowler he had seen. Both Merchant and Mankad received fulsome praise in the pages of *Wisden.*

Well, what about the captain, the Nawab of Pataudi? He was 36 and had last played in England in 1938. In five Test innings he made a total of 55 but he was third in the tour averages with 981 runs at 46.71. He was not an inspiring captain and had made a few decisions bordering on the absurd.

First Test – Lord's. India, 200. Bedser ripped through the side with figures of seven for 49. England replied with a massive 428, Hardstaff clobbering 205. Amarnath took five wickets for 118. India replied with 275; Mankad, 63, and Amarnath, 50. England made up the deficit runs and won by ten wickets.

What else did you expect? It was January and the weather must have defeated the Indians as much the players.

Second Test – Manchester. England, 294; Mankad – five for 101 – and Amarnath – five for 96 – shared the wickets equally. India, 170, Merchant the only one fighting, with 78. Pollard five for 24. England replied with 153 for five declared and India managed to hold out to a draw with 152 for nine, Hazare making 44. Bedser scalped seven for 52.

Third Test – Oval. India made a creditable 331, Merchant playing a gritty 128. England made 95 for three before the skies opened and it was a draw.

England won the rubber 1-0.

* * * * * * * *

Independence

Lord Louis Mountbatten, the last Viceroy of India, called for a press conference. It was only the second time in the history of British India that such a conference was held. It was also the last. Some 300 journalists were there from all over the world. After he had answered or parried all their questions, Mountbatten was asked one final question.

"Sir, if all agree that there is a most urgent need for speed between today and the transfer of power, surely you should have a date in mind?"

"Yes, indeed," replied Louis.

"And if you have chosen a date, sir, what is that date?"

"The final transfer of power to Indian hands will take place on the 15th of August 1947."

With typical arrogance he had not consulted a single Indian.

India was stunned. So were Downing Street and Buckingham Palace. As soon as All-India Radio announced Louis' bombshell, the Indian astrologers ran for their almanacs.

On the 15th of August 1947, India would lie under the zodiacal sign of inauspicious Capricorn passing through the influence of Saturn under the star Rahu. Saturn, Jupiter and Venus would all be in the ninth house of Karmasthan, the most accursed site in the heavens. Swami Madananand of Calcutta wrote to Mountbatten; "For the love of God, do not give India her independence on the 15th of August. If floods, drought, famine and massacres follow, it will be because free India was born on a day cursed by the stars."

Subsequent history has proved that the forecast was true. India did suffer from all those calamities, immediately starting with the massacre of at least a million people on both sides as more than ten million refugees started their painful trek across the borders of India.

Congress insisted that their new country retain the original name, India, and not be called Hindustan. That was right of them. The name India was derived from the river Indus. Partition saw it going to Pakistan. That was wrong. The great river should have been given to India. Undue haste and lack of historical knowledge are to blame.

Every government possession had to be divided – 20% to Pakistan, 80% to India. And they had exactly 73 days in which to do it. Tables, chairs, hat pegs, hat pegs with mirrors, book shelves, iron safes, table lamps, typewriters, fans, clocks, bicycles, inkstands, staff cars, sofas, chamber pots, spittoons, pincushions, dishes, silverware, portraits, calendars, turbans, leggings, rifles, bullets, lathis, musical instruments, bulldozers, wheelbarows, shovels, locomotives, artillery, ponies, camels, encyclopaedias, dictionaries, library books – everything had to be divided. India kept the only printing press and Pakistan had to rubber stamp its currency 'Pakistan'. The Muslims wanted to dismantle the Taj Mahal and cart it over to Pakistan as it was built by a Muslim; India told them where to go. India is now universally recognized by the Taj Mahal, a Muslim creation. The gold and white viceregal train came to India, the private cars of the commander-in-chief of the Indian army and the governor of Punjab went to Pakistan. The Viceroy had 12 horse-drawn carriages, six trimmed in gold, six in silver. Mountbatten's ADC, Lieutenant Commander Peter Howes, flipped a coin before Pakistan's Major Yacoub Khan and India's Major Gobind Singh. Singh shouted, 'Heads!' – and was lucky. Harnesses, whips, coachman's boots, wigs, uniforms, etc. were divided. The Indian army had 1.2 million Hindus, Muslims and Sikhs. Jinnah did not want the Hindus and Sikhs. The Muslims had to make a choice; some decided to stay on in India, some went over to Pakistan. In many families, a brother elected to stay while another elected to go; a father served India, while a son served Pakistan. Many of them came to fight each other soon after partition when Pakistan invaded Kashmir.

The House of Lords. The Clerk of Parliament reached for his pile of bills.

"The South Metropolitan Gas Bill."

"Le Roi le veult," replied the Clerk of the Crown.

"The Felixstowe Pier Bill."

"Le Roi le veult."

"The Indian Independence Bill."

"Le Roi le veult."

Prime Minister Clement Attlee, at the head of a 38-member delegation from the House of Commons, flushed and lowered his eyes as four words of archaic French consigned Britain's 'Jewel in the Crown' to the pages of history – and memory.

Gandhi asked Mountbatten to stay on after partition and be India's first Governor General. Mountbatten was overwhelmed. "We've jailed him, we've humiliated him, we've scorned him. We've ignored him and he still had the greatness of spirit to do this."

Jinnah said, "In Pakistan, I will be Governor General and the Prime Minister will do what I tell him to do."

The Union Jack was lowered and the Indian tricolour unfurled.

Nehru made his famous extempore speech.

He later came to Mountbatten, who poured him a glass of port.

"To India," said Louis.

"To King George VI," said Nehru.

"What a man!" thought Louis. "After all he's been through, on this, of all nights, he has the elegance, the grandeur of soul to make a gesture like that."

* * * * * * * *

CHAPTER 37
1947 – 1955

Communal cricket rightly came to an end after partition as political and religious frenzy spilled over onto the playing fields of India.

Ranji Trophy final – Baroda versus Holkar
Holkar was bundled out for just over 200, with Hazare scalping six enemy wickets for 85. Baroda was a reasonable 91 for three when Gul Mohammed strolled in from the pavilion to join Hazare. The record for any Indian wicket was 410, held by Amarnath and Modi. The world record stand for any wicket was a massive 574 by Worrall and Walcott at Port of Spain. Well, these records were not in the minds of Mohammed and Hazare when they came together. They batted and batted and batted for the incredible stand of 577, when Mohammed was out for a tired 319. Hazare went later for 288. This record still stands.

1947-48 – India tour to Australia
De Mello was now president of the board. Merchant backed out. Mushtaq's brother died and he opted out. The Maharaja of Holkar persuaded him to go but De Mello told him that it was too late. So India went to Australia with no recognized openers.

First Test – Brisbane. Australia, 382 for eight; Bradman, 185. India folded like a pack of cards for 58, with only Sarwate, Hazare and Amarnath reaching double figures. Toshack had the incredible figures of five for two! India followed on but did not do much

better and were out for 98, this time with four Indians –
Sarwate, Mohammed, Adhikari and Hazare – reaching
double figures. Toshack helped himself to another six
Indian scalps for 29.

Australia won by an innings and 226 runs. A
humiliating defeat for India.

Second Test – Sydney. This petered out to a
draw due to inclement weather. The only significant
thing to note is that Bradman was bowled by Hazare for
only 13.

Third Test – Melbourne. Australia 394, the Don
making 132. Amarnath and Mankad took four wickets
each. India replied with 291, Mankad making 116 of
them. Australia replied with 255 for four declared in
their second innings, with the Don making another ton –
127 – and Barnes 100. India folded for 125. Australia
won by another huge margin of 233 runs.

And so we come to the fourth Test at Adelaide.
Australia, 674. India, 381, Hazare's contribution a
studied 116. India followed on. Hazare made 145. Thus
he joined the coterie of batsmen who scored a century in
each innings – Bradman, Hammond, Compton, Sutcliffe,
Headley, Bardsley.

So once again, while India, as a team, fared
badly, an individual had covered himself in glory.

Fifth Test – Melbourne. Australia, 575, with
Bradman retiring hurt at 57, but Harvey helped himself
to 153. India replied with 331, Mankad making 111, and
followed on and collapsed for 67, thus giving Australia
another innings win besides 177 runs.

Australia won the rubber 4-0.

1948-49 – the West Indians come to India.

Nehru was keen on cricket and wanted a match in Delhi. So the first Test to be played in India after independence was in the capital.

First Test – Delhi. The West Indies scores a massive 631; Walcott, 152, Gomez, 101, Weekes, 128, Christiani 107. That must be some record. Rangachari took five for 107 – very creditable under the circumstances.

India replied with 454 – on any other occasion, a very good score; Adhikari, 114.

The match eventually petered out into a draw.

Second Test – Bombay. The West Indies scores another massive 629 for six declared; Rae, 104, Weekes, 194. India, 273, only Phadkar making 74. India followed on and made 333 for three, with two centurions: Modi, 112, and Hazare, 134.

Another draw.

Third Test – Calcutta. The West Indies scores a paltry 266. Weekes was enjoying his tour and made 101; Walcott was also on form, with 108. India replied with 325 for three, with Mushtaq making 106 and Modi 87.

Again a draw.

Fourth Test – Madras. The West Indies made another big score – 582. This time the high scorers were Rae, 109, and Stollmeyer, 160. But Phadkar took seven West Indian scalps for 159. India replied with 245 and 144 and lost the match by an innings and 193 runs.

Final Test – Brabourne Stadium, Bombay. West Indies, 286. India, 193. West Indies, 267. India had to score 361 in 395 minutes; a gettable score. End of fourth day, India 90 for three, with Hazare and Modi at the crease. So 271 runs had to be scored on the final day in 300 minutes; still an eminently achievable chore. Hazare and Modi were still together at lunch; 175. Slowly the score crept to 200. The West Indies panicked. They switched to Jardine's bodyline tactics; they bowled short on the leg side and packed the leg side field with six players. Modi departed after a gritty 86. Hazare was hit by a short ball and couldn't even stand. He was out for 122. The Indians had their tea hoping to score 72 runs with four wickets in hand. Adhikari and Banerjee fell; 40 runs with two wickets in hand. The crowd was silent. The bush telegraph sent out the message that India could win. Bombayites rushed excitedly to the ground.

Fifteen minutes; 21 runs needed. The West Indians were desperate. They called for drinks and loitered between every ball. Fourteen balls remaining; 11 runs for a historic win. You would have thought that the stadium was empty. Everyone stopped breathing.

Ball 1 – Leg side. No stroke.

Ball 2 – Short ball. Phadkar sent it to the boundary.

Ball 3 – A single.

Ball 4 – No run.

Ball 5 – Bouncer. No run.

Ball 6 – Was not bowled!!

The bloody umpire, a nitwit called Joshi, in his excitement had lost count and called the end of the over. He not only called a premature end of the over but to the whole match! He removed the bails and the teams returned to the pavilion.

Can you ever believe that?

What was the other umpire doing? What were the players and the idiots in the pavilion doing? And the crowd – why didn't they react?

Who is more guilty? The West Indians who resorted to bodyline and wasted time shamelessly, contrary to the spirit of the game; or the incompetent Indian umpire? Thus was India deprived of a very possible win and a squaring of the series.

Umrigar made his debut against the West Indies but didn't set the world on fire.

* * * * * * * *

Let us leave cricket for a while and turn to a bit of gossipry. The West Indians claimed that the 'servants'allotted to them during the tour were thieves or halfwits – something that I can very well believe. They also claimed that the Indian board gave them a paltry ten quid despite the full attendances over the country – this too I can well believe. They also made a fuss about the appalling state of the hotels they stayed in; this also could be true. They also grumbled over the long, tiring distances they had to travel by train; they were given air travel despite the fact that India was involved in a war with the Pakistanis soon after independence and the military had air priority.

What about the Indian team? They were put up in even more shoddy hotels and made to travel third class in trains. And they were paid sums that could hardly keep body and soul together. Amarnath lost his shirt and rightly complained. De Mello was furious and sacked him from the captaincy. He brought back Merchant as captain; but Merchant was just a pale shadow of his former self.

* * * * * * * *

The MCC couldn't make it so soon after the war as Britain was in dire straits; so De Mello brought over a Commonwealth team. Nothing much happened except the battle between Worrall and Hazare. The former scored 684 runs in nine innings at 97.71, while the latter amassed 677 runs in ten innings at 96.71. Kanpur held its first match.

The next year another Commonwealth team toured India. Once again Hazare topped the averages; 634 runs at 79.25. The Commonwealth players were given better accommodation and food, whilst the Indians lodged in wretched hotels with inadequate blankets, appalling food, with cockroaches as bed-mates.

* * * * * * * *

In August 1951 the Indian board ensconsed themselves in the Imperial Hotel, New Delhi. Armed with alcohol and malice, they set about sacking De Mello, installing A J C Mukherjea as president – and remember Vizzy? He was now a vice-president. Amarnath was still the bad boy; Merchant had come to the end of his tether; Hazare was made captain for the forthcoming England tour of India.

India had now played 20 Tests in 20 years. No wins. Nine draws.

1951-52 – MCC visits India

The MCC sent not a second-rate team but a third-rate team to India.

First Test – Delhi. England, 203; Shinde, six for 91. India, 418 for six declared; Merchant 154, Hazare 164. England 368, Watkins making 137; Mankad, four for 58. Draw.

Merchant retired from Test cricket. He had played all his 18 Tests against England, scoring 859 runs at a creditable 47.72.

Second Test – Bombay. India, 485 for nine declared; Pankaj Roy, 140, Hazare, 155. England replied well with 456, Tom Graveney making 175; Mankad again four for 91. The second time around, India made 208 and England 55 for two, and it ended in a tame draw.

Third Test – Calcutta. England, 342; Mankad again four for 89. India, 344; Phadkar, 115. England 252for five.

Draw.

Fourth Test – Kanpur. India made a paltry 121, with only Roy, Mankad and C S Nayudu reaching double figures. Tatersall was the one who made India look tattered with six for 48. England were bowled out for 203, with Ghulam Ahmed taking five for 70 and – yes – Mankad, four for 54. India, 157, Hilton taking five for 61. England made the required runs for the loss of two wickets and won the match.

Fifth Test – Madras. First innings: England, 266; Mankad,this time, eight for 55. India a good 457; Roy, 111, and Umrigar, 130. This was India's chance for a win, if ever there was one. England folded for 183; Mankad, four for 53; Ghulam Ahmed, four for 77.

It had come to pass. An Indian win by an innings and eight runs.

The rubber was a draw 1-1.

Hazare was not a dashing captain by any stretch of the imagination. He was a man who played safe – even when there were no ghosts in the dark. The selectors didn't particularly aid him as they played lucky dip with the players. They used three wicketkeepers, four opening pairs and four opening bowlers, chopping and changing according to their whims and fancies.

V L Manjrekar made his debut quietly.

1952 – Indian tour to England

A Lancashire club, Haslingdon, offered a £1,000 contract to Mankad. Mankad approached the board and asked about his place in the Indian team to tour England. The board could not give him the word of guarantee. Can you believe that? A player of Mankad's calibre, the hero of the only Test that India had won, and that too against England, was made to languish!

India had no specialist opening batsmen – no Mankad, no Amarnath, no Mushtaq. To top it all, Hazare, the captain, decided that the 'seniors' would play all the pre-Test fixtures; the 'juniors' would have to sit them out, watch the seniors and learn the game. Absurd!

First Test – Leeds   India, 293; new boy Manjrekar, 133. England, 334; Ghulam Ahned took five for 100. India faltered the second time around with 165, only Hazare 56, Phadkar 64 and Ghulam 14 reaching double figures, with five players out for ducks. Trueman and Jenkins enjoyed themselves immensely with four for 27 and four for 50 respectively. England made the required runs for the loss of three wickets and won comfortably.

Second Test – Lord's. Let me just give the statistics first. India, 235; Mankad, 72, and Hazare, 69. England, 537; Hutton, 150, Evans, 104; Mankad, five for 196.

India, 378; Mankad, 184. England, 79 for two. England won by eight wickets. But this Test has gone down in the annals of Indian history as heroic – despite the loss. Why? Because of Vinoo Mankad.

It was plain for even a moron to see that Mankad had to be reinstalled. Haslingdon wanted £300 to release him. After a lot of humming and hawing the Indian board coughed up the sum. Mankad seemed to play with a vengeance; he wanted to rub the noses of the Indian selectors in the English mud. He opened the innings and top-scored with a brilliant 72. India, 235. Then he bowled and bowled and bowled 73 overs for five for 196. England's first innings score was a huge 537. After bowling 31 of his overs on the Saturday, he came out to open the innings again. He once again pulverized the England bowlers. He was still at the crease at the end of the day with India's score at 137 for two. On Monday, the Queen came to see the match. Mankad must have planned a special treat for her. He demonstrated what batting was all about. It was not mindless slogging. It was a clinical display of cold, controlled, classic cricket. He was finally out four and half hours later for 184 – the highest for an Indian in Tests, surpassing Hazare's 164. In the process he and his partner, Hazare – who was almost a nonentity on that day, letting Mankad have his moment of glory – equalled the third wicket record partnership of 211 established by Merchant and Hazare. Hazare made a mere 49. India's final score was 378.

England had to score just 77 to win. Just 80 minutes of the day's play remained. Mankad on again. He scrubbed the ball on the turf and sent down 24 meticulous overs for just 35 runs, denying England a win that day. The English batsmen thought that they were wearing straitjackets, not England sweaters. They managed only 40 runs. The following morning England made the required runs and won by eight wickets.

The second Test at Lord's is now referred to in cricketing circles as 'England versus Mankad' – and quite rightly so. The others simply folded.

Third Test – Manchester. England, 347; Hutton, 104. India scored just 58, with only Hazare, Manjrekar and Mankad reaching double figures. Fiery Fred Trueman ran through the Indians like a hot knife through butter, taking eight wickets for 31. Following on, India scraped together 82, with Adhikari, Hazare and Mankad reaching double figures. This time around, Alec Bedser and Tony Lock did the damage, taking five for 27 and four for 36 respectively.

England won by an innings and 207 runs.

Fourth Test – Oval. England, 326; David Shepperd, 119. India were slaughtered for 98 by Bedser and Trueman, and English weather saw to a draw.

Manjrekar made a brilliant century in the first Test, proving his class, but achieved nothing else thereafter.

It was Umrigar who was the shame of the Indian contingent. His tour statistics show that he made 1,688 runs at 48.22, proof of a master batsman. But in seven Test innings he made a measly 43 at 6.14. He was absolutely terrified of Trueman running towards him like a half-crazed gorilla. He just shivered in his cricketing boots and sought refuge behind the square-leg umpire.

England won the series 3-0.

* * * * * * * *

1952-53 – India versus Pakistan

The war with Pakistan was over. The bunch of fanatic converts had usurped a sizeable chunk of Indian territory. The United Nations continued to be a somnolent cliché of morons. Nehru fiddled aimlessly.

The Indian selectors were up to their tricks. Vizzy was the puppeteer. Hazare was demoted; Amarnath was not only recalled from the wilderness but made captain.

First Test – Delhi. India made a decent score of 372, and Pakistan were apparently shell-shocked and mesmerized by Mankad and collapsed for 150 with only four batsmen reaching double figures. Mankad got eight for 52. Following on, Pakistan managed to score two more runs and were bowled out for 152, Mankad again taking five for 79.

India won the match comfortably by an innings and 70 runs.

Second Test – Lucknow. What was going to happen now? Hazare, Mankad and Adhikari did not play in the second Test. I suppose they thought that the Pakistanis did not deserve India's best. They paid the price.

This time, India were shot out for 106, with only four of them reaching double figures. They simply could not handle Fazal Mohammed; five for 52. Pakistan made a handsome 331, with Nazar Mohammed scoring a century, 124. The Indians folded again in the second innings for 182, this time five managing double digits. Fazal scalped seven Indian heads for 42.

Pakistan won the match by an innings and 43 runs. So, you see, even in those days the Pakistanis were excellent fighters.

Third Test – Bombay. India had to salvage her pride in front of the knowledgeable Bombay crowd. Amarnath called for a team meeting and asked Mankad what they should do if he won the toss. "Put the bastards in," said Mankad. But Kardar, the Pakistan captain, won the toss and put his team in to bat. The third Test marks the debut of Gupte, who took five wickets.

Pakistan, 186. India, 387; Hazare, 146, Umrigar, 102. Pakistan, 242; Hanif, 96; Mankad, five for 72. India made the remaining paltry runs without losing a wicket and won the match by ten wickets.

The fourth Test at Madras and the fifth Test at Calcutta were drawn due to inclement weather. So, India won the rubber 2-1. It was a good series.

So, bad boy Amarnath led India to her first series victory.

Mankad had achieved the double of 1,000 runs and 100 wickets in 23 Tests – a record that was to last until 1979, when Botham burst onto the cricket scene like D'Artagnan.

Amarnath was discarded by the Indian board. He retired after a turbulent 24 Tests, 878 runs at a statistically unremakable 24.38; he had also taken 45 wickets at 32.91. The memories he left behind far surpassed his achievements.

1952-53 – Indian tour of the West Indies

It was hardly a month since the Pakistanis had left India. The Indian team flew to London, drove down to Southampton and caught the boat to the islands 'discovered' by Columbus.

The Indians had been transported to British Guiana – the West Indies – in shiploads as indentured labour to work on the sugar plantations. Their lot was unenviable in India; their lot was equally unenviable in the new land. They were dumped in the old slave quarters with amenities not even fit for the animal species and treated like cattle. They were slaves; they could not return to India. After the white oppressors left, the black ones took over and, more often than not, ruled with comparable callousness. Now several generations had passed. The lot of the Indian was marginally better but racial discrimination – black/brown – still openly prevailed in all spheres of life. The Indians maintained their ancient customs and handed over their memories of India to successive generations, but many of the emigrant Indians had not seen a 'true' Indian in their lifetime. The Indian team visiting them was like a visitation from the gods. The West Indies board did not really want the Indian team to visit their islands as they believed that it would be a financial loss. What transpired made them open their eyes. The cricket grounds were filled at all matches; thousands and thousands of Indians from all over the place – people who had not moved out of their villages and towns during their entire lifetime – now boarded buses or trudged along dusty roads towards the playing fields like so many iron filings drawn to a magnet. They smiled, talked, embraced and invited the Indians into their homes. One of them even made love to an Indian cricketer. A Trinidadian of Indian blood fell in love with Subhash Gupte, the prestidigitator who displayed his skill with the spinning ball, and married him.

The great Rohan Kanhai, Joe Solomon and Ramadhin were of Indian descent. After they passed away, the Indian disappeared from the West Indian team for decades. Now we have Chanderpaul – and the West Indian board took a long time to show him the green flag.

Hazare was back as captain, Mankad as vice-captain. You didn't expect the Indians to win, did you? The West Indians won the second Test; the others were drawn. But India did have something to show.

Firstly, they won over the West Indian population – a rapport that has lasted to this day. They did this with some splendid batting, bowling and scintillating fielding. Don't laugh. That Indian side impressed everyone with their alacrity and precision when fielding.

Umrigar made 560 runs at 62.22; Madhav Apte, 460 runs at 51.11; Pankaj Roy, 383 at 47.87; Manjrekar blossomed into the class batsman that he was. Gupte bagged 50 wickets on the tour; in Tests he took 27 wickets at 29.22. Mankad took 15 wickets at an expensive 53.06. And the best fielders were Umrigar, Apte, Gaekwad and Ghorpade. They moved about like bolts of lightning, cutting out what seemed like inevitable boundary shots, then picked up the ball and threw it cleanly over the stumps in one classic, smooth action.

This was when Gupte became the hero for India. Every schoolboy wanted to be Gupte – a spinner.

First Test – Port of Spain. India, 417; Umrigar, 130. The West Indies replied with 438; Weekes, 207, and an unknown chap called Pairandeau, 115. Gupte mesmerized the crowds with seven for 162. India, 294. The West Indies, 142 for no wicket.

Draw.

Second Test – Bridgetown. The West Indies made a modest 296. India a modest 253. The West Indies a modest 228. And India collapsed for 129, Ramadhin spinning them out and taking five for 26.

The West Indies won by 142 runs.

Third Test – Port of Spain. India, 279; King, five for 74. The West Indies, 315; Weekes again with 161, Gupte again with five for 107. India 362 for seven declared, Apte making 163 not out. The West Indies 192 for two with Stollmeyer, 104.

Draw.

Fourth Test – Georgetown. India, 262; Valentine, five for 127. The West Indies, 364, the two Ws – Walcott, 125, Weekes, 86 – making the runs, with Gupte picking up another four wickets for 122. India 190 for five.

Draw.

Fifth Test – Kingston. India, 312; Umrigar, 117. The West Indies made a massive 576, with the three Ws – Worrall 237, Weekes 109 and Walcot 118 – scoring highly and Gupte hauling in another five for 180. India,

444; Pankaj Roy, 150, and Manjrekar, 118. The West Indies 92 for four.

Draw.

So the rubber was won by the West Indies 1-0.

* * * * * * * *

In 18 months, India had played 18 Tests and won once against England and twice against Pakistan.

They played a meaningless series against a stupid Commonwealth side and won 2-1. Everyone, including the captaincy, was juggled around and Apte, a batsman who had established his class in the West Indies, played no further part in Indian cricket. The Indian board is the 'voice of God'. Just as God does not give any reasons for the various cock-ups He apparently makes, the Indian board does not give any explanations for its behaviour and decisions.

Hazare bid farewell to Test cricket after 30 Tests, 53 innings, 2,192 runs at an average of 47.65 – and 20 wickets.

1955 – India tours Pakistan

This was the second Test series between the two nations after the traumas of 1947 and the needless bloodshed that followed. And it was the first time in Test history that all the five matches were drawn.

Mankad was now captain. But he seemed to have left his thinking cap behind. He was a pretty pathetic captain. Maybe the Pakistani girl with whom he had madly fallen in love had something to do with it. Gupte enhanced his reputation. He bagged 21 wickets at 22.61. Only Hanif Mohammed for Pakistan and Umrigar for

India managed to score centuries. On the whole, it was a pretty boring tour – what with umpire bias and wicked living conditions.

* * * * * * * *

CHAPTER 38
1955 – 1960

Well, it is boring to go through the entire history of Indian test cricket in detail. So let me touch on the highlights and drama to sustain the reader's interest.

1955-56 – India versus New Zealand
India won two.

Umrigar becomes the first Indian to score a double century, 223.

Madras, New Corporation Stadium. India won the toss and elected to bat. It is customary for the first few batsmen to pad up and be ready to take the field at the fall of a wicket. Well, no one needed to have padded up that opening day when Mankad and Pankaj Roy strolled onto the new turf. The world record for an opening stand was 359 by England's Hutton and Washbrook against South Africa at Johannesburg. At the close of the first day Mankad and Pankaj were still together, with centuries against their names. The next day they came out to slog and found that they were still together at lunch. Someone got out the records book and told them that they could do it. They did it. Our two chaps batted for eight hours and made 413; the record still stands. The match ended as the inevitable draw.

India won the second Test at Bombay by an innings and 27 runs, Mankad making merry with 223 runs. The third and fourth Tests were drawn.

1956-57 – India versus Australia
Australia won two.

Gupte couldn't do much, especially against the left-handed Neil Harvey, who treated him with impunity. Ghulam Ahmed fared better. But Benaud was the best of the bowlers. The third Test at Calcutta was a funny one. It was low-scoring match, Australia making 177 and 169 for seven declared and India 136 and 136 again.

1958-59 – India versus West Indies
The West Indies won three.

Mankad retires. Borde comes in. This was the series that established the malevolent tactics of West Indian pace spearheaded by Hall and Gilchrist, who sent down an unending barrage of bouncers and beamers, whose intention was to frighten, pulverize and maim; legal dismissal of the batsmen was only incidental. They looked like black demons escaped from hell as they ran towards the batsmen from almost the far side screen. The Indian umpires, the Indian press and even the Indian board did nothing to stop the sickening thud of leather against flesh and bone. It was mayhem, it was war – not a game of cricket.

The first Test at Bombay was a draw, the hero being Garfield Sobers, who scored 142. The second Test at Kanpur was won by the West Indians by 203 runs, Sobers again making 198 runs. The only curiosity about this game is that both India and the West Indies made 222 in their first innings. The third Test at Calcutta was an even more humiliating defeat for the Indians, by an innings and 336 runs. The West Indies, 614 runs; Kanhai, 256, Butcher, 103, the inevitable Sobers, 106.

1959 – England versus India

England won all five.

Abbas Ali Baig was a fair-skinned, handsome student at Oxford who had rattled the scoreboards playing for his university. He was drafted in by the Indian tourists for a match against Middlesex. He gleefully accepted the invitation and showed the Indians how to play in England. He scattered the opposition with a masterly century. He was picked for the fourth Test. First innings, 26. Second innings he lit up the faces of his team-mates with a flashy 112, thus joining Amarnath and Ranji, who also made centuries on their debuts.

The first Test at Nottingham was won by England by an innings and 59 runs; the second at Lord's by eight wickets; the third at Leeds by an innings and 173 runs; the fourth at Manchester by 171 runs; and the fifth at the Oval by an innings and 27 runs. It was a total rout. The Indians didn't know what hit them; but they had a hero – Abbas Ali Baig, and they were happy. That was the only century he made in 18 innings, though. He disappeared with 428 to his credit at an average of 23.77 – a flash in the pan.

1959-60 – India versus Australia

First Test – Delhi. India, a meagre 135. Australia, 468; Harvey, 114. India once again a poor reply of 206, with Pankaj Roy missing out by a run on his century. Benaud was the chief wrecker with five for 76.

Australia won by an innings and 127 runs.

Second Test – Kanpur. India posted a paltry 152, Davidson scalping five hapless Indians for only 31 runs. Might as well pack up and go home. If you had you would have missed the match of a lifetime. Australia folded for 219 due to the wizardry of Jesu Patel, who ended with the incredible figures of nine for 69. India answered with another meagre total of 291 and Australia collapsed for 105, with only three reaching double digits. Patel once again was the chief wrecker with five for 55.

Jesu Patel was himself surprised when he was called for duty. Amarnath thought that he could do the trick with his unusual action, bowling curious off-spinners. Patel mesmerized the Australians and engineered the first win against Australia. Fortune smiled on Patel just for that one Test. Like Baig, he mysteriously disappeared after ten innings, taking 29 wickets at an average of 21.96.

Third Test – Bombay. India, 289; Nari Contractor, 108. Australia, 387; Harvey, 102, and O'Neill, 163. Nadkarni, the slow plodder, six for 105. India 226 for five declared and Australia 34 for one. It was a dreary affair.

Fourth Test – Madras. Australia, 342; Favell, 101. India, 149, once again felled by Benaud, who got five for 43. India, 138. Only four reached double figures in either Indian innings.

Budhi Kunderan, a black version of Dumas' D'Artagnan. He was a wicketkeeper batsman – in spite of parental objections to the game. He embodied all that is good about maidan cricket – cricket for sheer pleasure, cricket that is spontaneous, unharnessed, cricket that emanates from the very soul, cricket that knows no fear. He slammed a double century in his first school match, later played with Merchant at the Fort Vijay Cricket Club, and joined the Railways. Amarnath was at the time the coach for the Railways team. He immediately saw Kunderan's potential and recommended him for the team against the Australians. He was 12th man in the first two Tests, came on in Bombay and scored 19 and two. He didn't exactly set the ground on fire. But did he make up for it in Madras! Boy, oh boy! The regular opener, Contractor, was unwell and opted to come in later. Ramchand, the captain, asked young Kunderan to open. Well, why not? He was unafraid, completely devoid of 'nerves' – and had nothing to lose. The Madras crowd saw the black, diminutive unknown walk to the crease along with bespectacled Pankaj Roy. They couldn't see the sparkle in the young man's eyes, the rippling muscles under his shirt and the rash bravado in his heart.

First over – Pankaj Roy, maiden over from Davidson.

Second over – Kunderan. Meckiff bowling. At the end of the first over, the scoreboard read 14. The Madras crowd went berserk. The entire ground was screaming; they couldn't believe that an unknown could come along and slog the feared Australian fast bowlers in the very first over he faced. His mates in the pavilion had to pinch themselves.

The Australians were nonplussed. They were swearing and fuming in the Madras sun and flung their balls with increased venom. But Kunderan just stood and slashed them over the slips and over the covers for magical fours. That was how he used to play, you see. He made 71 and 33 in that match and became a hero. His nonchalant attitude, his skill and mastery made a forceful dent in the dull, crippling ethos of Indian cricket.

India lost by an innings and 55 runs – but what the hell? They had darling Kunderan to croon over... But even such a character as Kunderan seemed only a transient star on the Indian horizon. He made a couple of centuries in 34 innings for a total of 981 runs at an average of 32.70.

Fifth Test – Calcutta. India, 194. Australia, 331; O'Neill, 113. India, 339. Australia 121 for two.

Draw.

So, Australia won the series 2-1.

* * * * * * *

Cricket fever becomes endemic in the Indian subcontinent. The virus infects every citizen without discrimination – men, women, children, plebeians and patricians, city-dwellers and village rustics. Women are arguing about 'leg-befores' and 'run outs' and screaming about 'good shots' and 'googlies'. Life comes to a standstill all over the nation. The sale of radios and transistor sets soars. The inhabitants of the entire nation acquire an electrical appendage and strive to perform their jobs with their ears glued to their receiver sets. The streets that used to vibrate to film music now splutter forth with cricket commentaries; the din of the crowd's cheering and howling, the sound of bat against ball, ecstasy and despair, joy and agony. The street corners are jammed with pedestrians listening to the destiny of their teams at the *bidi* (indigenous rolled tobacco leaves favoured by rural folk– mini-cigars, if you like; I smoke them), betel-nut, bhaji, *bonda* and samosa stalls – the last three are all delicious savouries. The Indians have a new entertainment besides the cinema houses. Five days of tamasha. Five days of living and breathing cricket. It is a truly heady atmosphere. No longer are tickets sold for each day; the counters simply cannot cope with the endless queues. They introduce the 'season' ticket for the entire match. Radio commentary is now in English, Hindi, Marathi and Bengali to enable the masses to follow the game in their own languages. It is sheer intoxication. It is a phenomenon that cannot be explained.

The 1960s saw the start of cricket 'stars'. C K, Hazare, Merchant were cricketers, not people in the firmament. But now people recognized the ethereal glamour of Abbas Ali Baig, Salim Durrani, M L Jaisimha, Budhi Kunderan and others who seemed to play for the express purpose of entertaining the people, not merely to win matches. Women ran to them and hugged and kissed them in public – something that was unimaginable in India, where even a kiss is banned in the cinema; kisses are still prohibited on the Indian screen.

Of the lot, Salim Durrani was the undisputed hero. He couldn't help it with a name like 'Salim', the famous son of Akbar the Great, who fell in love with a commoner and went on to become Emperor Jehangir. Tall, lithe, handsome with an enticing air of insouciance, he was reputed to slam sixes on request – irrespective of the team's predicament. Both he and Jaisimha were, however, flawed heroes. They could not sustain the fight while entertaining the crowd. Durrani made only 1,202 runs in 50 innings at an average of 25.04, with just one hundred to his credit. Jaisimha made 2,056 runs in 71 innings at an average of 30.68, with three centuries. Neither of these heart-throbs, as their averages show, lived up to their adoring fans' expectations.

* * * * * * * *

CHAPTER 39
1960 – 1970

1960-61 – India versus Pakistan

All Tests were drawn.

1961-62 – India versus England
India won two.

Gupte retires. But what were the circumstances? Pretty absurd, really. It shows, once again, the hideboundness of the Indian board. The Indian team was staying at the Imperial Hotel, New Delhi. Kripal Singh wanted to make a date with the hotel receptionist. He telephoned her from his room, which he was sharing with Gupte. The silly cow complained to the Indian manager. By this time Kripal had left for the airport. Gupte was collared by the captain, Contractor. Gupte rushed to the airport and informed Kripal of what was going on. Both of them had to answer to a board of enquiry at Madras and, despite Kripal owning up and clearing Gupte, both were suspended... Gupte was penalized because he did not try and stop Kripal from making the call! Thus was the career of India's greatest spinner ended, just because his room-mate wanted to have a chit-chat with a girl.

Gupte had had enough by now and retired. He emigrated to the West Indies and settled down with his West Indian wife.

In 1960, an ugly, horse-faced Oxford freshman piled up a century against the traditional rival,

Cambridge. During the following year he had amassed a dazzling 1,216 runs at the pretty good average of 55.27.

On the 1st of July 1961, he was involved in a car accident. A splinter of glass entered the lens of his right eye and blinded it. What he lacked in looks he more than made up with breeding and grit. He was the young Nawab of Pataudi, whose father had played for both England and India. Within months of the accident, he was playing cricket again – such was his pertinacity. Try pouring water into a glass with one eye shut. I always remember my grandmother missing the glass by six inches after her cataract operation.

The nawab played for the President's XI against Dexter's England team in India and whipped up 70 runs. He was named for the Delhi Test and made a quiet 13. He showed his capabilities in the Calcutta Test with a creditable 64 and 32. But it was in Madras that he showed his potential. Until then, none of the Indian batsmen used the hook shot; nor did they lift the ball over the cordon of fielders. The last one who delighted the crowds was part of memory – the great C K Nayudu. The Merchant-Hazare era had heralded the safe, along-the-ground shot. Pataudi now seemed to take a leaf out of C K's book and he lifted his shots to the open parts of the ground. The crowd drew in its breath. This was something quite new. In two and a half hours Pataudi made 103 spectacular runs and laid the foundation for a well-deserved win against the mighty England.

E A S Prasanna makes his debut with one wicket in the fifth Test.

The details are as follows.

First Test – Bombay. Draw.

Second Test – Kanpur – Draw.

Third Test – Delhi. Draw.

Fourth Test – Calcutta. India, 380; Allen, five for 67. England, 212; Salim Durrani, five for 47. India, 252. England, 233. India won 187 runs.

Fifth Test – Madras. India, 428; Nawab of Pataudi, 103. England, 281; Durrani another six for 105. India, 190, Lock spearing six Indians for 65 runs. England, 209, once again Durrani taking four for 72, with Borde chipping in with three for 89. India won the Test by 128 runs.

This was a historic series win indeed.

Ken Barrington helped himself to three centuries along the way.

1961-62 – West Indies versus India
The West Indies won all five.

Sandwiched between the second and third Tests was a match against Barbados. Frank Worrall had warned the Indians that amongst the enemy ranks was a chap called Charlie Griffith, who was really fast. The Indians suspected that he chucked the ball. But, by the time they could object, the deed was done. Nari Contractor, the Indian captain, was knocked out of Test cricket. Griffith sent down a missile that pitched and rose viciously. Contractor probably saw it a bit late and could not judge the height. He bent back at the last moment but by then it was too late. The ball crashed into his skull just above the right ear. Contractor was a doughty cricketer and stood his ground, but after some time decided to come in, retired hurt. He was in the Indian dressing room. Meanwhile Manjrekar had gone in and received a similar ball that whizzed past his nose. It flew out of the hands of the wicketkeeper and injured the slip fielder. The Indian players now started to notice Griffith's bowling action. But now they heard a terrifying scream from the dressing room. They rushed in to see their captain writhing in agony. He was taken to the hospital and operated upon; the blood clot was removed and an iron plate inserted in the skull. Griffith was in tears. Frank Worrall donated blood. The Indian contingent was in shock.

Charlie didn't play in any more of the Tests.

Pataudi took over as captain; the youngest, at 21. But the Indians lost the series. They had no answers against illegitimate cricket. But they were not beaten. The youngsters, Jaisimha, Durrani, Pataudi and even Umrigar, salvaged some dignity and respect with their pertinacious displays in the third and fourth Tests. Umrigar and Durrani scored 172 and 104 respectively in the fourth Test. Where was Kunderan? you may ask. Farokh Engineer kept wickets in the first three Tests and Kunderan for the last two. He didn't do much.

The details are as follows.

First Test – Port of Spain. India, 203. The West Indies, 289. India, 98. The West Indies, 15 for no wicket. Win by ten wickets.

Second Test – Kingston. India, 395. The West Indies, 631 for eight declared. India, 218; Hall, six for 49. Win by innings and 18 runs.

Third test – Bridgetown. India, 258. The West Indies, 475. India, 187; Gibbs, eight for 38. Win by innings and 30 runs.

Fourth Test – Port of Spain. The West Indies, 444; Kanhai, 139. India, 197; Hall, five for 20. India, 422; Durrani, 104, Umrigar, 172. The West Indies, 176 for three. Win by seven wickets.

Fifth Test – Kingston. The West Indies, 253, Sobers at last making 104. India, 178, King doing the damage with five for 46. The West Indies, 283. India, 235, Sobers doing the damage with five wickets for 63. Win by 123 runs.

1963-64 – *India versus England*
All the Tests were drawn.

But three men made good. Kunderan was back and made a carefree 'club cricket' 170; Hanumant Singh made 105 on his debut; and Pataudi cracked the highest score by an Indian against England – 203 not out. Hanumant Singh, by the way, never repeated his feat, played in 24 innings, clocked up 686 runs at an average of just 31.18 – and disappeared.

Chandrasekhar made his debut quietly with ten wickets in the series. He was the unorthodox, unpredictable, medium pace, hardly turning, leg-breaker who bowled his balls with a polio-withered, full-sleeved right arm and who had an almost unplayable googly. He was a 'freak' bowler.

The story goes that, after four draws, Mike Smith, the England captain, with his side well placed at 271 for three, parleyed with Pataudi to inject some life into the proceedings. He offered to declare if India would reciprocate and make a match of it. But Pataudi dithered. He consulted the Indian board – a foolish thing to do. Of course, they objected, and the match petered out into a tame draw.

1964-65 – India versus Australia
First Test – Madras. Australia, 211; Nadkarni, five for 31. India, 276, with Pataudi making 128; only three others managed double figures. McKenzie reaped a harvest of six wickets for 58. Australia, 347; Nadkarni again scalping six for 91. India folded for 173, only five reaching double figures. McKenzie reaped four for 33.

Australia won by 139 runs.

Second Test – Brabourne Stadium, Bombay. Australia, first innings, 320. Chandrasekhar scalped four enemies. India replied with 341; Jaisimha, 66, Manjrekar, 59, Pataudi, 86, with Surti, Nadkarni and wicketkeeper Indrasinghji contributing collectively a valuable 78 runs to give India a lead of 21 runs. Australia made 274 in their second innings, with Chandra adding four more scalps to his tally; Nadkarni helped with four to his name. Now India had to make 254 runs with more than a day in hand. The stage was set for an Indian win. But the citizens of India knew how capricious their heroes could be; they could lose spectacularly or play for a boring draw. Sardesai and Jaisimha opened. Before one could go to the toilet and return, India were four for one, with Jaisimha trudging back to the pavilion for a duck. Romantic Salim joined Sardesai. Normally the crowd would have erupted with demands for a six. This time, the entire ground was as silent as the graveyard; only the susurrus of the wind could be heard. "Salim, play safe, play steady," the crowd seemed to pray. But that was not Salim's game.

He tried to confine himself in a mental straitjacket for some time, but the effort was too great for so mercurial a personality. After a patient, sensible 31, he lost his head, took a swipe and was caught.

It was nearing the end of the fourth day's play. Pataudi sent in Nadkarni as nightwatchman. After all, he had made 52 and 122 against England at Kanpur. Nadkarni was soon making his sad way back to the pavilion for a duck. Pataudi sent in Surti, another fair batsman. Surti survived. India went home that evening on 74 for three.

The whole of India was agog. What would happen? Would India win? The next day was an excruciating, maddening religious holiday that no Indian really enjoyed.

Final day. Vievers removed Surti for a measly ten and McKenzie went berserk. He trapped Sardesai lbw for a solid 56 and bowled Hanumantsingh for 11with an unplayable yorker. The whole of India groaned. Manjrekar was the best of the lot. He now came in at number eight. and joined his captain. They played sensible cricket and stayed together until lunch – and tea. India started to breathe again. India was 215 for six. Manjrekar and Pataudi were nearing a century partnership when the former was caught for 39. Next man in was Borde, another experienced, solid batsman. He epitomized calm confidence. Pataudi slashed viciously at a loose ball outside the off stump. Luckily he caught it with the meat of his bat, a solid contact. A four was already being chalked up. But Burge had performed an incredible piece of magic. He appeared at point and took a brilliant catch. Pataudi out for 53. India

224 for eight. Indrajitsinghji joined Borde. Why did India pick him when it had Engineer and Kunderan, who were good batsmen? Maybe because he was a relation of the Ranji family. The Aussies knew that Borde was a good player. So they threw everything they had at Indra. But Borde was playing an inspired and responsible game that day. He shielded the junior player and took on the bulk of the bowling. Thirty minutes to go; two runs to win; two wickets in hand. Still the Indian people refused to celebrate. They waited. Vievers bowled. Borde calmly on-drove him to the boundary. The stadium erupted like a volcano.

The third Test at Calcutta ended in a draw. So the series ended evenly for both sides, 1-1.

1964-65 – India versus New Zealand
The first three Tests ended in draws.

The fourth Test at Delhi produced an Indian win by seven wickets. New Zealand, 262, with new boy Venkataraghavan taking eight wickets for 72. India made a huge 465 with Sardesai, 106, and Pataudi, 113. The New Zealanders replied with 273, with Venkat taking four more wickets, and India made the required runs for the loss of three wickets.

1966-67 – India versus West Indies
The West Indies won two.

Bedi comes into the team. Prasanna, who went AWOL, now rejoins the Indian team.

First Test – Bombay. India, 296, with only Borde making 121. The West Indies notched up 421; Hunte, 101. Chandra's figures were seven for 157. India the second time around made 316. The West Indies made up the deficit for the loss of four wickets and won the match.

Second Test – Calcutta. The West Indies, 390. India, 167 and 178. The West Indians won by an innings and 45 runs.

Though the game was disheartening for the Indians, life bubbled outside the stadium, with riots caused by the authorities selling 70,000 tickets for the then Eden Gardens, which had a capacity of 50,000. Both the teams had to run for their lives and the West Indians rightly thought of returning home, but were cajoled into staying. How can you keep a public riot a secret? Yet the fools at All-India Radio lied to the nation that play was stopped due to 'fog'!

1967 – England versus India
England won all three.

India's spin quartet play together for the first time in the third Test.

India lost the series outside the playing grounds of England. Their manager, an obsequious oaf called Tarapore, all but prostrated himself before the mighty English, saying that his team had come to learn from them. The Indian board did not provide any equipment; can you believe that? As soon as they arrived, the Indian cricketers had to beg and borrow money to go to the sports shops. Everyone knows how cold it can get in England; your fingers freeze on the field. Yet they were supplied only with gaberdine flannels that stick to the skin and sleeveless sweaters. The players had to buy themselves appropriate wear. And food. It is difficult to survive in England if you are a vegetarian; only bread and fruit are available. No arrangements were made for wholesome food for the likes of Venkat and Prasanna, who were orthodox vegetarians. The allowances were so diabolical that they couldn't even afford to go to an Indian hotel for nourishment.

I am not going to give you more facts and figures. It can get a bit boring.

1967-68 – Australia versus India. Australia won all four.

1967-68 – New Zealand versus India. India won three; New Zealand won one.

1969-70 – India versus New Zealand. India won one; New Zealand won one.

1969-70 – India versus Australia. Australia won three; India won one.

Viswanath makes an entry with a century; 137 in the second Test.

Pataudi is hounded out. Borde, the chap who should have really followed Contractor as captain, is now too old at 37. He retires. Wadekar, by default, is given the captaincy.

The team sets off for the West Indies.

* * * * * * * *

Let us look at the era of the 1950s and 1960 and compare the three batsmen – Umrigar, Manjrekar and Borde.

	Innings	Runs	Hundreds	Average
Umrigar	94	3,631	2	42.22
Manjrekar	92	3,208	7	39.12

Borde   97   3,061   5   35.59

Borde was was my idol during my schooldays. He was a handsome bloke and a stylish player. I used to mimic the way he used to stand at the bowler's end, leaning on his bat with the toe of one boot crossed over the other. My great-uncle and I went to see him play at the Corporation Stadium, Madras, during the 1960-61 series against Pakistan, where he made that brilliant 177. That was perhaps the highlight of my schooldays with regards to cricket.

* * * * * * * *